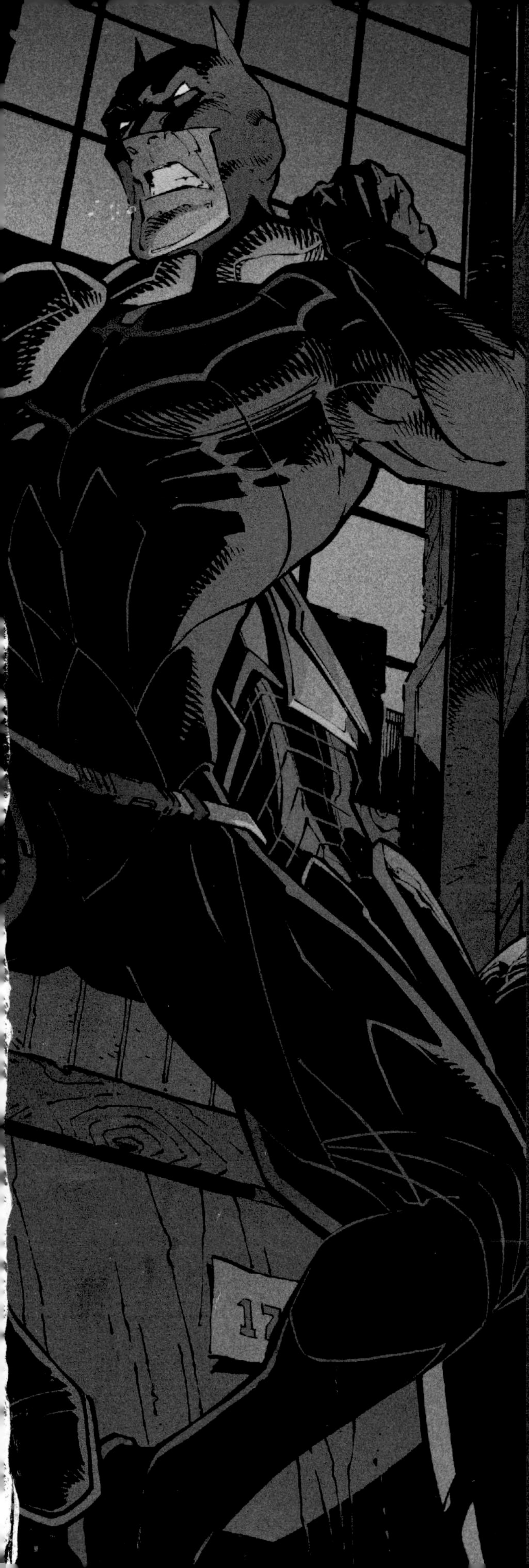
17

BATMAN

VOLUME 9
BLOOM

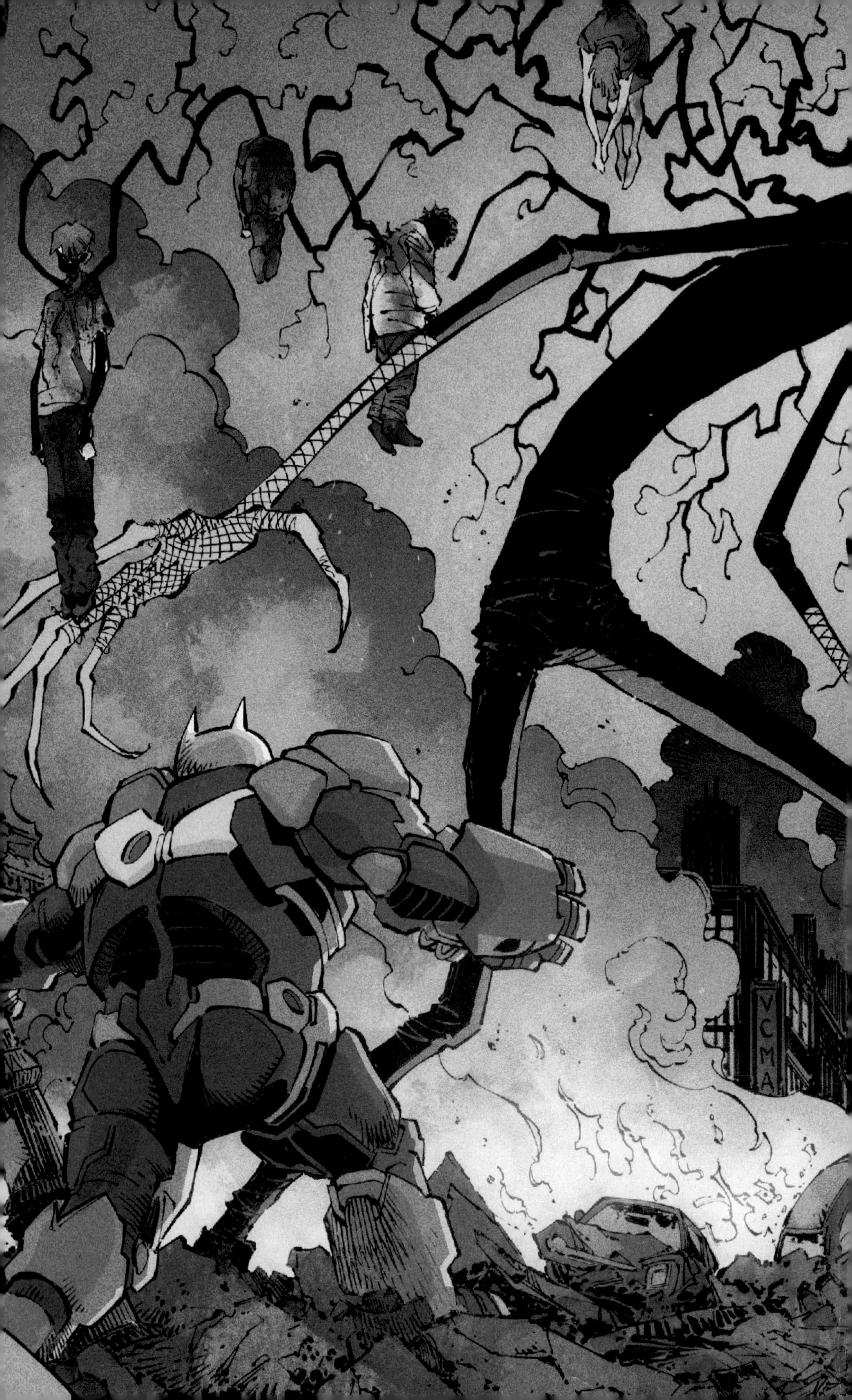
VCMA

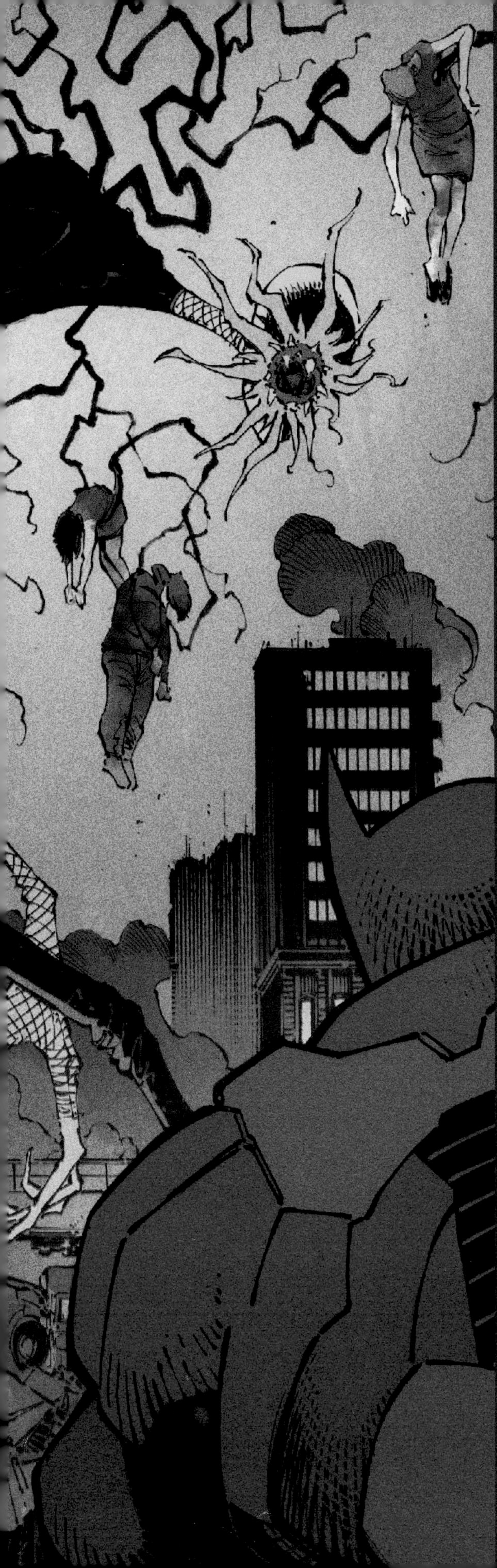

BATMAN

VOLUME 9
BLOOM

WRITTEN BY
SCOTT SNYDER
JAMES TYNION IV

ART BY
GREG CAPULLO
DANNY MIKI
YANICK PAQUETTE
SEAN MURPHY

COLOR BY
FCO PLASCENCIA
NATHAN FAIRBAIRN
MATT HOLLINGSWORTH

LETTERS BY
STEVE WANDS

COLLECTION COVER ART BY
GREG CAPULLO, DANNY MIKI
& FCO PLASCENCIA

BATMAN CREATED BY
BOB KANE with **BILL FINGER**

MARK DOYLE Editor – Original Series
REBECCA TAYLOR Associate Editor – Original Series
JEB WOODARD Group Editor – Collected Editions
ROBIN WILDMAN Editor – Collected Edition
STEVE COOK Design Director – Books
DAMIAN RYLAND Publication Design

BOB HARRAS Senior VP – Editor-in-Chief, DC Comics

DIANE NELSON President
DAN DIDIO and JIM LEE Co-Publishers
GEOFF JOHNS Chief Creative Officer
AMIT DESAI Senior VP – Marketing & Global Franchise Management
NAIRI GARDINER Senior VP – Finance
SAM ADES VP – Digital Marketing
BOBBIE CHASE VP – Talent Development
MARK CHIARELLO Senior VP – Art, Design & Collected Editions
JOHN CUNNINGHAM VP – Content Strategy
ANNE DEPIES VP – Strategy Planning & Reporting
DON FALLETTI VP – Manufacturing Operations
LAWRENCE GANEM VP – Editorial Administration & Talent Relations
ALISON GILL Senior VP – Manufacturing & Operations
HANK KANALZ Senior VP – Editorial Strategy & Administration
JAY KOGAN VP – Legal Affairs
DEREK MADDALENA Senior VP – Sales & Business Development
JACK MAHAN VP – Business Affairs
DAN MIRON VP – Sales Planning & Trade Development
NICK NAPOLITANO VP – Manufacturing Administration
CAROL ROEDER VP – Marketing
EDDIE SCANNELL VP – Mass Account & Digital Sales
COURTNEY SIMMONS Senior VP – Publicity & Communications
JIM (SKI) SOKOLOWSKI VP – Comic Book Specialty & Newsstand Sales
SANDY YI Senior VP – Global Franchise Management

BATMAN VOLUME 9: BLOOM

DC Comics, 2900 West Alameda Ave., Burbank, CA 91505
Printed by RR Donnelley, Salem, VA, USA. 8/5/16. First Printing.
ISBN: 978-1-4012-6462-8

Library of Congress Cataloging-in-Publication Data is available.

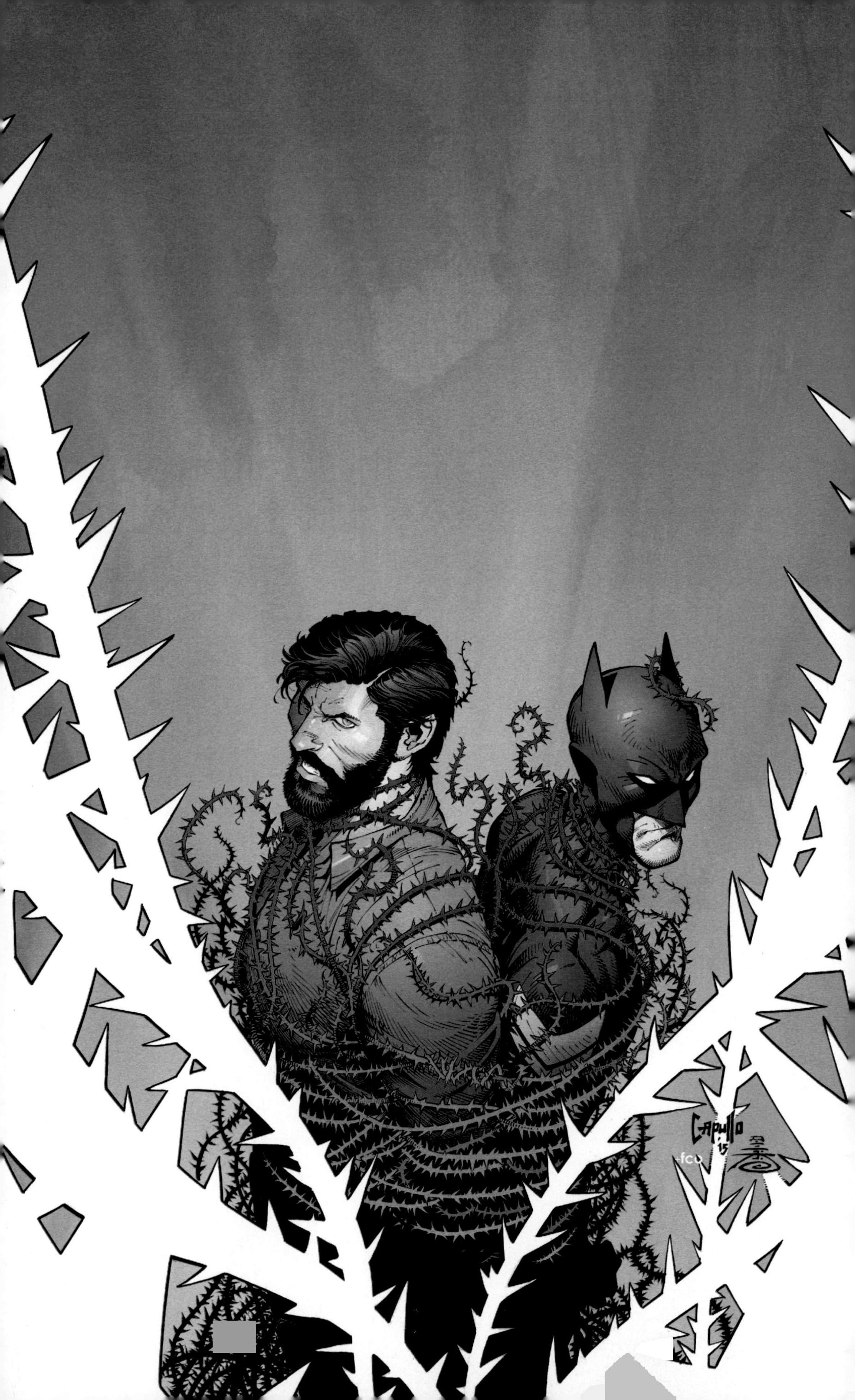

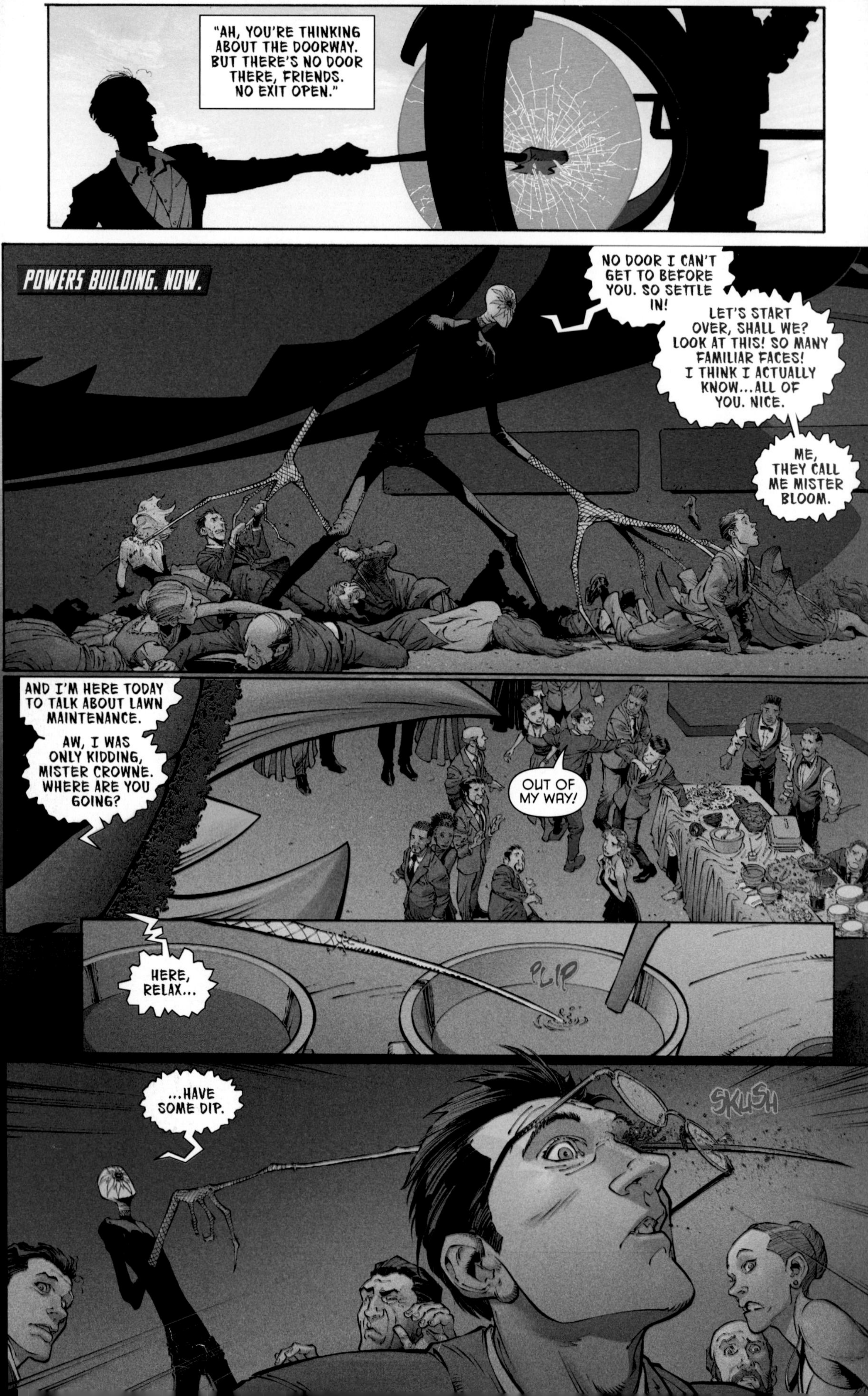
"AH, YOU'RE THINKING ABOUT THE DOORWAY. BUT THERE'S NO DOOR THERE, FRIENDS. NO EXIT OPEN."
POWERS BUILDING. NOW.
NO DOOR I CAN'T GET TO BEFORE YOU. SO SETTLE IN!
LET'S START OVER, SHALL WE? LOOK AT THIS! SO MANY FAMILIAR FACES! I THINK I ACTUALLY KNOW...ALL OF YOU. NICE.
ME, THEY CALL ME MISTER BLOOM.
AND I'M HERE TODAY TO TALK ABOUT LAWN MAINTENANCE.
AW, I WAS ONLY KIDDING, MISTER CROWNE. WHERE ARE YOU GOING?
OUT OF MY WAY!
HERE, RELAX...
PLIP
...HAVE SOME DIP.
SKUSH

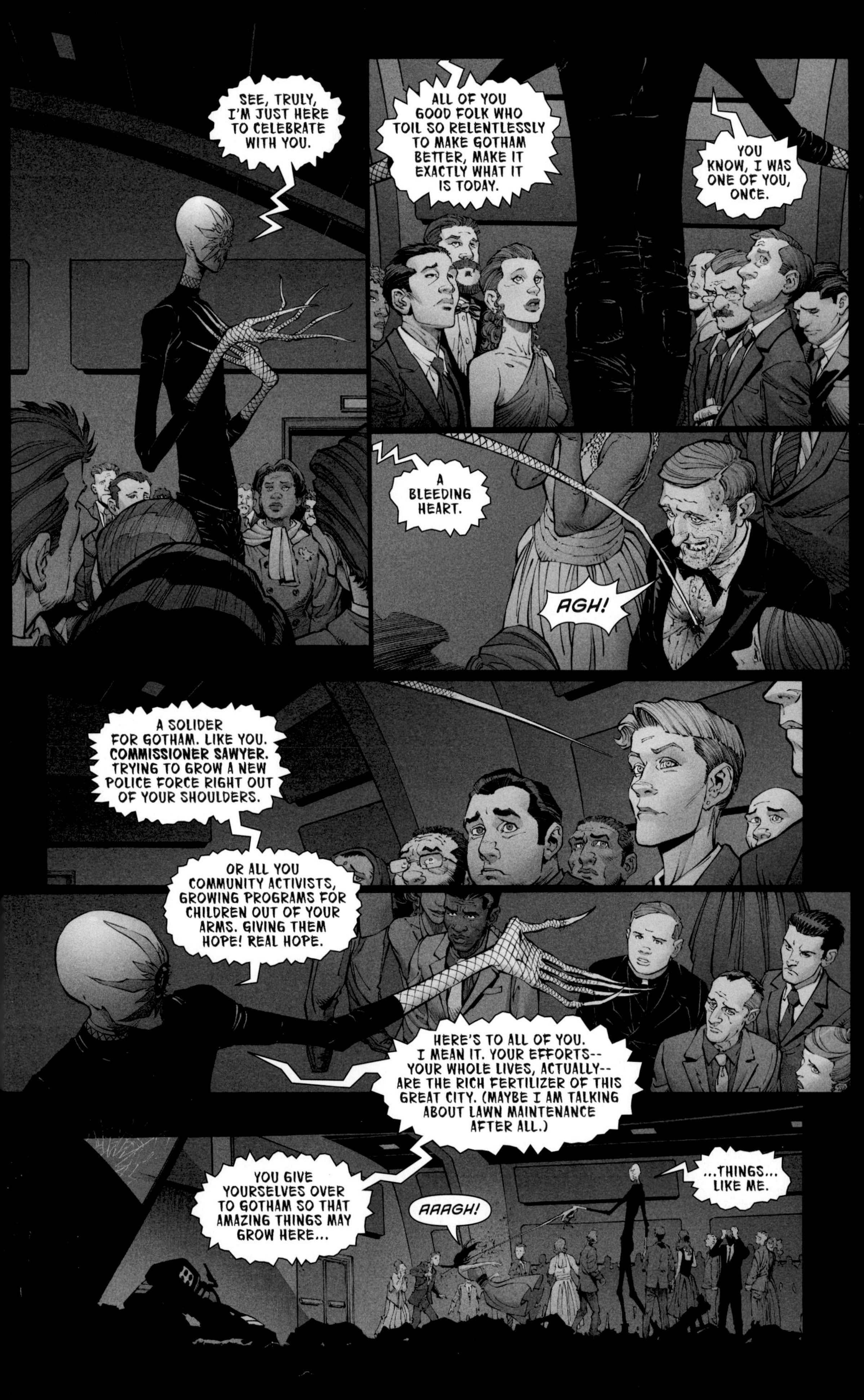
SEE, TRULY, I'M JUST HERE TO CELEBRATE WITH YOU.
ALL OF YOU GOOD FOLK WHO TOIL SO RELENTLESSLY TO MAKE GOTHAM BETTER, MAKE IT EXACTLY WHAT IT IS TODAY.
YOU KNOW, I WAS ONE OF YOU, ONCE.
A BLEEDING HEART.
AGH!
A SOLIDER FOR GOTHAM. LIKE YOU. COMMISSIONER SAWYER. TRYING TO GROW A NEW POLICE FORCE RIGHT OUT OF YOUR SHOULDERS.
OR ALL YOU COMMUNITY ACTIVISTS, GROWING PROGRAMS FOR CHILDREN OUT OF YOUR ARMS. GIVING THEM HOPE! REAL HOPE.
HERE'S TO ALL OF YOU. I MEAN IT. YOUR EFFORTS-- YOUR WHOLE LIVES, ACTUALLY-- ARE THE RICH FERTILIZER OF THIS GREAT CITY. (MAYBE I AM TALKING ABOUT LAWN MAINTENANCE AFTER ALL.)
YOU GIVE YOURSELVES OVER TO GOTHAM SO THAT AMAZING THINGS MAY GROW HERE...
AAAGH!
...THINGS... LIKE ME.

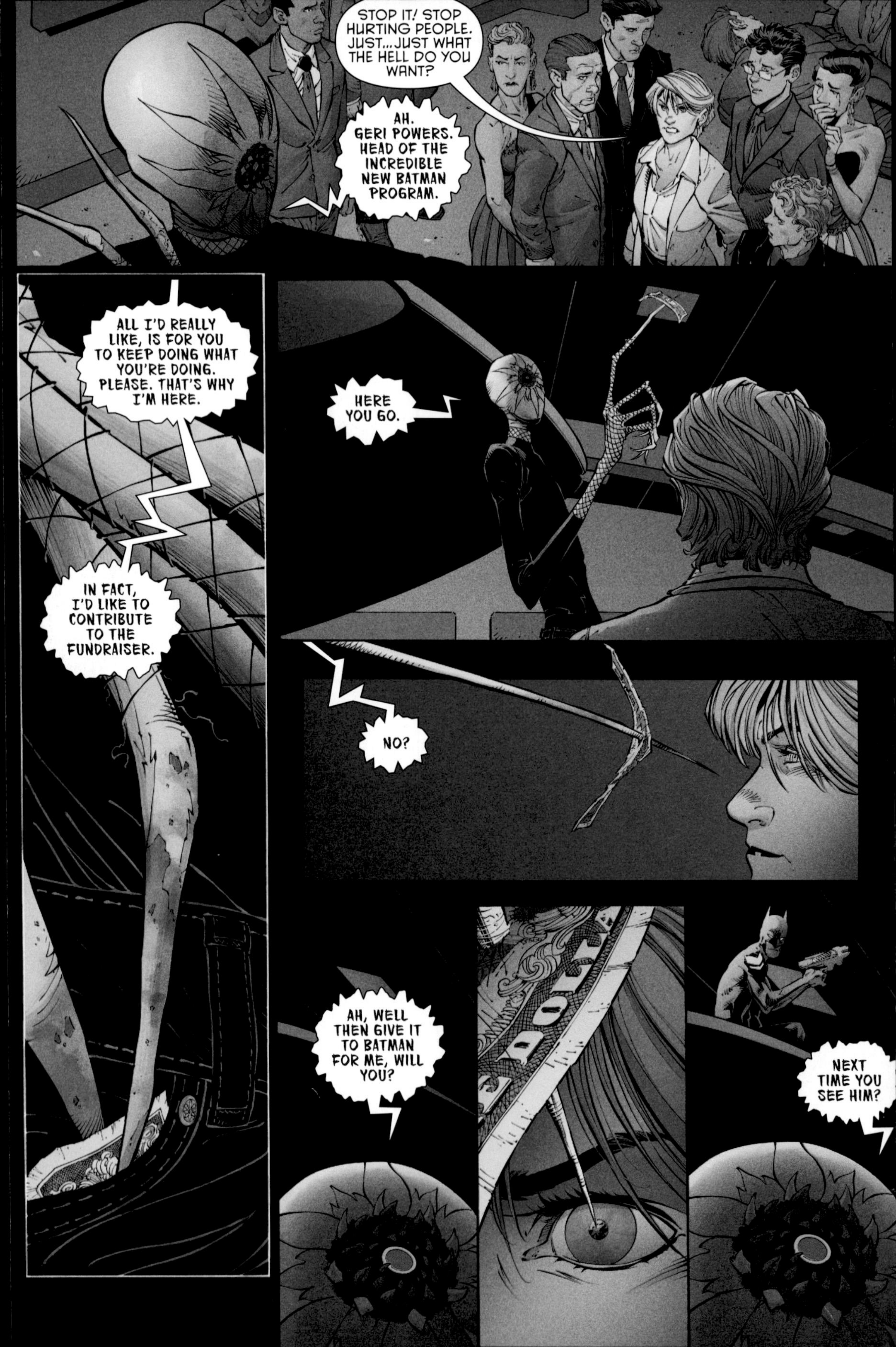
STOP IT! STOP HURTING PEOPLE. JUST...JUST WHAT THE HELL DO YOU WANT?
AH. GERI POWERS. HEAD OF THE INCREDIBLE NEW BATMAN PROGRAM.
ALL I'D REALLY LIKE, IS FOR YOU TO KEEP DOING WHAT YOU'RE DOING. PLEASE. THAT'S WHY I'M HERE.
IN FACT, I'D LIKE TO CONTRIBUTE TO THE FUNDRAISER.
HERE YOU GO.
NO?
AH, WELL THEN GIVE IT TO BATMAN FOR ME, WILL YOU?
NEXT TIME YOU SEE HIM?

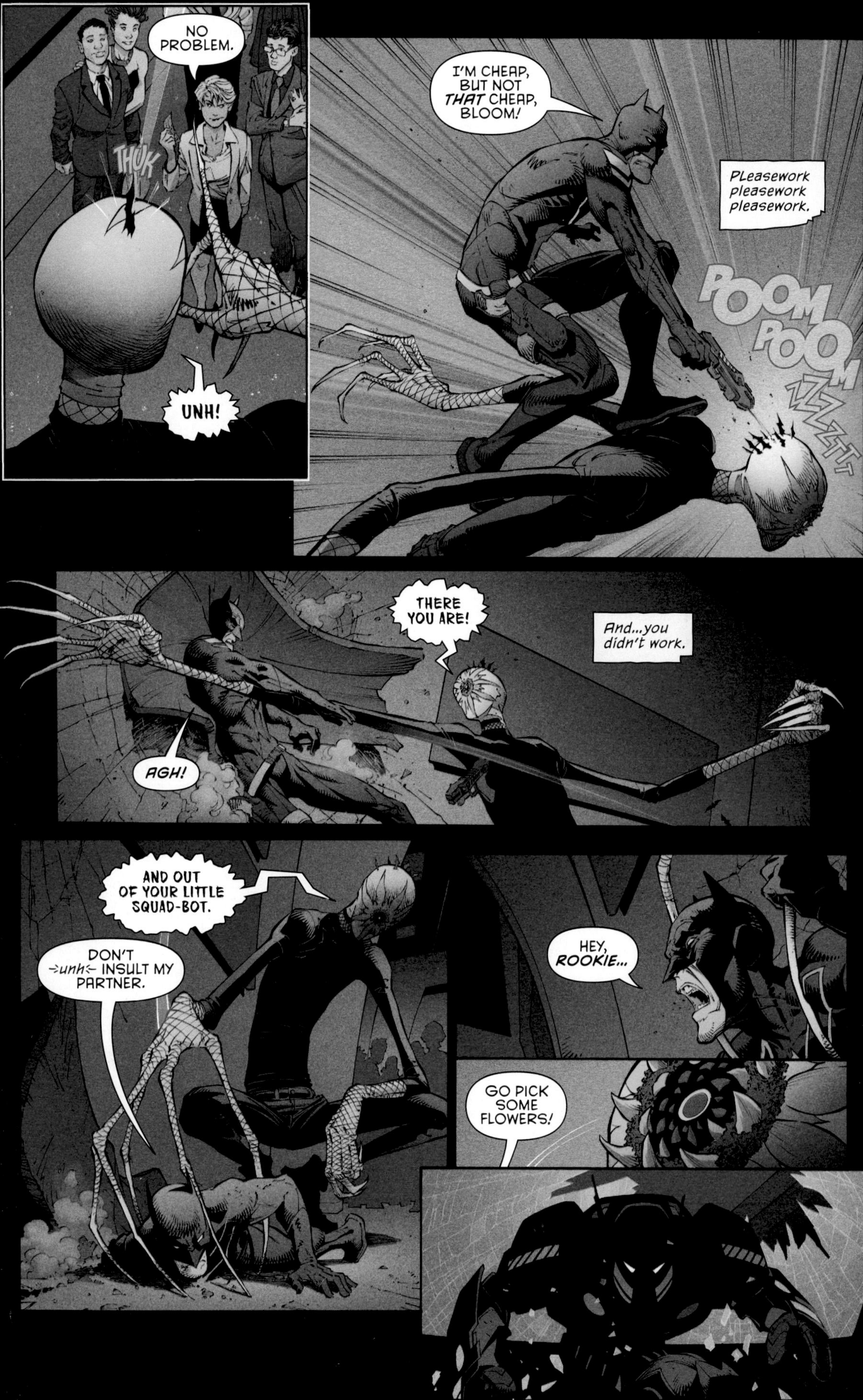
NO PROBLEM.
THUK
UNH!
I'M CHEAP, BUT NOT *THAT* CHEAP, BLOOM!
PLeasework pleasework pleasework.
POOM POOM
ZZZZTT
THERE YOU ARE!
And...you didn't work.
AGH!
AND OUT OF YOUR LITTLE SQUAD-BOT.
DON'T -unh- INSULT MY PARTNER.
HEY, *ROOKIE*...
GO PICK SOME FLOWERS!

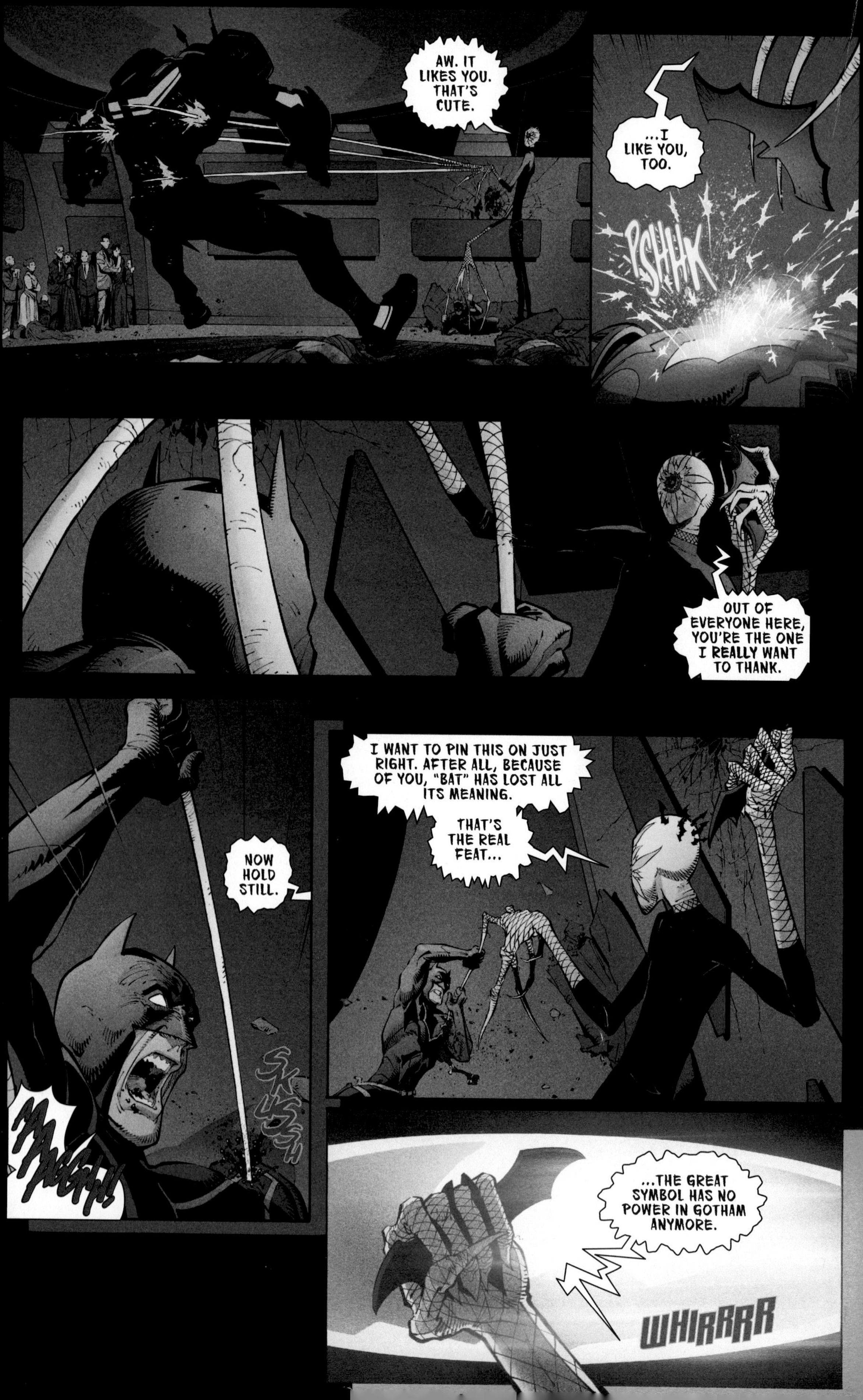
AW. IT LIKES YOU. THAT'S CUTE.
...I LIKE YOU, TOO.
PSHHK
OUT OF EVERYONE HERE, YOU'RE THE ONE I REALLY WANT TO THANK.
NOW HOLD STILL.
SKLUSSH
MNGH!!
I WANT TO PIN THIS ON JUST RIGHT. AFTER ALL, BECAUSE OF YOU, "BAT" HAS LOST ALL ITS MEANING.
THAT'S THE REAL FEAT...
...THE GREAT SYMBOL HAS NO POWER IN GOTHAM ANYMORE.
WHIRRRR

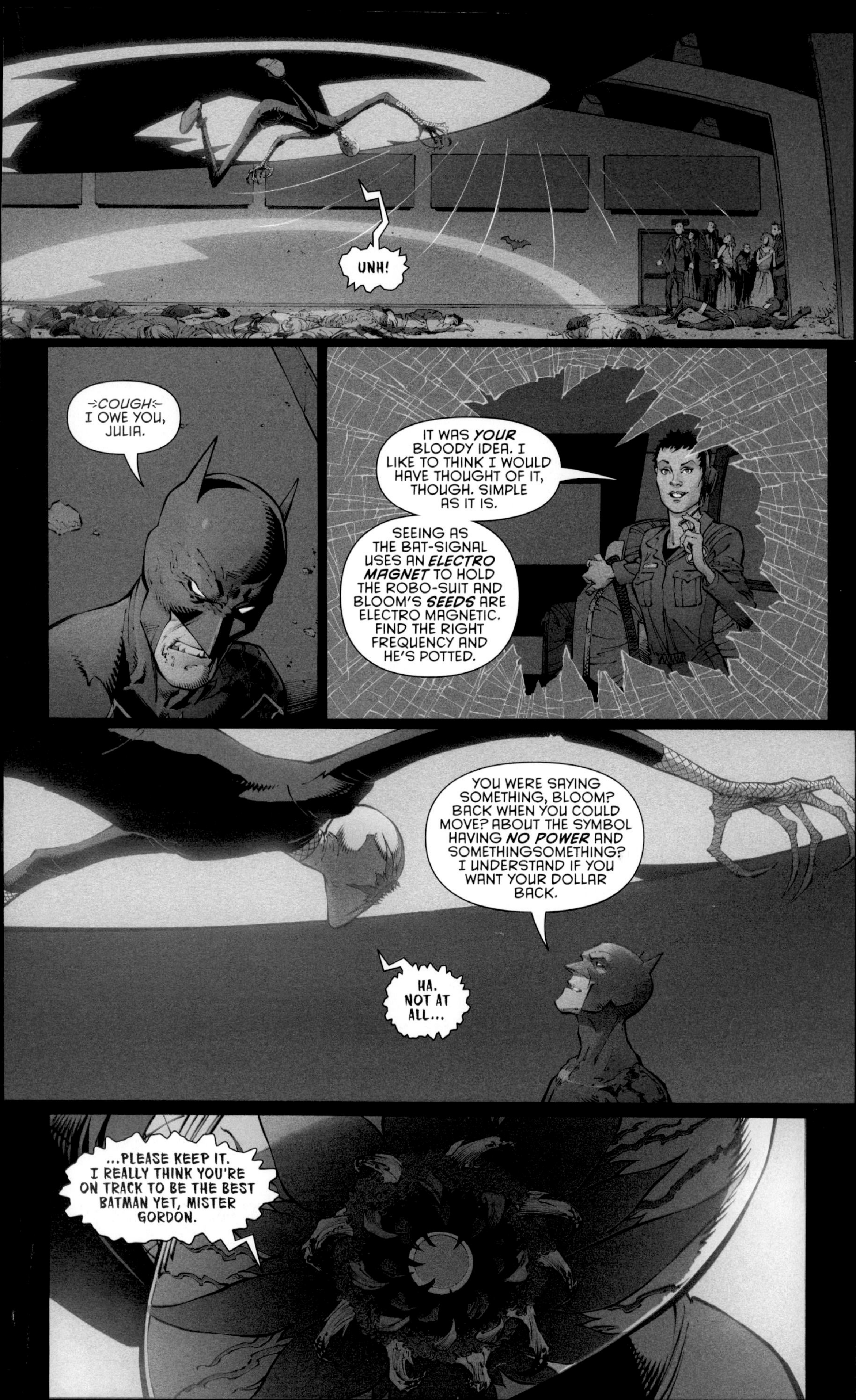
UNH!
-COUGH- I OWE YOU, JULIA.
IT WAS YOUR BLOODY IDEA. I LIKE TO THINK I WOULD HAVE THOUGHT OF IT, THOUGH. SIMPLE AS IT IS.
SEEING AS THE BAT-SIGNAL USES AN ELECTRO MAGNET TO HOLD THE ROBO-SUIT AND BLOOM'S SEEDS ARE ELECTRO MAGNETIC. FIND THE RIGHT FREQUENCY AND HE'S POTTED.
YOU WERE SAYING SOMETHING, BLOOM? BACK WHEN YOU COULD MOVE? ABOUT THE SYMBOL HAVING NO POWER AND SOMETHINGSOMETHING? I UNDERSTAND IF YOU WANT YOUR DOLLAR BACK.
HA. NOT AT ALL...
...PLEASE KEEP IT. I REALLY THINK YOU'RE ON TRACK TO BE THE BEST BATMAN YET, MISTER GORDON.

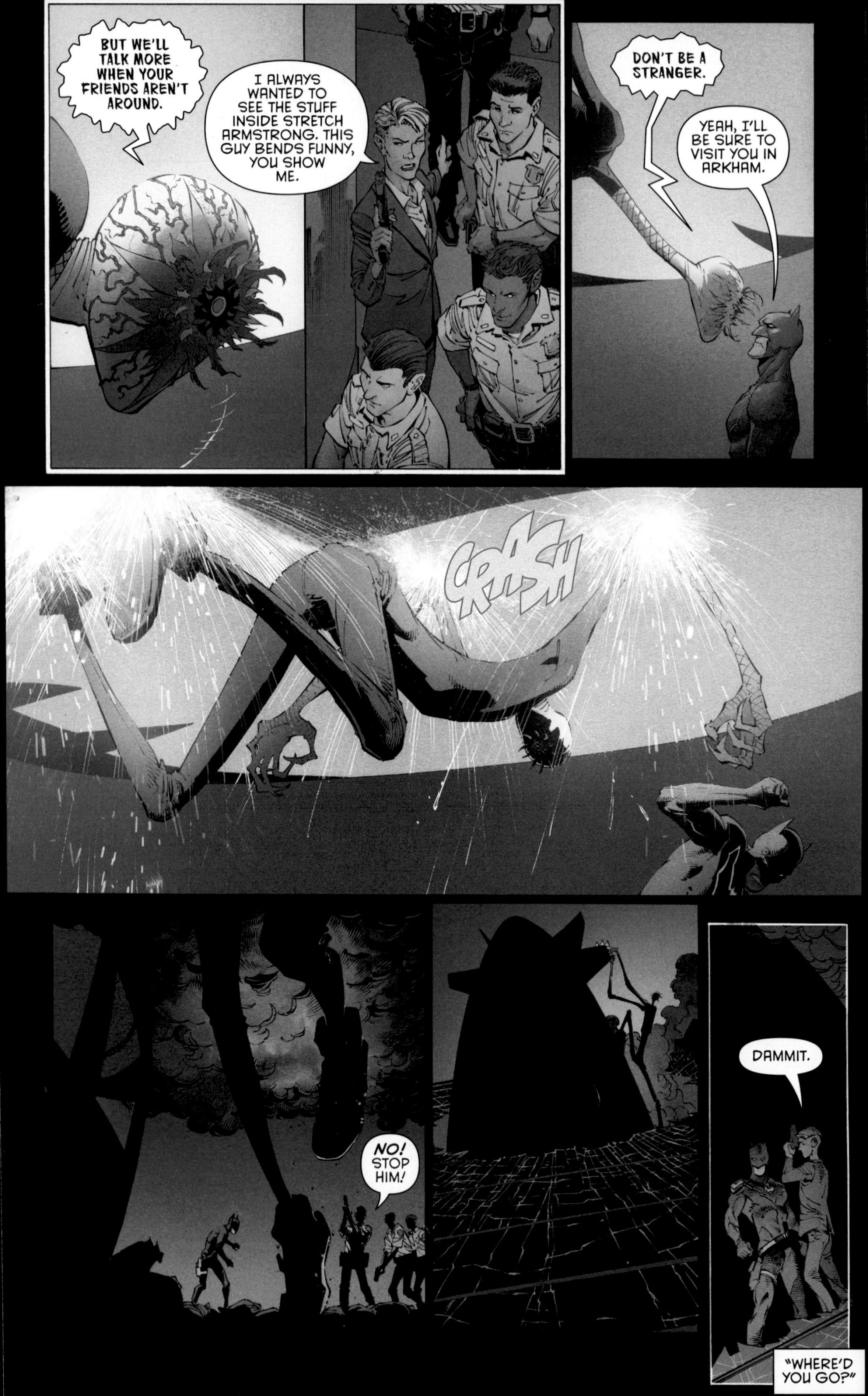
BUT WE'LL TALK MORE WHEN YOUR FRIENDS AREN'T AROUND.
I ALWAYS WANTED TO SEE THE STUFF INSIDE STRETCH ARMSTRONG. THIS GUY BENDS FUNNY, YOU SHOW ME.
DON'T BE A STRANGER.
YEAH, I'LL BE SURE TO VISIT YOU IN ARKHAM.
CRASH
NO! STOP HIM!
DAMMIT.
"WHERE'D YOU GO?"

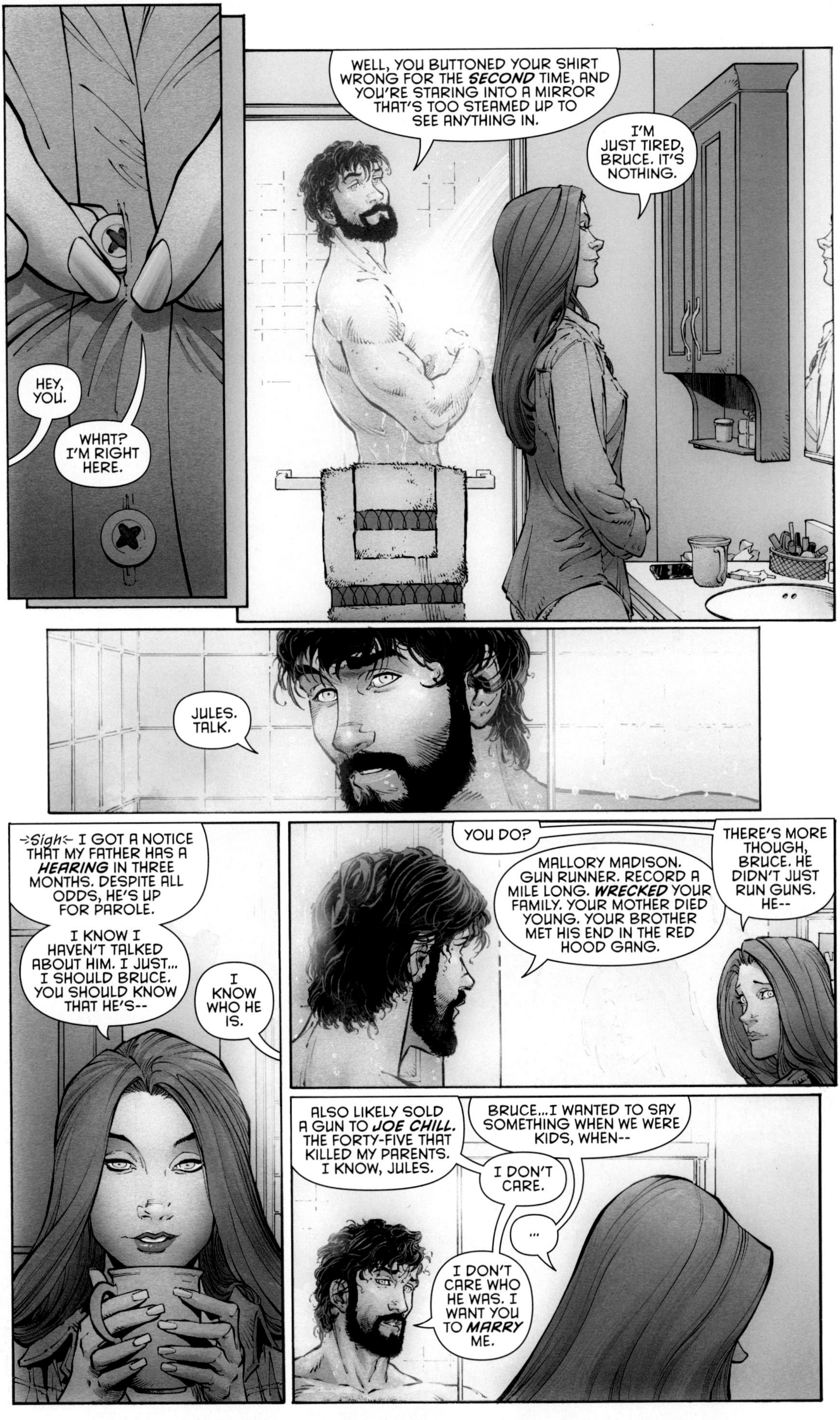
HEY, YOU.
WHAT? I'M RIGHT HERE.
WELL, YOU BUTTONED YOUR SHIRT WRONG FOR THE SECOND TIME, AND YOU'RE STARING INTO A MIRROR THAT'S TOO STEAMED UP TO SEE ANYTHING IN.
I'M JUST TIRED, BRUCE. IT'S NOTHING.
JULES. TALK.
Sigh I GOT A NOTICE THAT MY FATHER HAS A HEARING IN THREE MONTHS. DESPITE ALL ODDS, HE'S UP FOR PAROLE.
I KNOW I HAVEN'T TALKED ABOUT HIM. I JUST... I SHOULD BRUCE. YOU SHOULD KNOW THAT HE'S--
I KNOW WHO HE IS.
YOU DO?
MALLORY MADISON. GUN RUNNER. RECORD A MILE LONG. WRECKED YOUR FAMILY. YOUR MOTHER DIED YOUNG. YOUR BROTHER MET HIS END IN THE RED HOOD GANG.
THERE'S MORE THOUGH, BRUCE. HE DIDN'T JUST RUN GUNS. HE--
ALSO LIKELY SOLD A GUN TO JOE CHILL. THE FORTY-FIVE THAT KILLED MY PARENTS. I KNOW, JULES.
BRUCE...I WANTED TO SAY SOMETHING WHEN WE WERE KIDS, WHEN--
I DON'T CARE.
...
I DON'T CARE WHO HE WAS. I WANT YOU TO MARRY ME.

...MARRY?

YOU'RE ACTING CRAZY. JUST THE OTHER DAY YOU SEEMED *UNSURE* ABOUT EVERYTHING. THE CENTER, ME, ALL OF IT.

I'M *NOT* ANYMORE. LISTEN TO ME.

WHEN I WAS FOUND, ALFRED THOUGHT IT WAS SOME KIND OF CIRCLE *CLOSING.* HE KEPT SAYING SO. BUT MAYBE...IT IS. YOUR FATHER, MY *PARENTS,* ALL OF IT. IT FEELS RIGHT, JULES. LIKE A WAY OUT.

NOW, I LOST ALL THESE YEARS OF MY LIFE. I DON'T WANT TO LOSE ANYMORE. SO IN THREE MONTHS, WHEN YOUR FATHER IS UP FOR PAROLE...

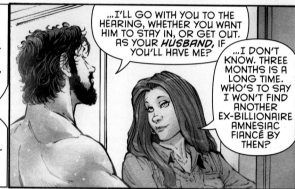

...I'LL GO WITH YOU TO THE HEARING, WHETHER YOU WANT HIM TO STAY IN, OR GET OUT. AS YOUR *HUSBAND,* IF YOU'LL HAVE ME?

...I DON'T KNOW. THREE MONTHS IS A LONG TIME. WHO'S TO SAY I WON'T FIND ANOTHER EX-BILLIONAIRE AMNESIAC FIANCÉ BY THEN?

Heh. COME HERE.

"THAT'S NOT SUPPOSED TO HAPPEN AROUND HERE..."

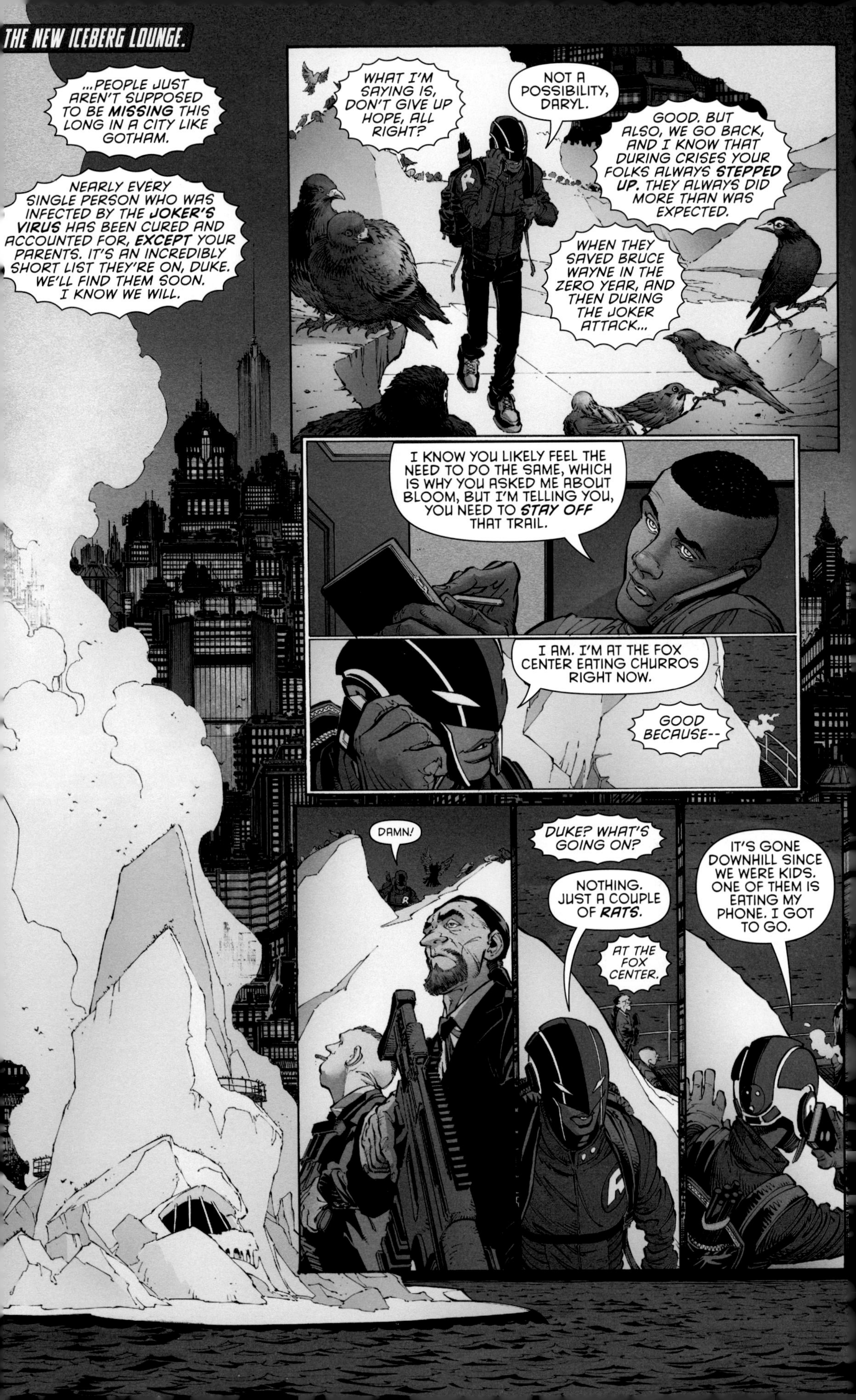
THE NEW ICEBERG LOUNGE.
...PEOPLE JUST AREN'T SUPPOSED TO BE MISSING THIS LONG IN A CITY LIKE GOTHAM.
NEARLY EVERY SINGLE PERSON WHO WAS INFECTED BY THE JOKER'S VIRUS HAS BEEN CURED AND ACCOUNTED FOR, EXCEPT YOUR PARENTS. IT'S AN INCREDIBLY SHORT LIST THEY'RE ON, DUKE. WE'LL FIND THEM SOON. I KNOW WE WILL.
WHAT I'M SAYING IS, DON'T GIVE UP HOPE, ALL RIGHT?
NOT A POSSIBILITY, DARYL.
GOOD. BUT ALSO, WE GO BACK, AND I KNOW THAT DURING CRISES YOUR FOLKS ALWAYS STEPPED UP. THEY ALWAYS DID MORE THAN WAS EXPECTED.
WHEN THEY SAVED BRUCE WAYNE IN THE ZERO YEAR, AND THEN DURING THE JOKER ATTACK...
I KNOW YOU LIKELY FEEL THE NEED TO DO THE SAME, WHICH IS WHY YOU ASKED ME ABOUT BLOOM, BUT I'M TELLING YOU, YOU NEED TO STAY OFF THAT TRAIL.
I AM. I'M AT THE FOX CENTER EATING CHURROS RIGHT NOW.
GOOD BECAUSE--
DAMN!
DUKE? WHAT'S GOING ON?
NOTHING. JUST A COUPLE OF RATS.
AT THE FOX CENTER.
IT'S GONE DOWNHILL SINCE WE WERE KIDS. ONE OF THEM IS EATING MY PHONE. I GOT TO GO.

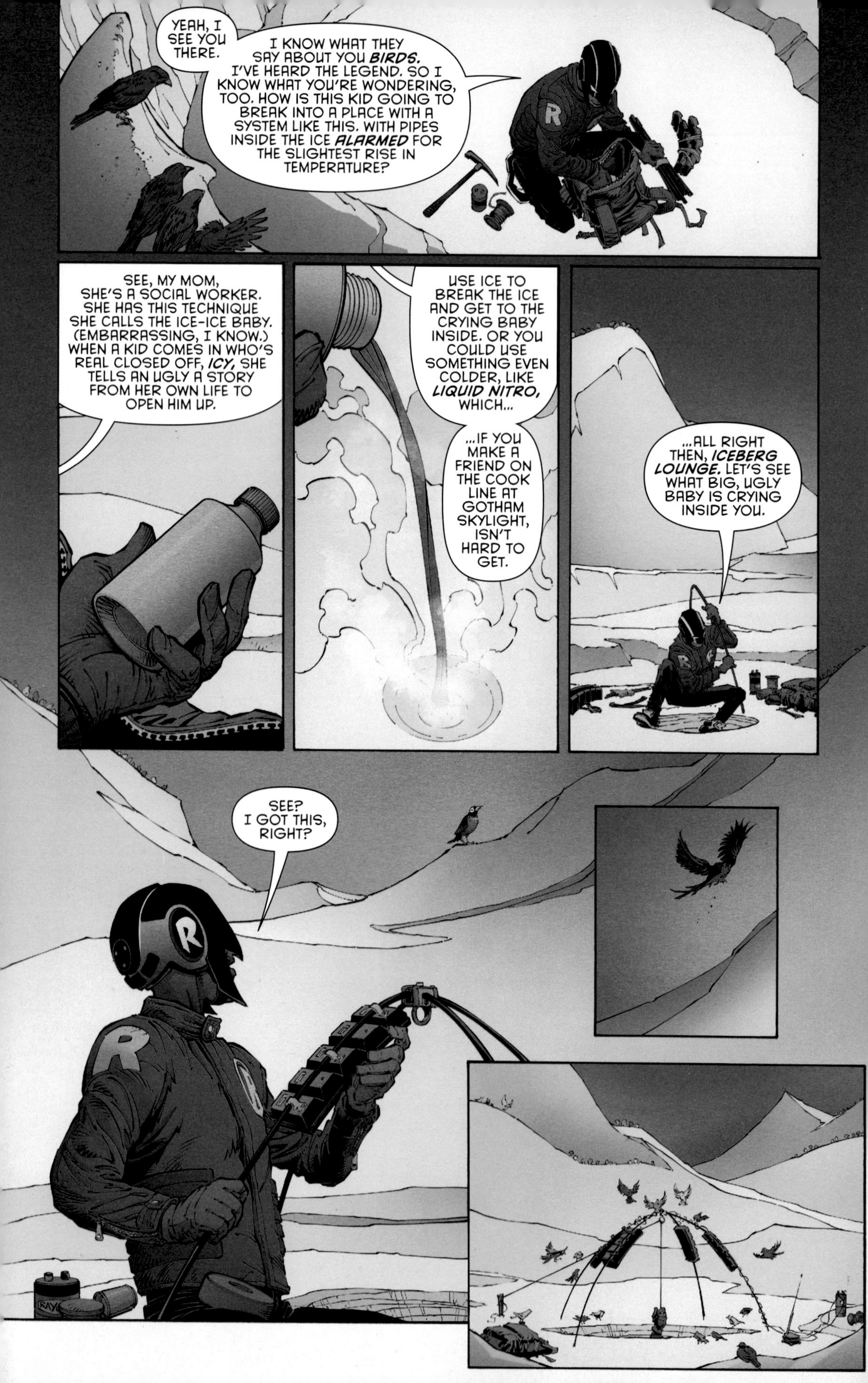
YEAH, I SEE YOU THERE.
I KNOW WHAT THEY SAY ABOUT YOU BIRDS. I'VE HEARD THE LEGEND. SO I KNOW WHAT YOU'RE WONDERING, TOO. HOW IS THIS KID GOING TO BREAK INTO A PLACE WITH A SYSTEM LIKE THIS. WITH PIPES INSIDE THE ICE ALARMED FOR THE SLIGHTEST RISE IN TEMPERATURE?
SEE, MY MOM, SHE'S A SOCIAL WORKER. SHE HAS THIS TECHNIQUE SHE CALLS THE ICE-ICE BABY. (EMBARRASSING, I KNOW.) WHEN A KID COMES IN WHO'S REAL CLOSED OFF, ICY, SHE TELLS AN UGLY A STORY FROM HER OWN LIFE TO OPEN HIM UP.
USE ICE TO BREAK THE ICE AND GET TO THE CRYING BABY INSIDE. OR YOU COULD USE SOMETHING EVEN COLDER, LIKE LIQUID NITRO, WHICH...
...IF YOU MAKE A FRIEND ON THE COOK LINE AT GOTHAM SKYLIGHT, ISN'T HARD TO GET.
...ALL RIGHT THEN, ICEBERG LOUNGE. LET'S SEE WHAT BIG, UGLY BABY IS CRYING INSIDE YOU.
SEE? I GOT THIS, RIGHT?

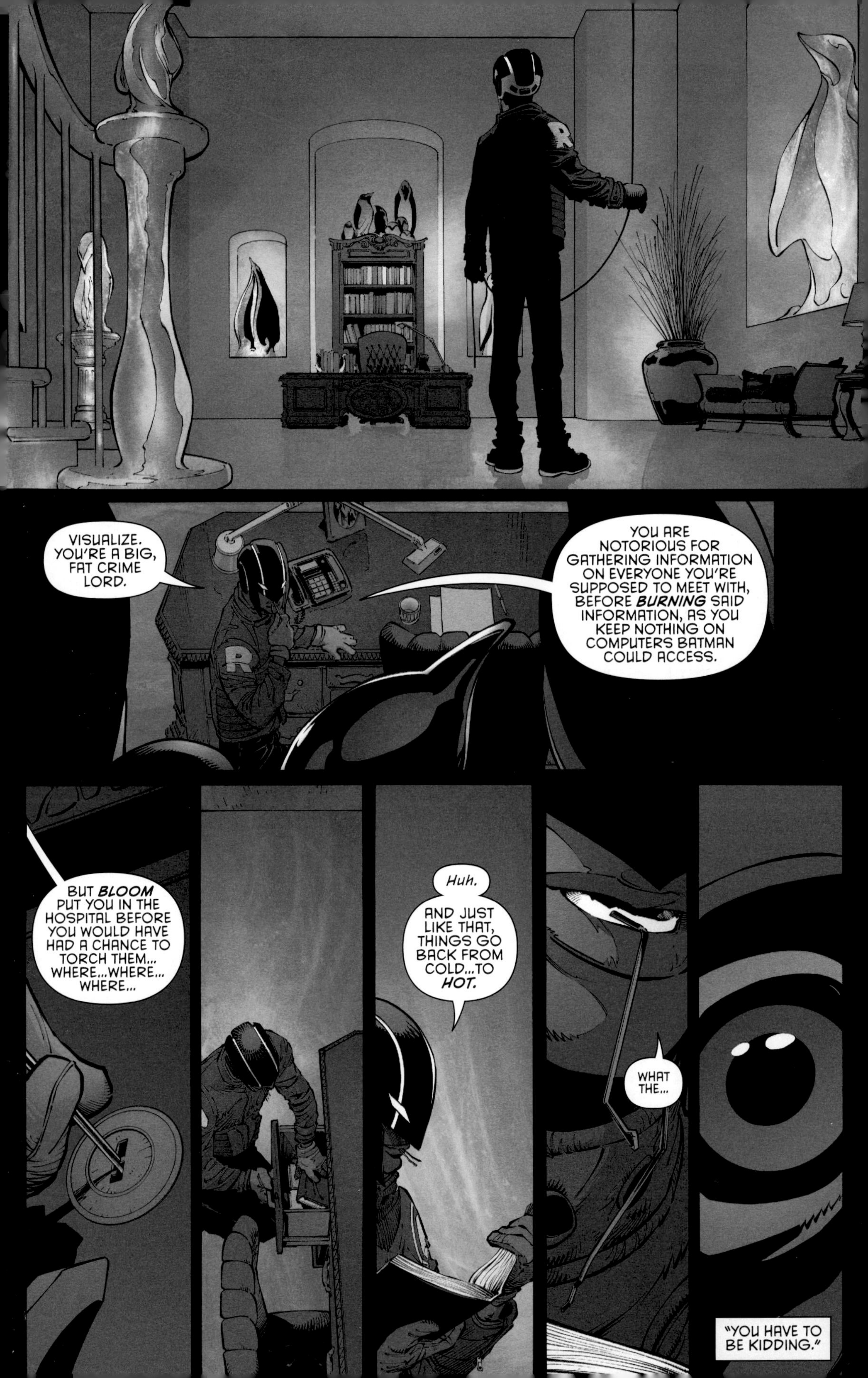
VISUALIZE. YOU'RE A BIG, FAT CRIME LORD.
YOU ARE NOTORIOUS FOR GATHERING INFORMATION ON EVERYONE YOU'RE SUPPOSED TO MEET WITH, BEFORE **BURNING** SAID INFORMATION, AS YOU KEEP NOTHING ON COMPUTERS BATMAN COULD ACCESS.
BUT **BLOOM** PUT YOU IN THE HOSPITAL BEFORE YOU WOULD HAVE HAD A CHANCE TO TORCH THEM... WHERE...WHERE... WHERE...
Huh.
AND JUST LIKE THAT, THINGS GO BACK FROM COLD...TO ***HOT.***
WHAT THE...
"YOU HAVE TO BE KIDDING."

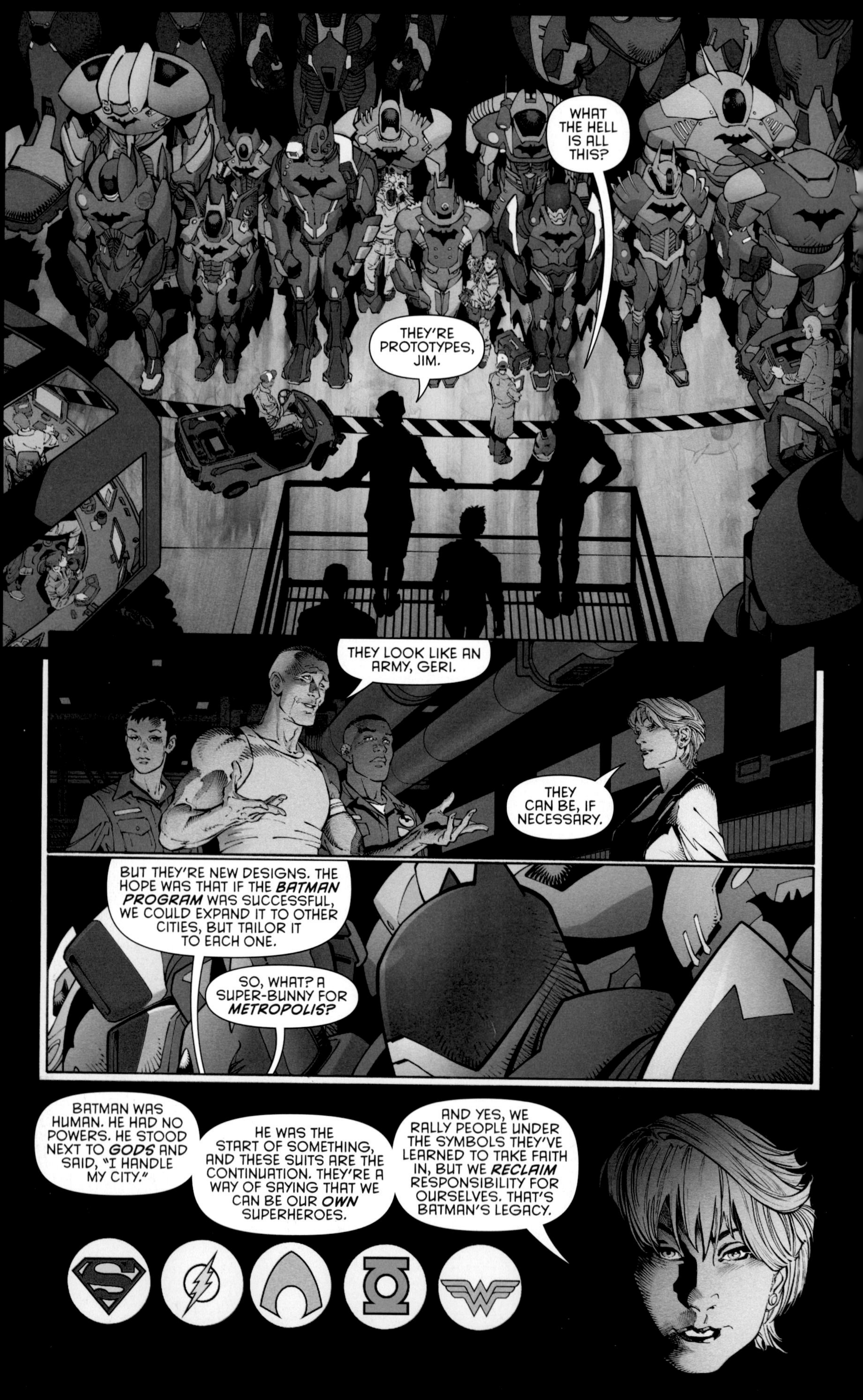
WHAT THE HELL IS ALL THIS?
THEY'RE PROTOTYPES, JIM.
THEY LOOK LIKE AN ARMY, GERI.
THEY CAN BE, IF NECESSARY.
BUT THEY'RE NEW DESIGNS. THE HOPE WAS THAT IF THE *BATMAN PROGRAM* WAS SUCCESSFUL, WE COULD EXPAND IT TO OTHER CITIES, BUT TAILOR IT TO EACH ONE.
SO, WHAT? A SUPER-BUNNY FOR *METROPOLIS?*
BATMAN WAS HUMAN. HE HAD NO POWERS. HE STOOD NEXT TO *GODS* AND SAID, "I HANDLE MY CITY."
HE WAS THE START OF SOMETHING, AND THESE SUITS ARE THE CONTINUATION. THEY'RE A WAY OF SAYING THAT WE CAN BE OUR *OWN* SUPERHEROES.
AND YES, WE RALLY PEOPLE UNDER THE SYMBOLS THEY'VE LEARNED TO TAKE FAITH IN, BUT WE *RECLAIM* RESPONSIBILITY FOR OURSELVES. THAT'S BATMAN'S LEGACY.

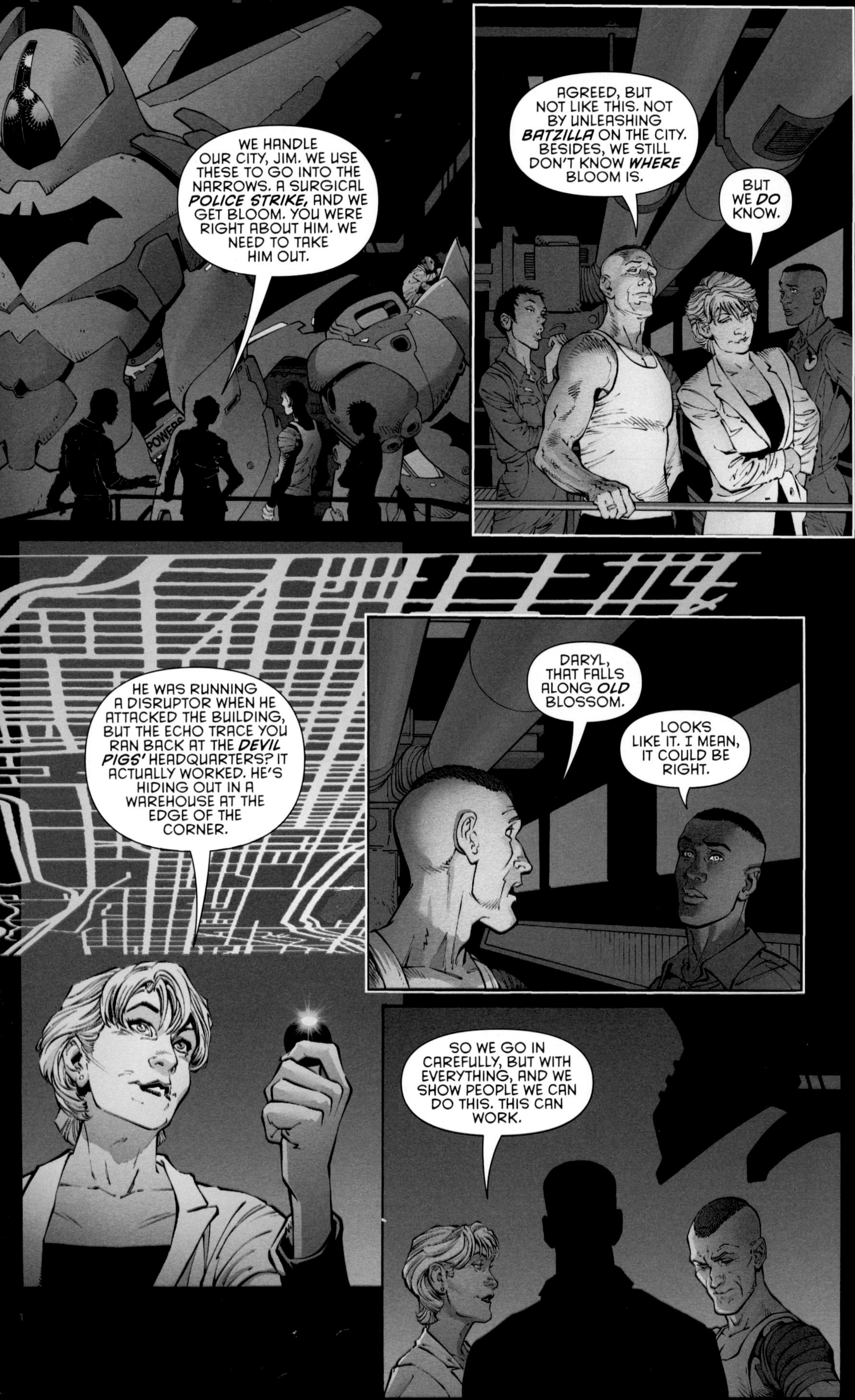
WE HANDLE OUR CITY, JIM. WE USE THESE TO GO INTO THE NARROWS. A SURGICAL POLICE STRIKE, AND WE GET BLOOM. YOU WERE RIGHT ABOUT HIM. WE NEED TO TAKE HIM OUT.
POWERS
AGREED, BUT NOT LIKE THIS. NOT BY UNLEASHING BATZILLA ON THE CITY. BESIDES, WE STILL DON'T KNOW WHERE BLOOM IS.
BUT WE DO KNOW.
HE WAS RUNNING A DISRUPTOR WHEN HE ATTACKED THE BUILDING, BUT THE ECHO TRACE YOU RAN BACK AT THE DEVIL PIGS' HEADQUARTERS? IT ACTUALLY WORKED. HE'S HIDING OUT IN A WAREHOUSE AT THE EDGE OF THE CORNER.
DARYL, THAT FALLS ALONG OLD BLOSSOM.
LOOKS LIKE IT. I MEAN, IT COULD BE RIGHT.
SO WE GO IN CAREFULLY, BUT WITH EVERYTHING, AND WE SHOW PEOPLE WE CAN DO THIS. THIS CAN WORK.

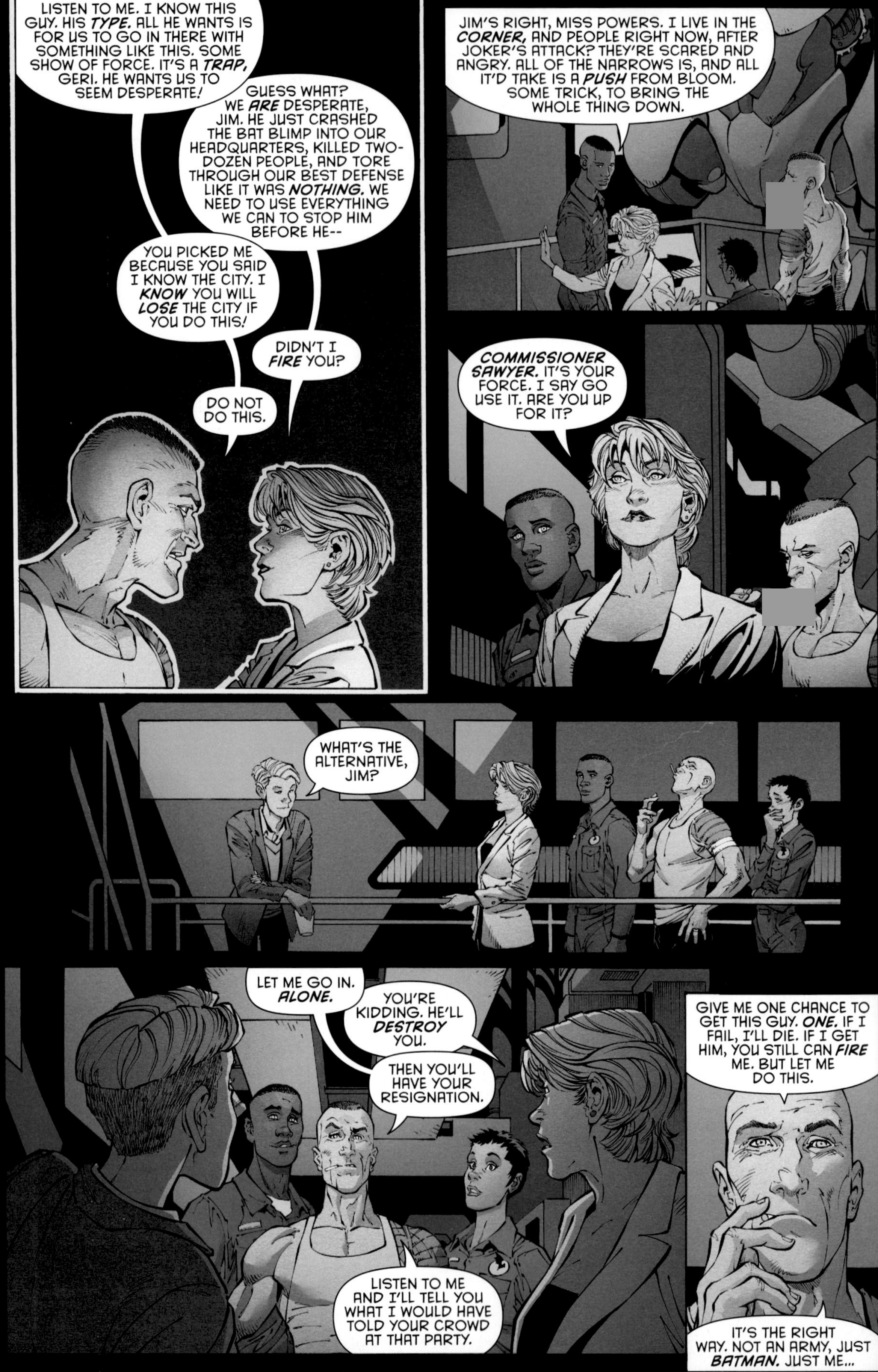
LISTEN TO ME. I KNOW THIS GUY. HIS TYPE. ALL HE WANTS IS FOR US TO GO IN THERE WITH SOMETHING LIKE THIS. SOME SHOW OF FORCE. IT'S A TRAP, GERI. HE WANTS US TO SEEM DESPERATE!
GUESS WHAT? WE ARE DESPERATE, JIM. HE JUST CRASHED THE BAT BLIMP INTO OUR HEADQUARTERS, KILLED TWO-DOZEN PEOPLE, AND TORE THROUGH OUR BEST DEFENSE LIKE IT WAS NOTHING. WE NEED TO USE EVERYTHING WE CAN TO STOP HIM BEFORE HE--
YOU PICKED ME BECAUSE YOU SAID I KNOW THE CITY. I KNOW YOU WILL LOSE THE CITY IF YOU DO THIS!
DIDN'T I FIRE YOU?
DO NOT DO THIS.
JIM'S RIGHT, MISS POWERS. I LIVE IN THE CORNER, AND PEOPLE RIGHT NOW, AFTER JOKER'S ATTACK? THEY'RE SCARED AND ANGRY. ALL OF THE NARROWS IS, AND ALL IT'D TAKE IS A PUSH FROM BLOOM. SOME TRICK, TO BRING THE WHOLE THING DOWN.
COMMISSIONER SAWYER. IT'S YOUR FORCE. I SAY GO USE IT. ARE YOU UP FOR IT?
WHAT'S THE ALTERNATIVE, JIM?
LET ME GO IN. ALONE.
YOU'RE KIDDING. HE'LL DESTROY YOU.
THEN YOU'LL HAVE YOUR RESIGNATION.
LISTEN TO ME AND I'LL TELL YOU WHAT I WOULD HAVE TOLD YOUR CROWD AT THAT PARTY.
GIVE ME ONE CHANCE TO GET THIS GUY. ONE. IF I FAIL, I'LL DIE. IF I GET HIM, YOU STILL CAN FIRE ME. BUT LET ME DO THIS.
IT'S THE RIGHT WAY. NOT AN ARMY, JUST BATMAN. JUST ME...

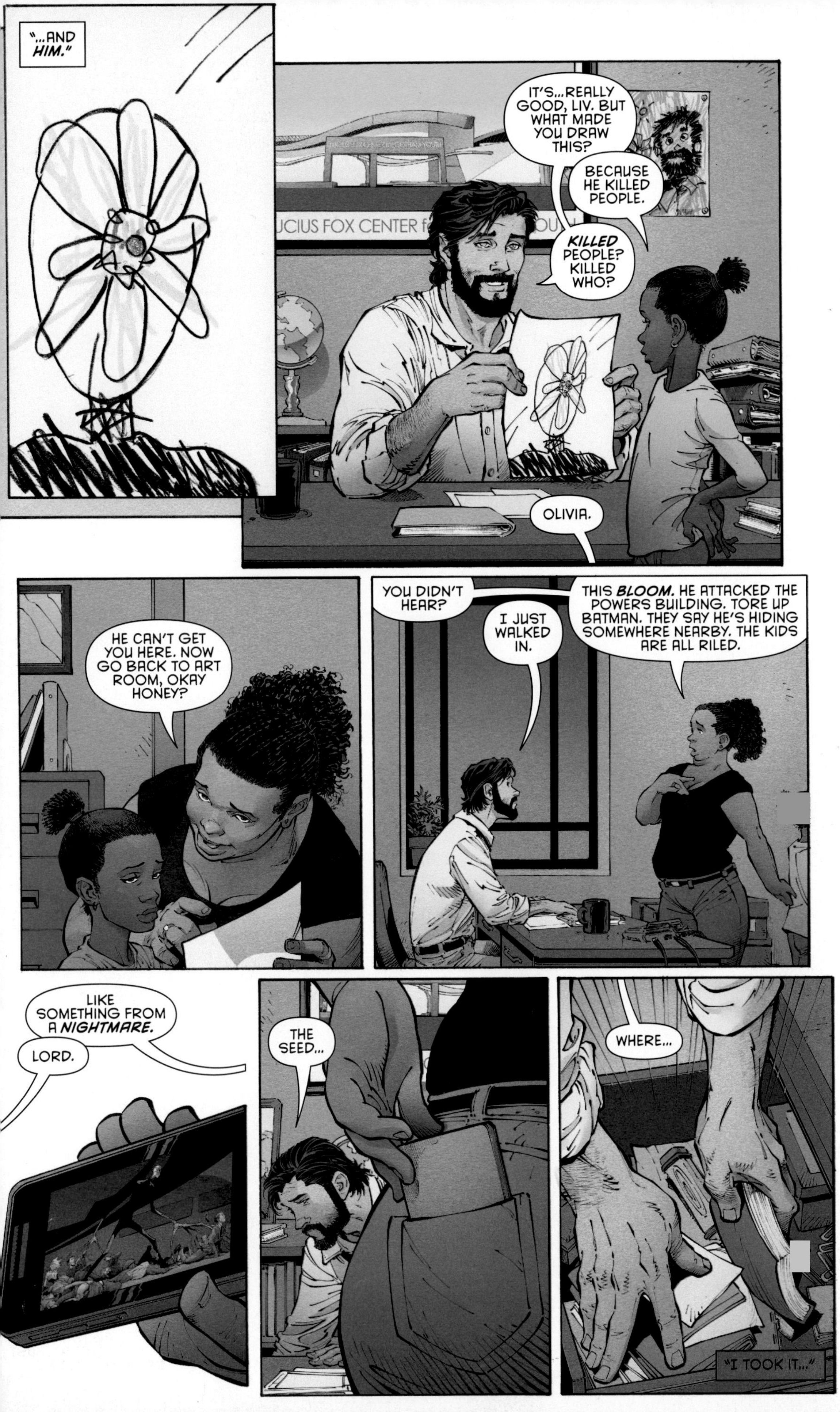
"...AND HIM."
IT'S...REALLY GOOD, LIV. BUT WHAT MADE YOU DRAW THIS?
BECAUSE HE KILLED PEOPLE.
KILLED PEOPLE? KILLED WHO?
OLIVIA.
UCIUS FOX CENTER f
HE CAN'T GET YOU HERE. NOW GO BACK TO ART ROOM, OKAY HONEY?
YOU DIDN'T HEAR?
I JUST WALKED IN.
THIS BLOOM. HE ATTACKED THE POWERS BUILDING. TORE UP BATMAN. THEY SAY HE'S HIDING SOMEWHERE NEARBY. THE KIDS ARE ALL RILED.
LIKE SOMETHING FROM A NIGHTMARE.
LORD.
THE SEED...
WHERE...
"I TOOK IT..."

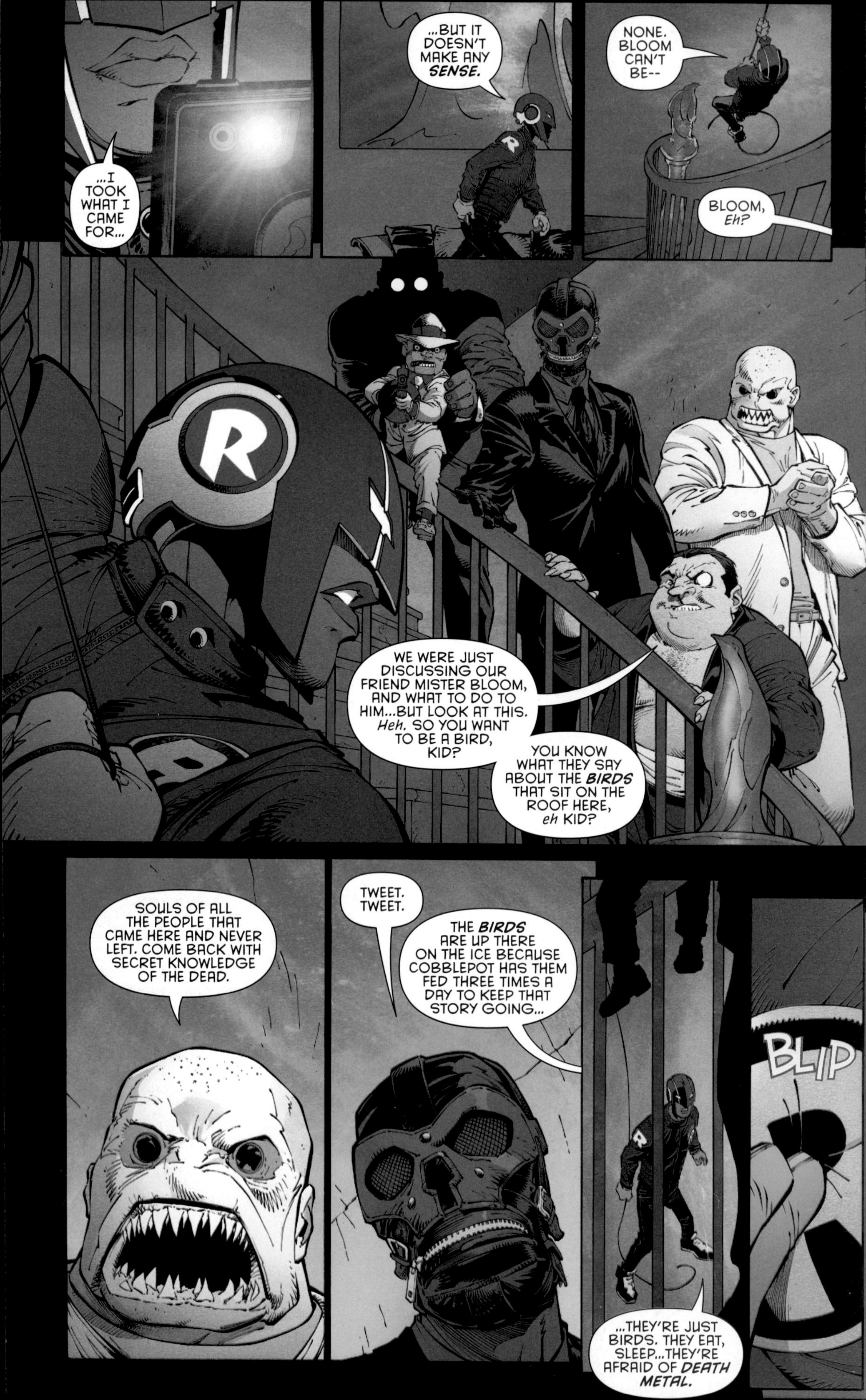
...I TOOK WHAT I CAME FOR...
...BUT IT DOESN'T MAKE ANY *SENSE.*
NONE. BLOOM CAN'T BE--
BLOOM, *Eh?*
WE WERE JUST DISCUSSING OUR FRIEND MISTER BLOOM, AND WHAT TO DO TO HIM...BUT LOOK AT THIS. *Heh.* SO YOU WANT TO BE A BIRD, KID?
YOU KNOW WHAT THEY SAY ABOUT THE *BIRDS* THAT SIT ON THE ROOF HERE, *eh* KID?
SOULS OF ALL THE PEOPLE THAT CAME HERE AND NEVER LEFT. COME BACK WITH SECRET KNOWLEDGE OF THE DEAD.
TWEET. TWEET.
THE *BIRDS* ARE UP THERE ON THE ICE BECAUSE COBBLEPOT HAS THEM FED THREE TIMES A DAY TO KEEP THAT STORY GOING...
...THEY'RE JUST BIRDS. THEY EAT, SLEEP...THEY'RE AFRAID OF *DEATH METAL.*
BLIP

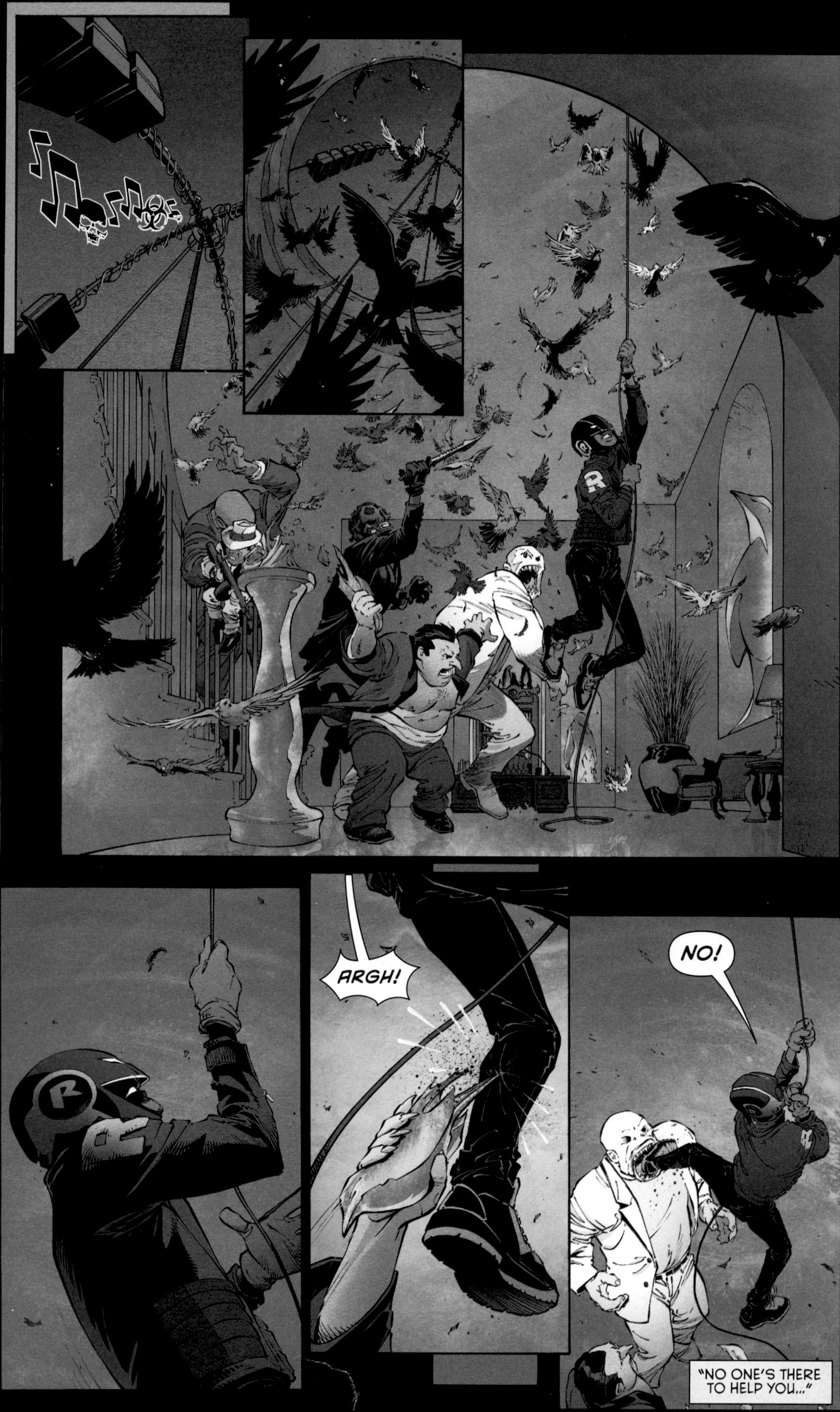
ARGH!
NO!
"NO ONE'S THERE TO HELP YOU..."

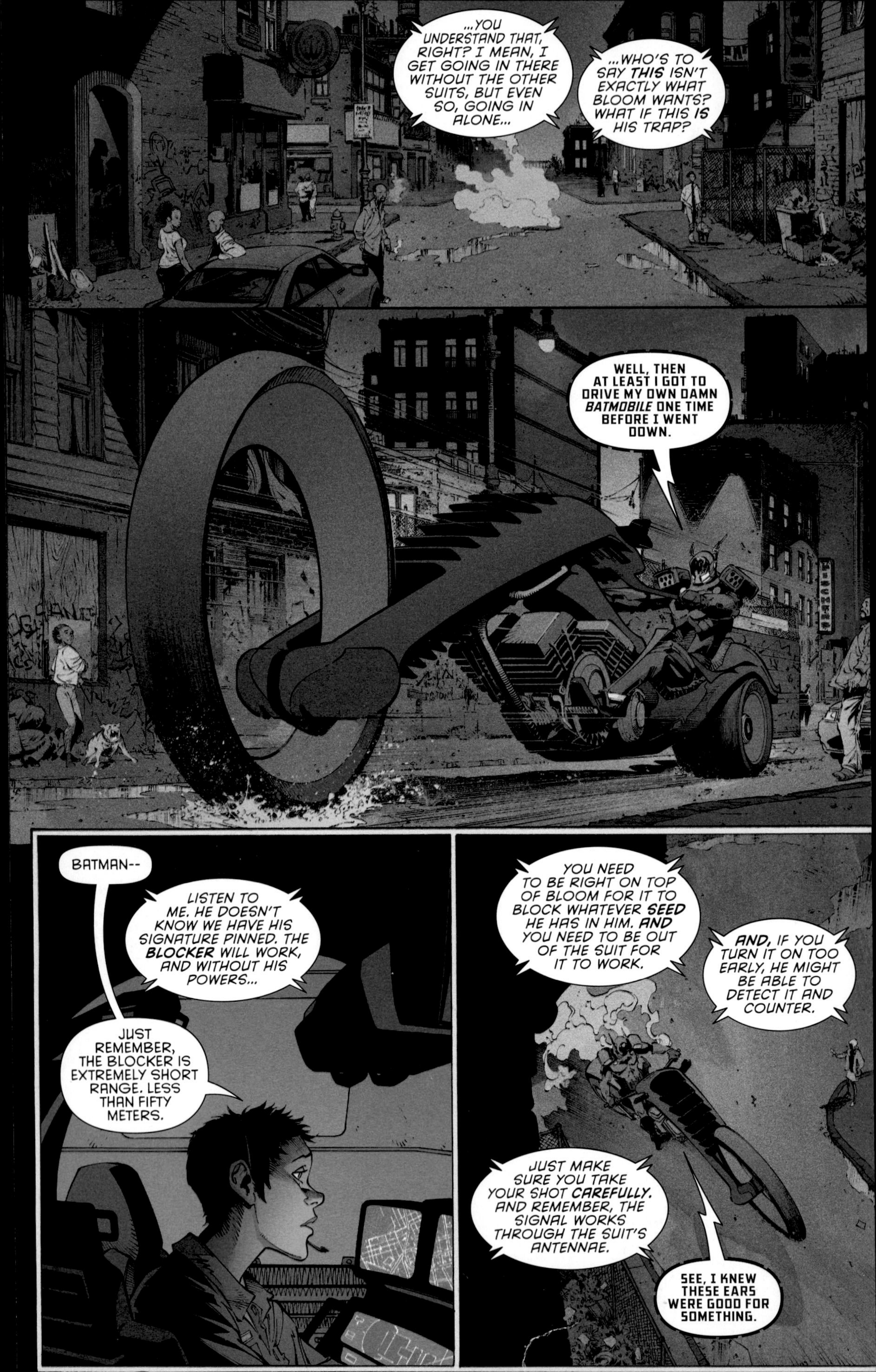
...YOU UNDERSTAND THAT, RIGHT? I MEAN, I GET GOING IN THERE WITHOUT THE OTHER SUITS, BUT EVEN SO, GOING IN ALONE...
...WHO'S TO SAY **THIS** ISN'T EXACTLY WHAT BLOOM WANTS? WHAT IF THIS **IS** HIS TRAP?
WELL, THEN AT LEAST I GOT TO DRIVE MY OWN DAMN *BATMOBILE* ONE TIME BEFORE I WENT DOWN.
BATMAN--
LISTEN TO ME. HE DOESN'T KNOW WE HAVE HIS SIGNATURE PINNED. THE **BLOCKER** WILL WORK, AND WITHOUT HIS POWERS...
JUST REMEMBER, THE BLOCKER IS EXTREMELY SHORT RANGE. LESS THAN FIFTY METERS.
YOU NEED TO BE RIGHT ON TOP OF BLOOM FOR IT TO BLOCK WHATEVER **SEED** HE HAS IN HIM. **AND** YOU NEED TO BE OUT OF THE SUIT FOR IT TO WORK.
AND, IF YOU TURN IT ON TOO EARLY, HE MIGHT BE ABLE TO DETECT IT AND COUNTER.
JUST MAKE SURE YOU TAKE YOUR SHOT **CAREFULLY.** AND REMEMBER, THE SIGNAL WORKS THROUGH THE SUIT'S ANTENNAE.
SEE, I KNEW THESE EARS WERE GOOD FOR SOMETHING.

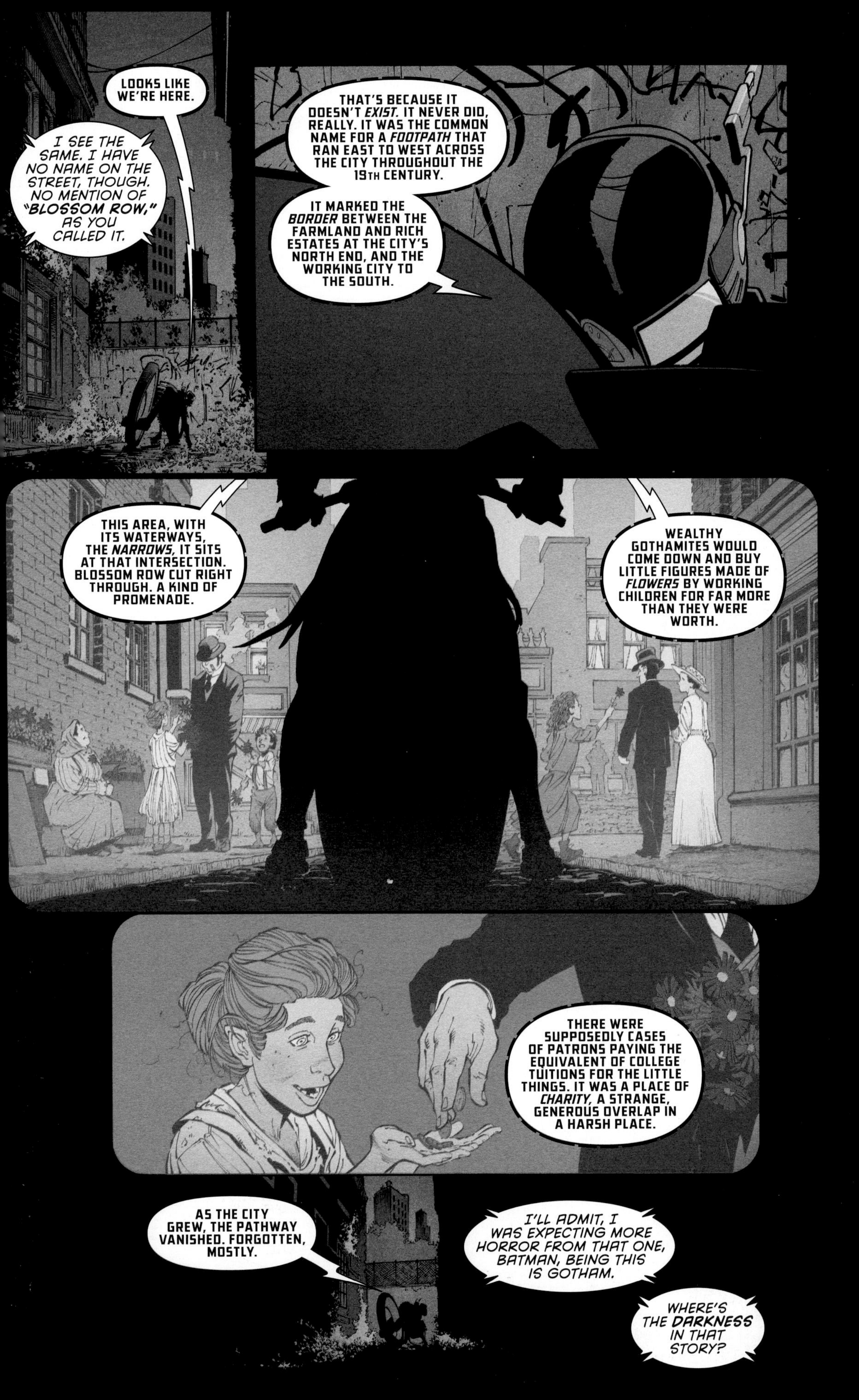
LOOKS LIKE WE'RE HERE.
I SEE THE SAME. I HAVE NO NAME ON THE STREET, THOUGH. NO MENTION OF "BLOSSOM ROW," AS YOU CALLED IT.
THAT'S BECAUSE IT DOESN'T *EXIST.* IT NEVER DID, REALLY. IT WAS THE COMMON NAME FOR A *FOOTPATH* THAT RAN EAST TO WEST ACROSS THE CITY THROUGHOUT THE 19TH CENTURY.
IT MARKED THE *BORDER* BETWEEN THE FARMLAND AND RICH ESTATES AT THE CITY'S NORTH END, AND THE WORKING CITY TO THE SOUTH.
THIS AREA, WITH ITS WATERWAYS, THE *NARROWS,* IT SITS AT THAT INTERSECTION. BLOSSOM ROW CUT RIGHT THROUGH. A KIND OF PROMENADE.
WEALTHY GOTHAMITES WOULD COME DOWN AND BUY LITTLE FIGURES MADE OF *FLOWERS* BY WORKING CHILDREN FOR FAR MORE THAN THEY WERE WORTH.
THERE WERE SUPPOSEDLY CASES OF PATRONS PAYING THE EQUIVALENT OF COLLEGE TUITIONS FOR THE LITTLE THINGS. IT WAS A PLACE OF *CHARITY,* A STRANGE, GENEROUS OVERLAP IN A HARSH PLACE.
AS THE CITY GREW, THE PATHWAY VANISHED. FORGOTTEN, MOSTLY.
I'LL ADMIT, I WAS EXPECTING MORE HORROR FROM THAT ONE, BATMAN, BEING THIS IS GOTHAM.
WHERE'S THE **DARKNESS** IN THAT STORY?

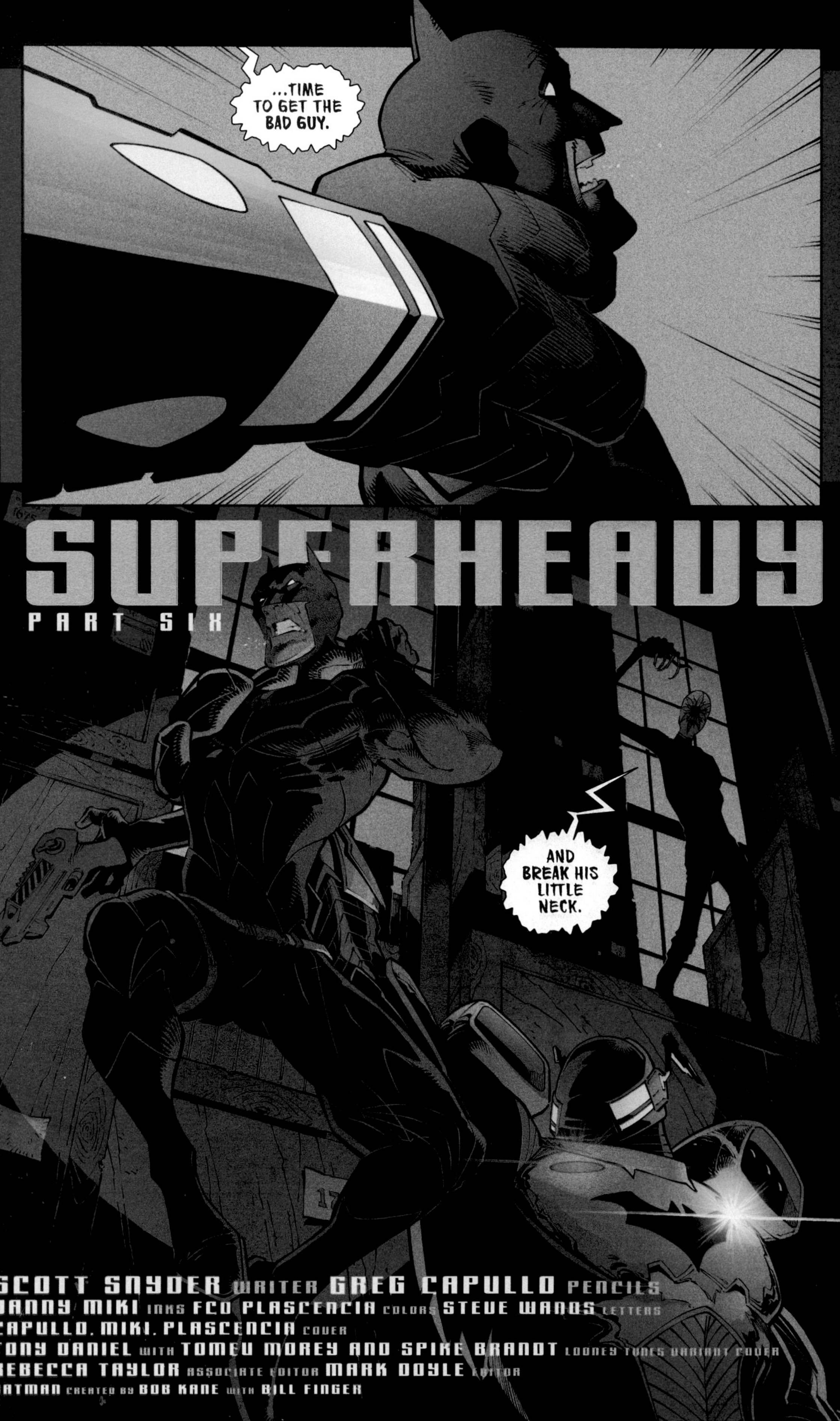
...TIME TO GET THE BAD GUY.
SUPERHEAVY
PART SIX
AND BREAK HIS LITTLE NECK.
SCOTT SNYDER WRITER GREG CAPULLO PENCILS
ANNY MIKI INKS FCO PLASCENCIA COLORS STEVE WANDS LETTERS
CAPULLO, MIKI, PLASCENCIA COVER
TONY DANIEL WITH TOMEU MOREY AND SPIKE BRANDT LOONEY TUNES VARIANT COVER
EBECCA TAYLOR ASSOCIATE EDITOR MARK DOYLE EDITOR
ATMAN CREATED BY BOB KANE WITH BILL FINGER

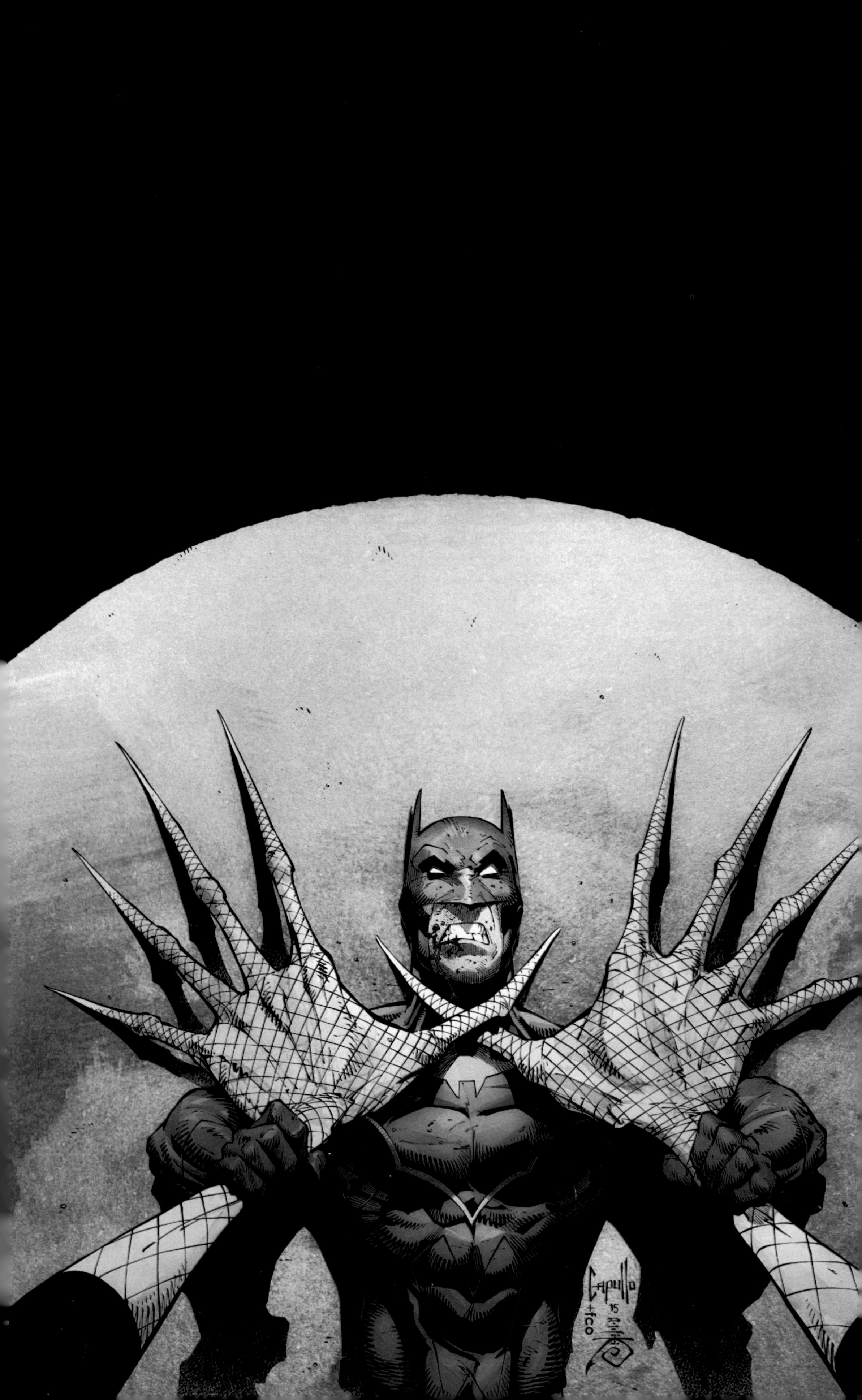

SCOTT SNYDER WRITER **GREG CAPULLO** PENCILS
DANNY MIKI INKS **FCO PLASCENCIA** COLORS **STEVE WANDS** LETTERS
CAPULLO, MIKI, PLASCENCIA COVER **ALEX ROSS** HARLEY'S LITTLE BLACK BOOK VARIANT COVER
REBECCA TAYLOR ASSOCIATE EDITOR **MARK DOYLE** EDITOR
BATMAN CREATED BY **BOB KANE** WITH **BILL FINGER**

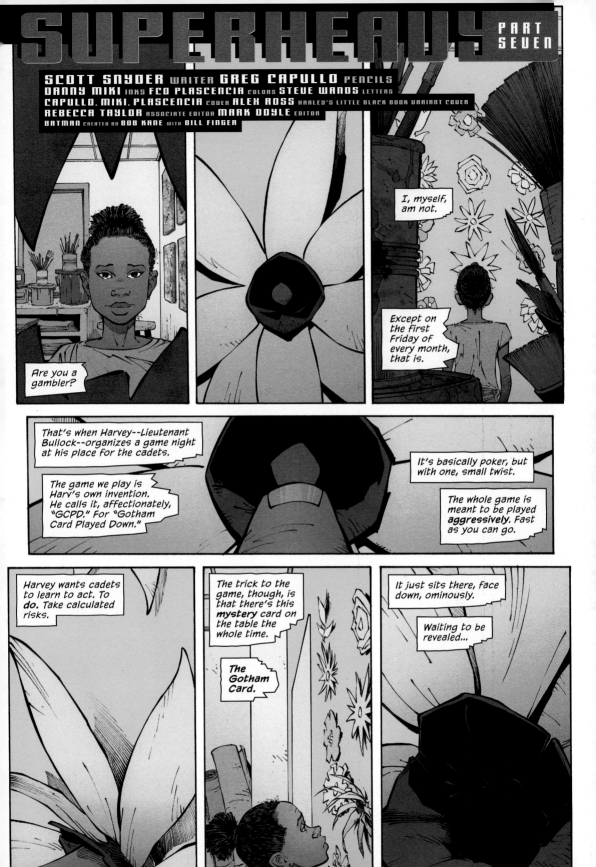

Are you a gambler?

I, myself, am not.

Except on the first Friday of every month, that is.

That's when Harvey--Lieutenant Bullock--organizes a game night at his place for the cadets.

The game we play is Harv's own invention. He calls it, affectionately, "GCPD." For "Gotham Card Played Down."

It's basically poker, but with one, small twist.

The whole game is meant to be played **aggressively**. Fast as you can go.

Harvey wants cadets to learn to act. To **do**. Take calculated risks.

The trick to the game, though, is that there's this **mystery** card on the table the whole time.

The Gotham Card.

It just sits there, face down, ominously.

Waiting to be revealed...

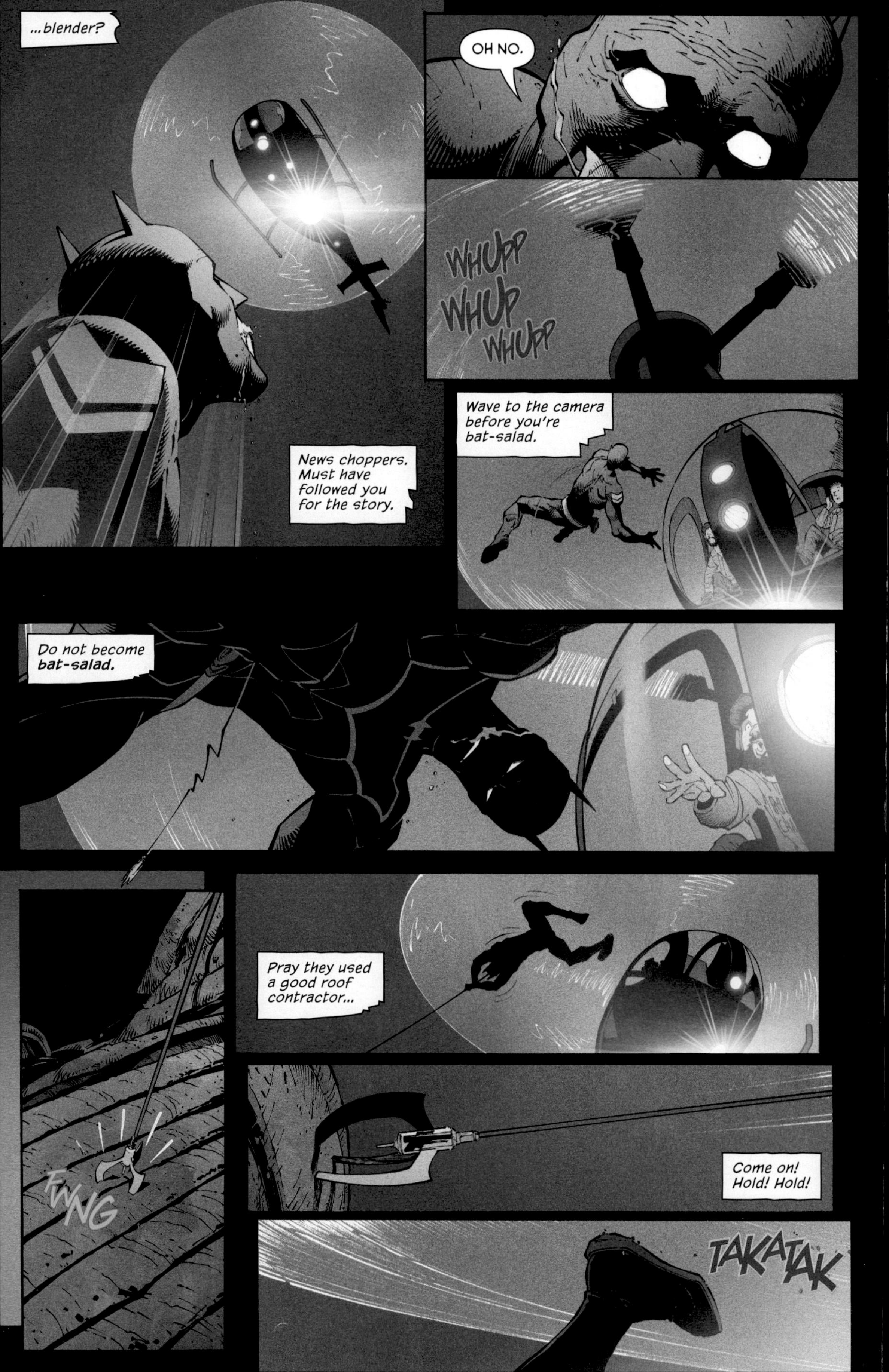
...blender?
OH NO.
WHUPP
WHUP
WHUPP
News choppers. Must have followed you for the story.
Wave to the camera before you're bat-salad.
Do not become **bat-salad.**
Pray they used a good roof contractor...
FWNG
Come on! Hold! Hold!
TAKATAK

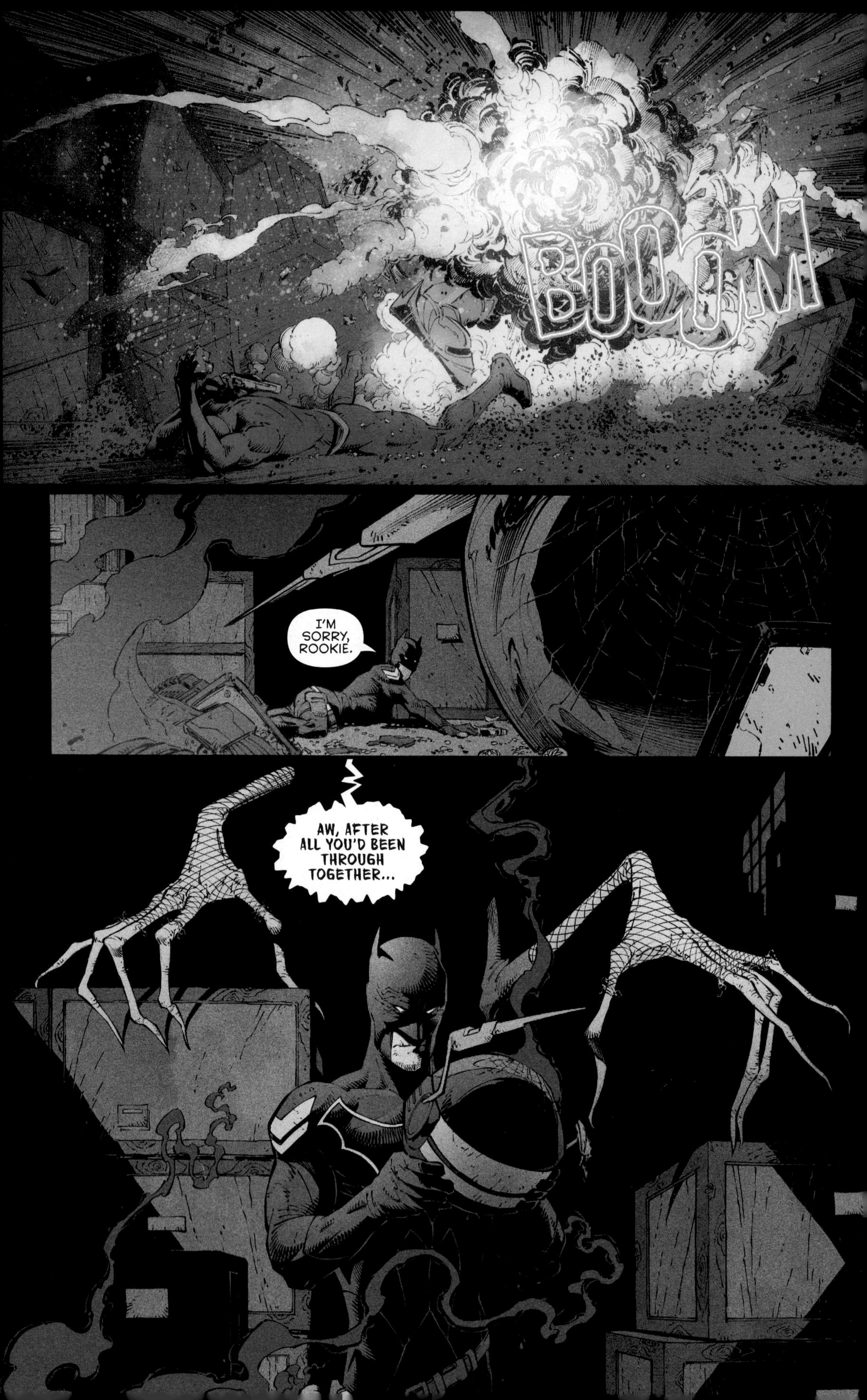
BOOOM
I'M SORRY, ROOKIE.
AW, AFTER ALL YOU'D BEEN THROUGH TOGETHER...

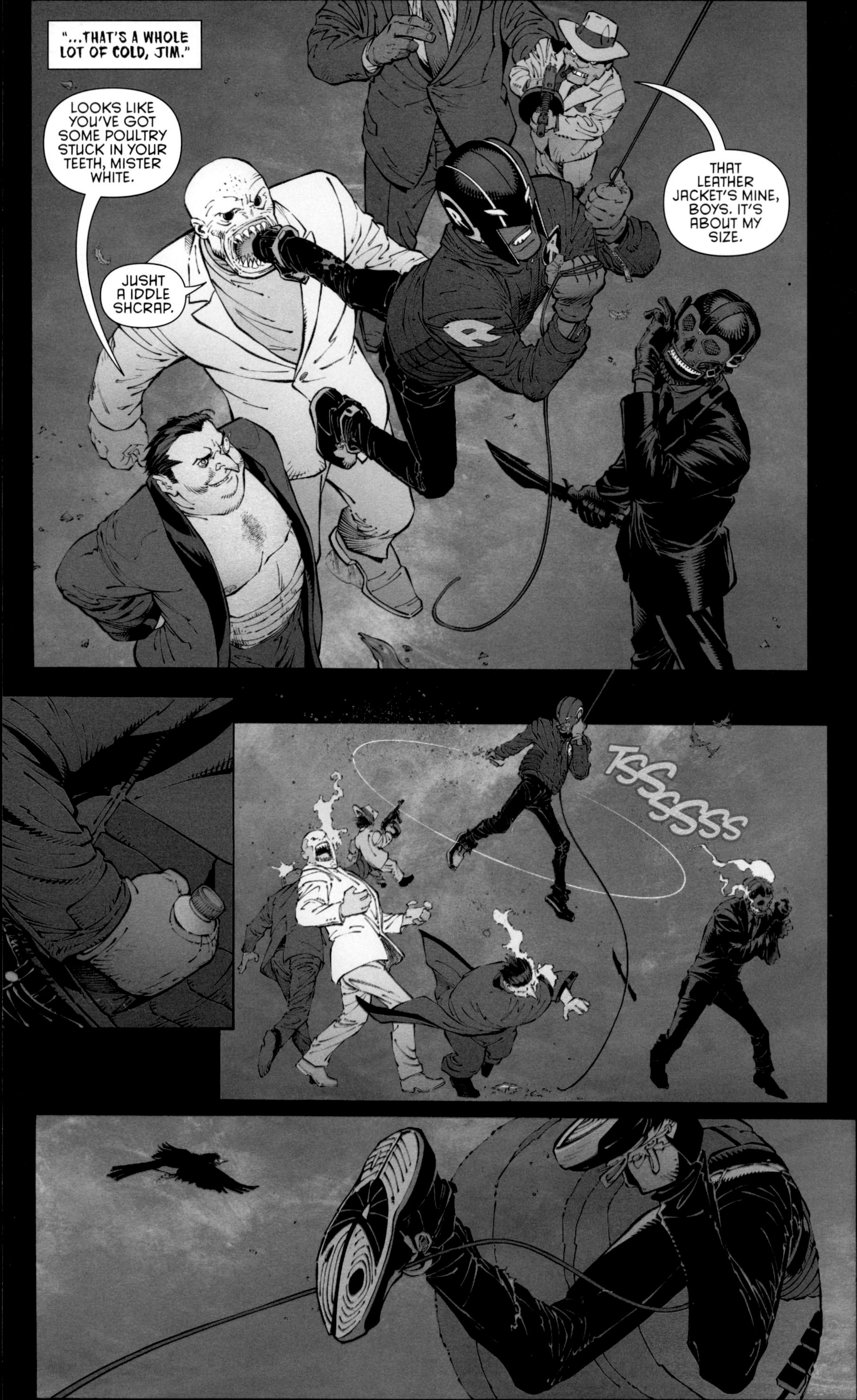
"...THAT'S A WHOLE LOT OF COLD, JIM."
LOOKS LIKE YOU'VE GOT SOME POULTRY STUCK IN YOUR TEETH, MISTER WHITE.
JUSHT A IDDLE SHCRAP.
THAT LEATHER JACKET'S MINE, BOYS. IT'S ABOUT MY SIZE.
TSSSSSS

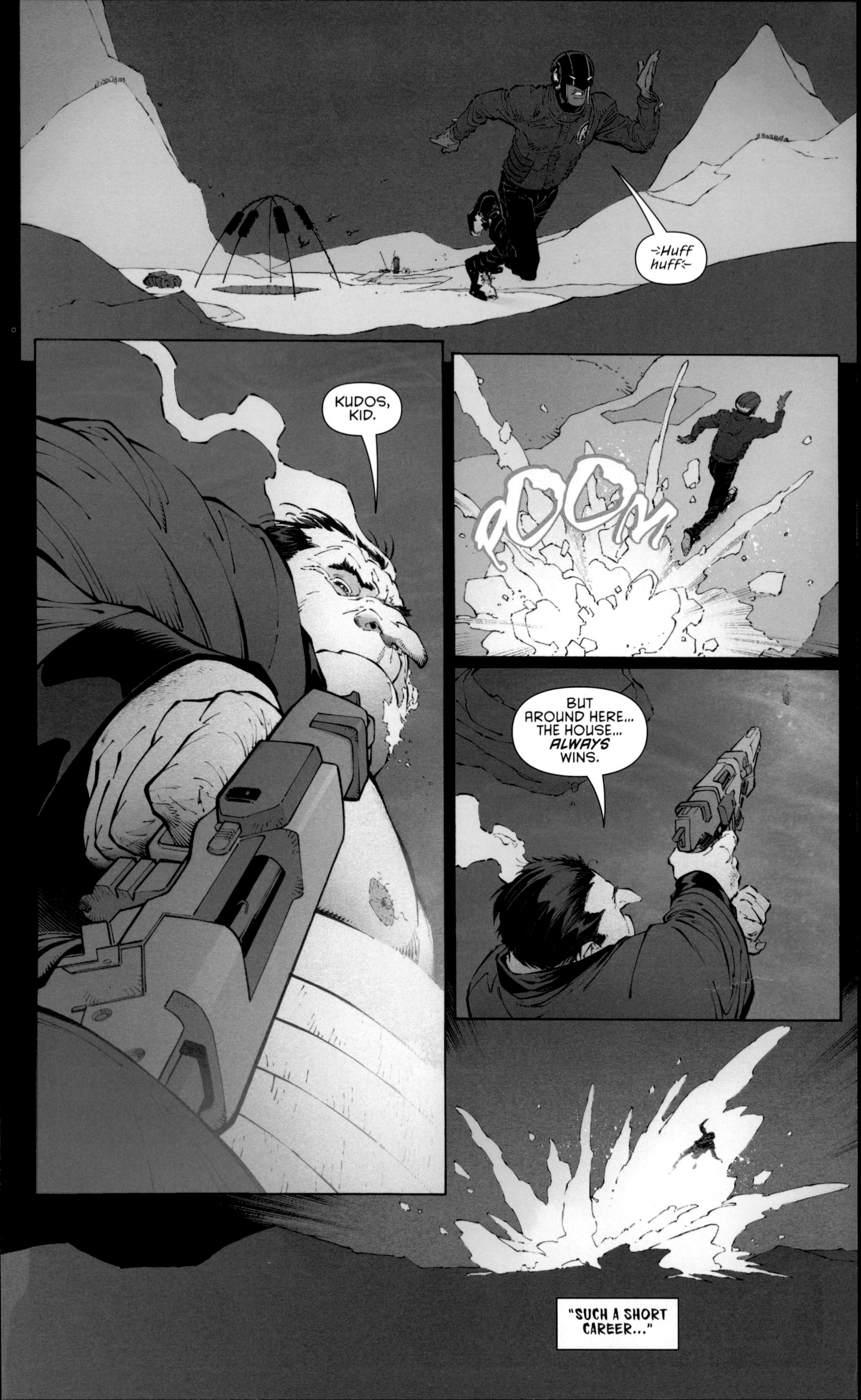
Huff huff
KUDOS, KID.
DOOM
BUT AROUND HERE... THE HOUSE... ALWAYS WINS.
"SUCH A SHORT CAREER..."

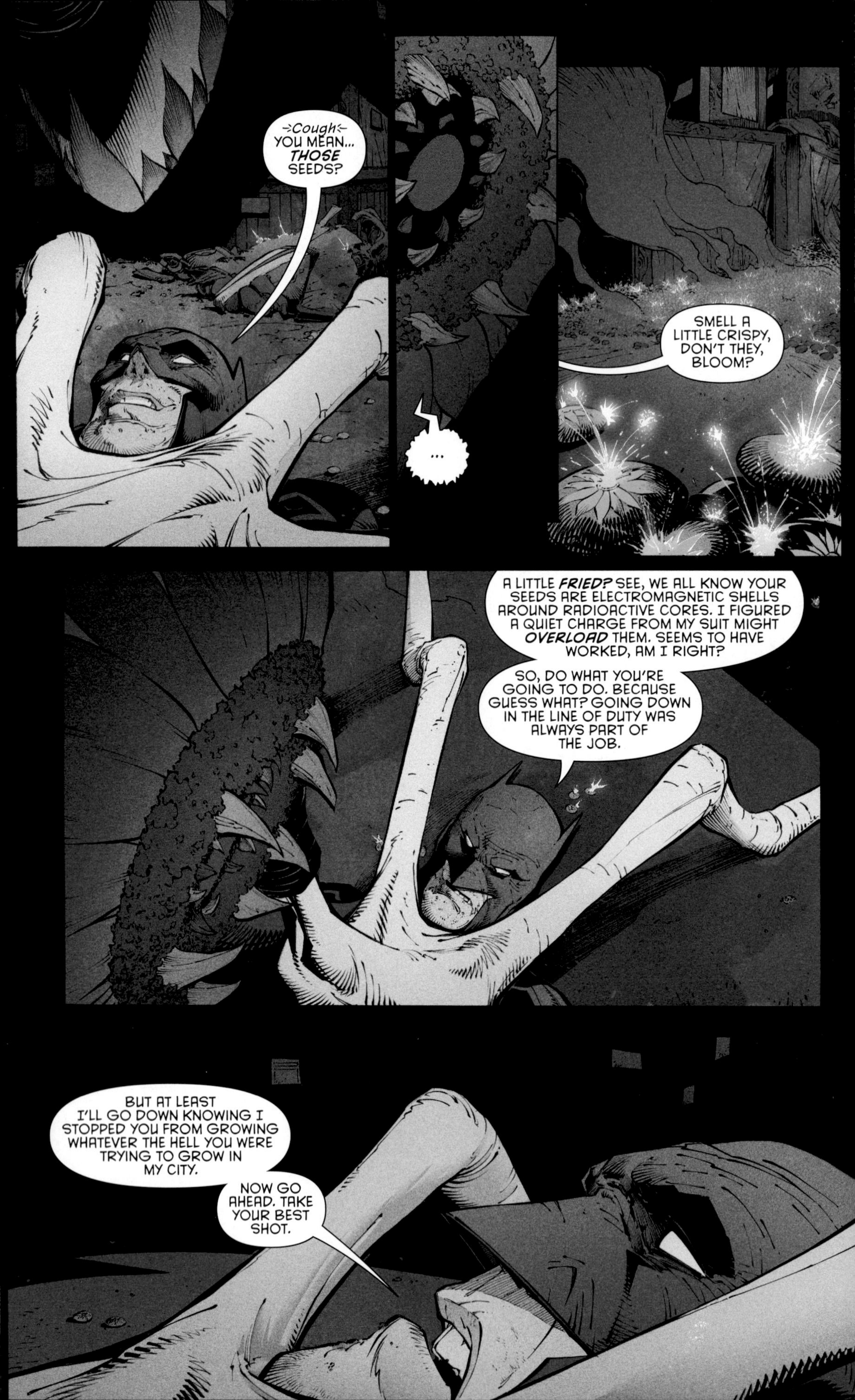
Cough YOU MEAN... THOSE SEEDS?
...
SMELL A LITTLE CRISPY, DON'T THEY, BLOOM?
A LITTLE FRIED? SEE, WE ALL KNOW YOUR SEEDS ARE ELECTROMAGNETIC SHELLS AROUND RADIOACTIVE CORES. I FIGURED A QUIET CHARGE FROM MY SUIT MIGHT OVERLOAD THEM. SEEMS TO HAVE WORKED, AM I RIGHT?
SO, DO WHAT YOU'RE GOING TO DO. BECAUSE GUESS WHAT? GOING DOWN IN THE LINE OF DUTY WAS ALWAYS PART OF THE JOB.
BUT AT LEAST I'LL GO DOWN KNOWING I STOPPED YOU FROM GROWING WHATEVER THE HELL YOU WERE TRYING TO GROW IN MY CITY.
NOW GO AHEAD. TAKE YOUR BEST SHOT.

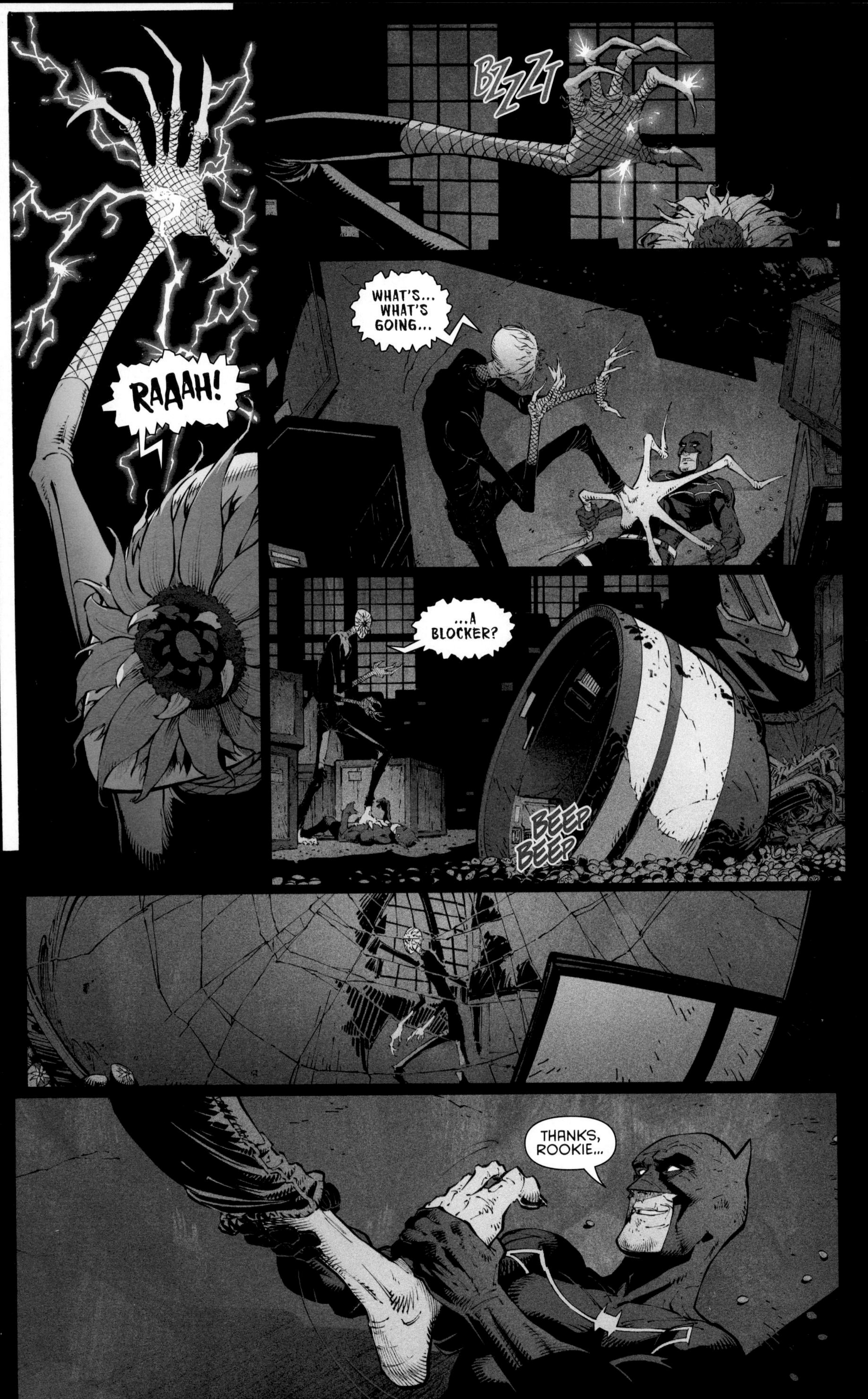
BZZZT
RAAAH!
WHAT'S... WHAT'S GOING...
...A BLOCKER?
BEEP BEEP
THANKS, ROOKIE...

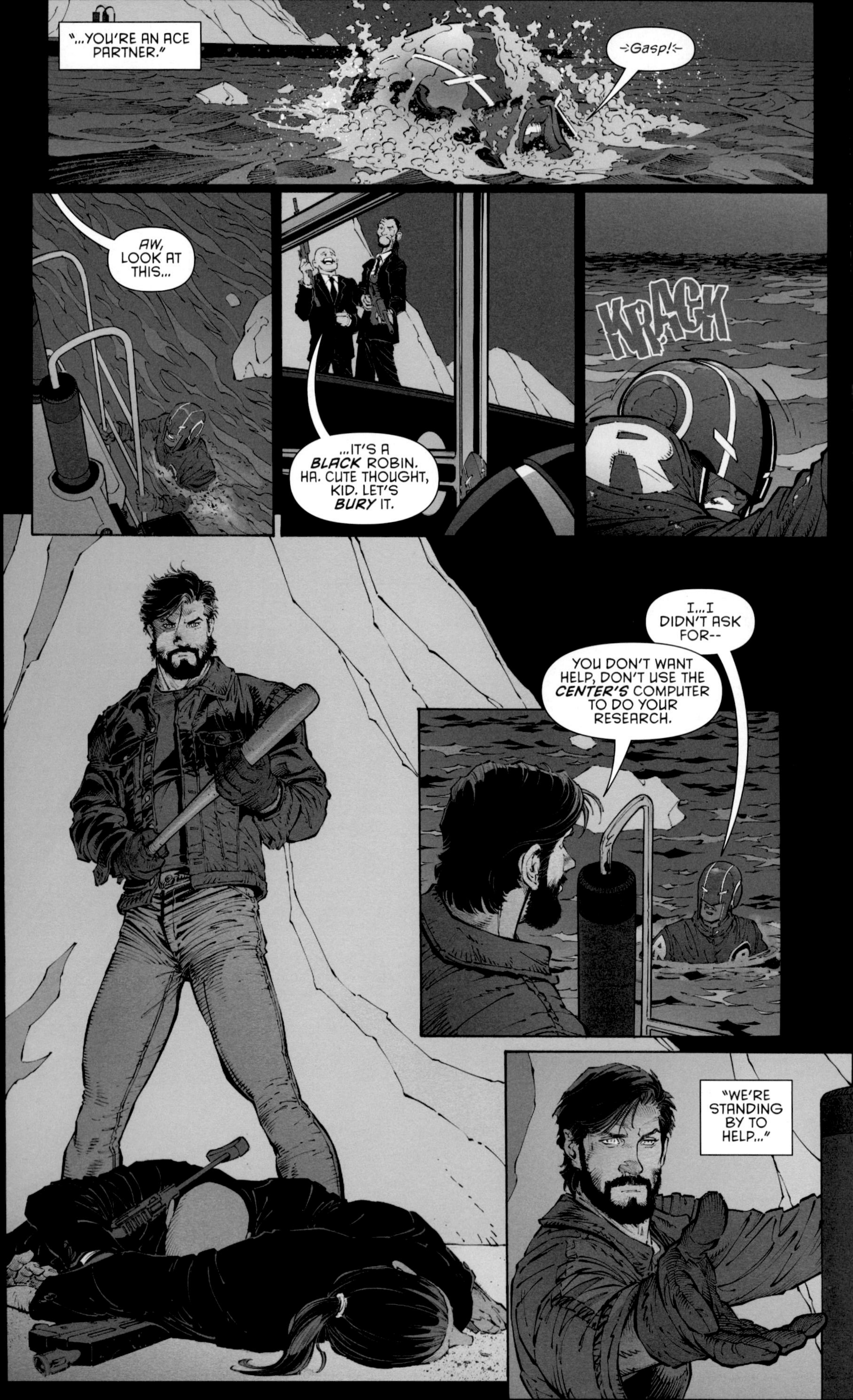
"...YOU'RE AN ACE PARTNER."
-Gasp!-
AW, LOOK AT THIS...
...IT'S A BLACK ROBIN. HA. CUTE THOUGHT, KID. LET'S BURY IT.
KRACK
I...I DIDN'T ASK FOR--
YOU DON'T WANT HELP, DON'T USE THE CENTER'S COMPUTER TO DO YOUR RESEARCH.
"WE'RE STANDING BY TO HELP..."

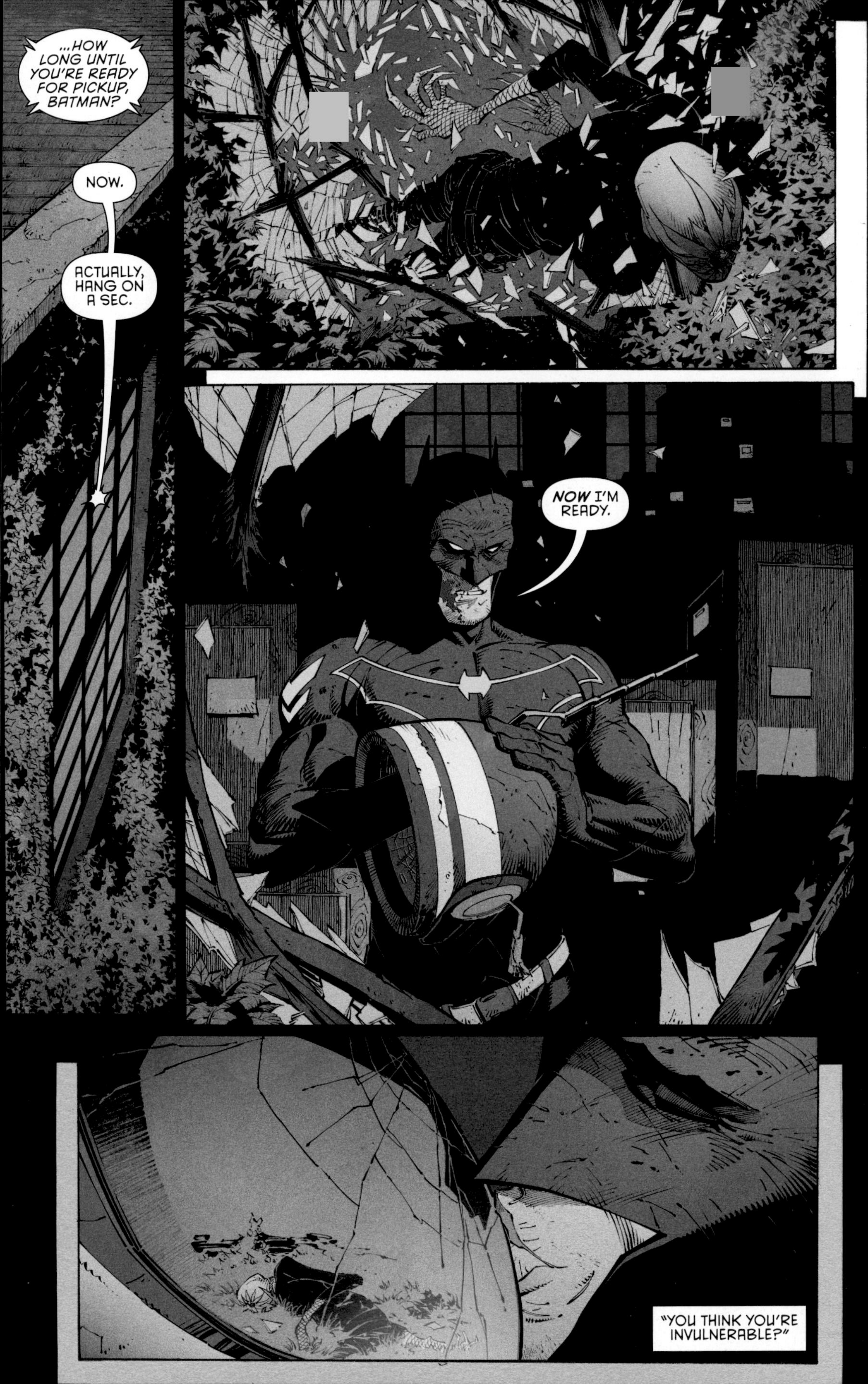
...HOW LONG UNTIL YOU'RE READY FOR PICKUP, BATMAN?
NOW.
ACTUALLY, HANG ON A SEC.
NOW I'M READY.
"YOU THINK YOU'RE INVULNERABLE?"

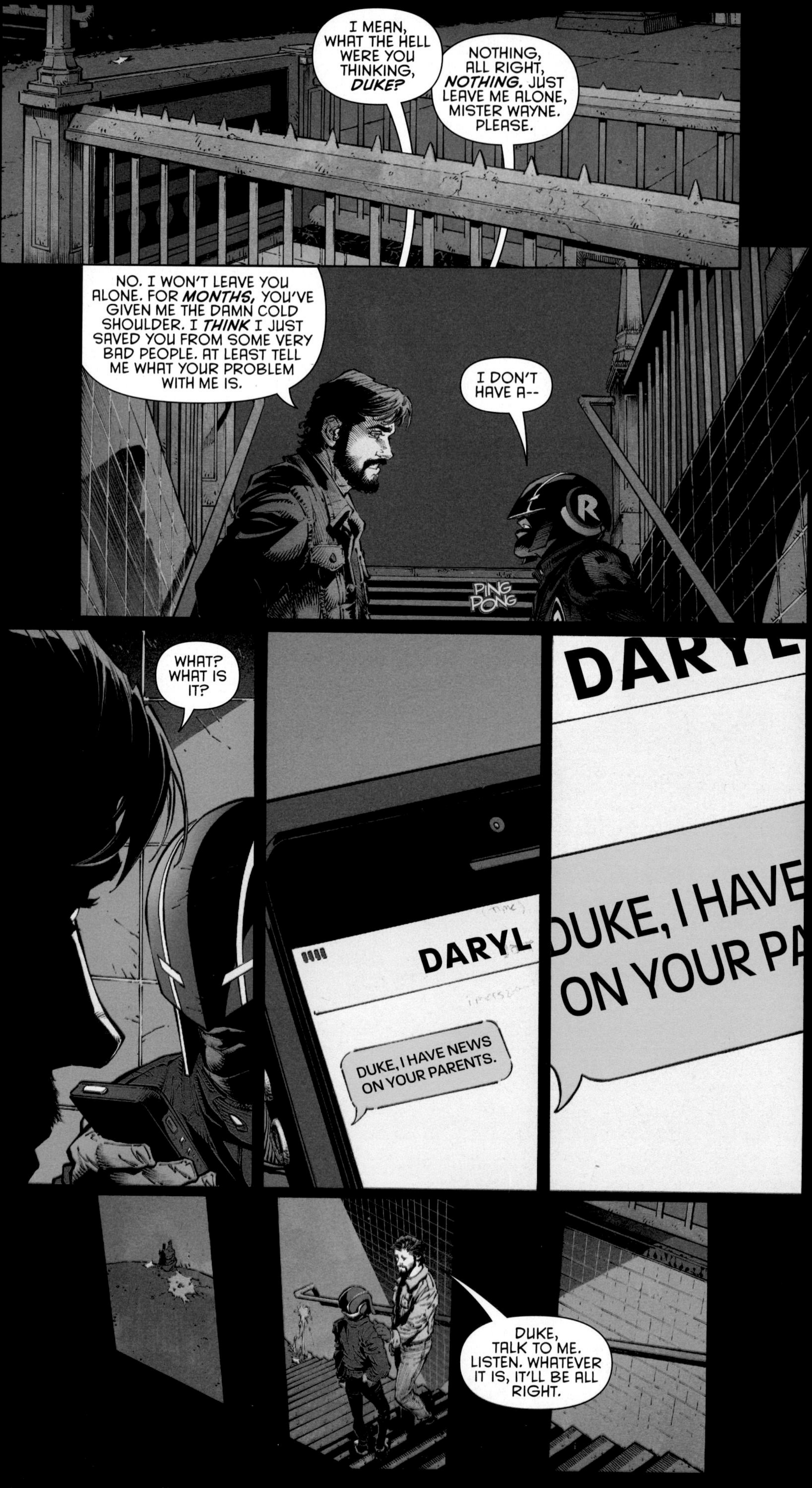
I MEAN, WHAT THE HELL WERE YOU THINKING, DUKE?
NOTHING, ALL RIGHT, NOTHING. JUST LEAVE ME ALONE, MISTER WAYNE. PLEASE.
NO. I WON'T LEAVE YOU ALONE. FOR MONTHS, YOU'VE GIVEN ME THE DAMN COLD SHOULDER. I THINK I JUST SAVED YOU FROM SOME VERY BAD PEOPLE. AT LEAST TELL ME WHAT YOUR PROBLEM WITH ME IS.
I DON'T HAVE A--
PING PONG
WHAT? WHAT IS IT?
DARYL
DUKE, I HAVE NEWS ON YOUR PARENTS.
DARYL
DUKE, I HAVE
ON YOUR PA
DUKE, TALK TO ME. LISTEN. WHATEVER IT IS, IT'LL BE ALL RIGHT.

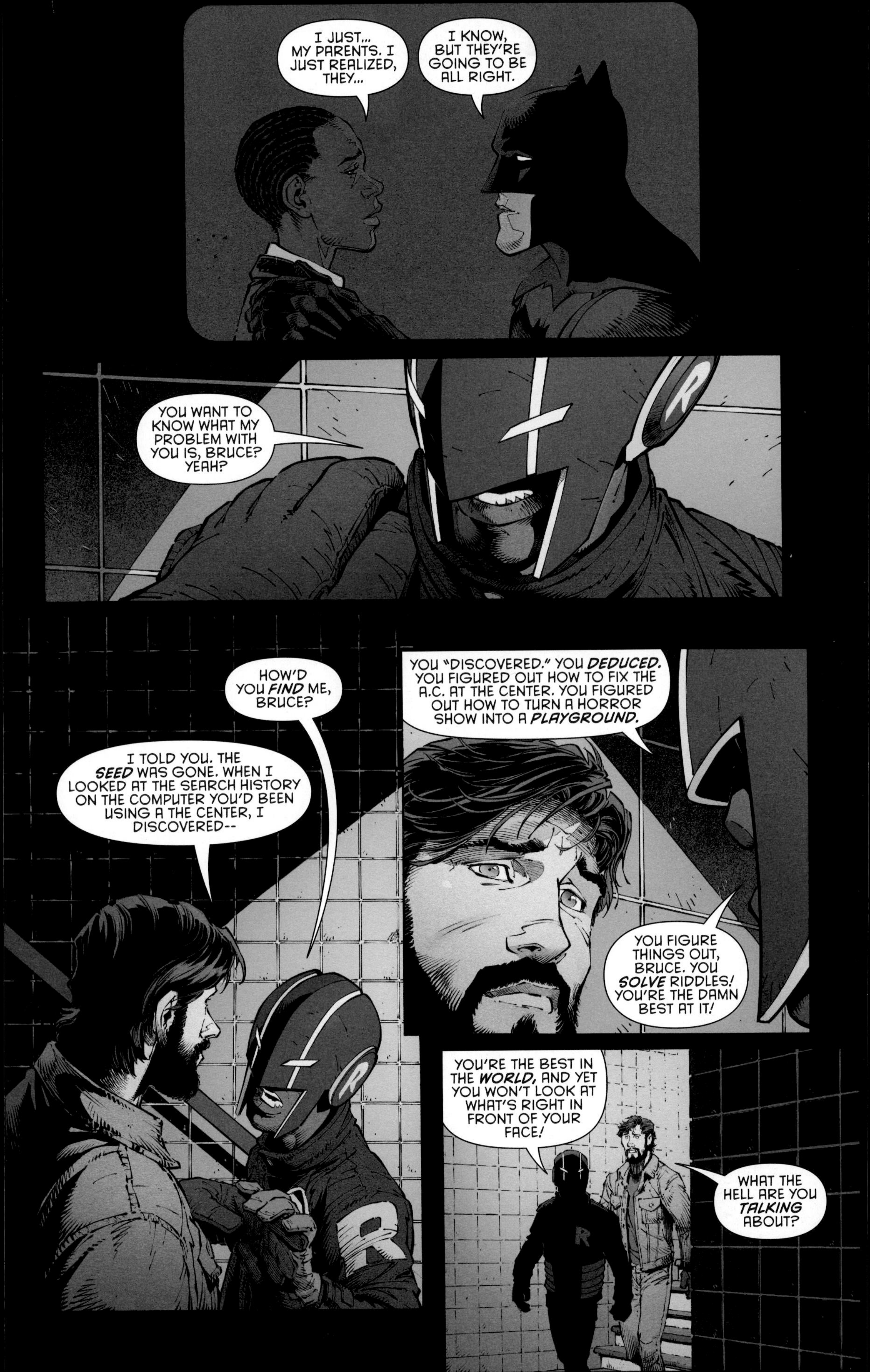
I JUST... MY PARENTS. I JUST REALIZED, THEY...
I KNOW, BUT THEY'RE GOING TO BE ALL RIGHT.
YOU WANT TO KNOW WHAT MY PROBLEM WITH YOU IS, BRUCE? YEAH?
HOW'D YOU *FIND* ME, BRUCE?
I TOLD YOU. THE *SEED* WAS GONE. WHEN I LOOKED AT THE SEARCH HISTORY ON THE COMPUTER YOU'D BEEN USING A THE CENTER, I DISCOVERED--
YOU "DISCOVERED." YOU *DEDUCED.* YOU FIGURED OUT HOW TO FIX THE A.C. AT THE CENTER. YOU FIGURED OUT HOW TO TURN A HORROR SHOW INTO A *PLAYGROUND.*
YOU FIGURE THINGS OUT, BRUCE. YOU *SOLVE* RIDDLES! YOU'RE THE DAMN BEST AT IT!
YOU'RE THE BEST IN THE *WORLD,* AND YET YOU WON'T LOOK AT WHAT'S RIGHT IN FRONT OF YOUR FACE!
WHAT THE HELL ARE YOU *TALKING* ABOUT?

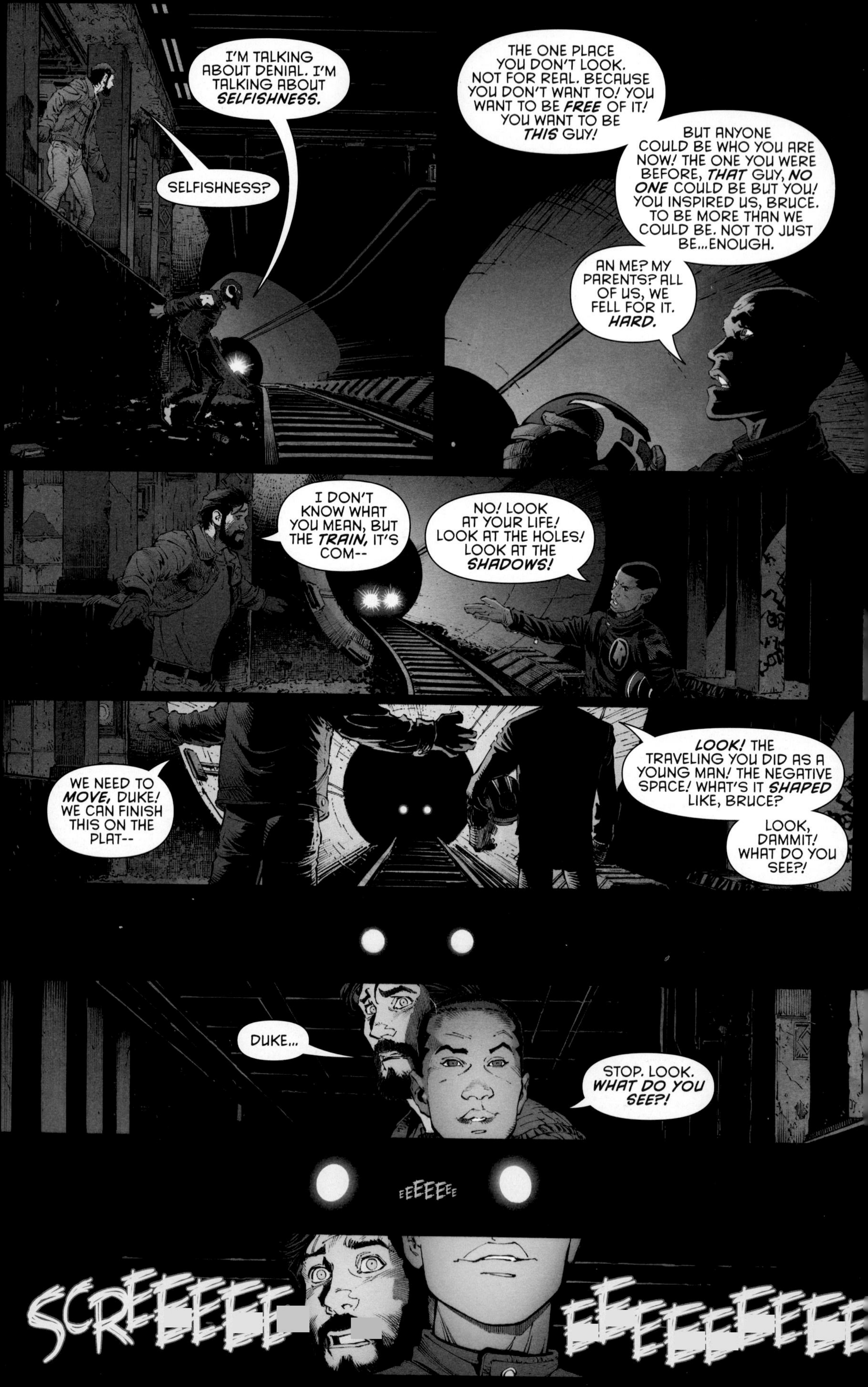
I'M TALKING ABOUT DENIAL. I'M TALKING ABOUT *SELFISHNESS.*
SELFISHNESS?
THE ONE PLACE YOU DON'T LOOK. NOT FOR REAL. BECAUSE YOU DON'T WANT TO! YOU WANT TO BE *FREE* OF IT! YOU WANT TO BE *THIS* GUY!
BUT ANYONE COULD BE WHO YOU ARE NOW! THE ONE YOU WERE BEFORE, *THAT* GUY, *NO ONE* COULD BE BUT YOU! YOU INSPIRED US, BRUCE. TO BE MORE THAN WE COULD BE. NOT TO JUST BE...ENOUGH.
AN ME? MY PARENTS? ALL OF US, WE FELL FOR IT. *HARD.*
I DON'T KNOW WHAT YOU MEAN, BUT THE *TRAIN,* IT'S COM--
NO! LOOK AT YOUR LIFE! LOOK AT THE HOLES! LOOK AT THE *SHADOWS!*
WE NEED TO *MOVE,* DUKE! WE CAN FINISH THIS ON THE PLAT--
LOOK! THE TRAVELING YOU DID AS A YOUNG MAN! THE NEGATIVE SPACE! WHAT'S IT *SHAPED* LIKE, BRUCE?
LOOK, DAMMIT! WHAT DO YOU SEE?!
DUKE...
STOP. LOOK. *WHAT DO YOU SEE?!*
EEEEEEE
SCREEEEEE--
EEEEEEEEE

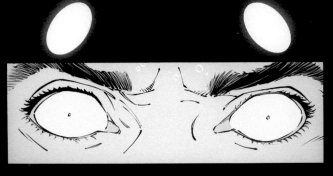

"WHAT DO YOU SEE?"

JUST...JUST STAY AWAY, BRUCE. I'M SORRY. STAY AWAY!

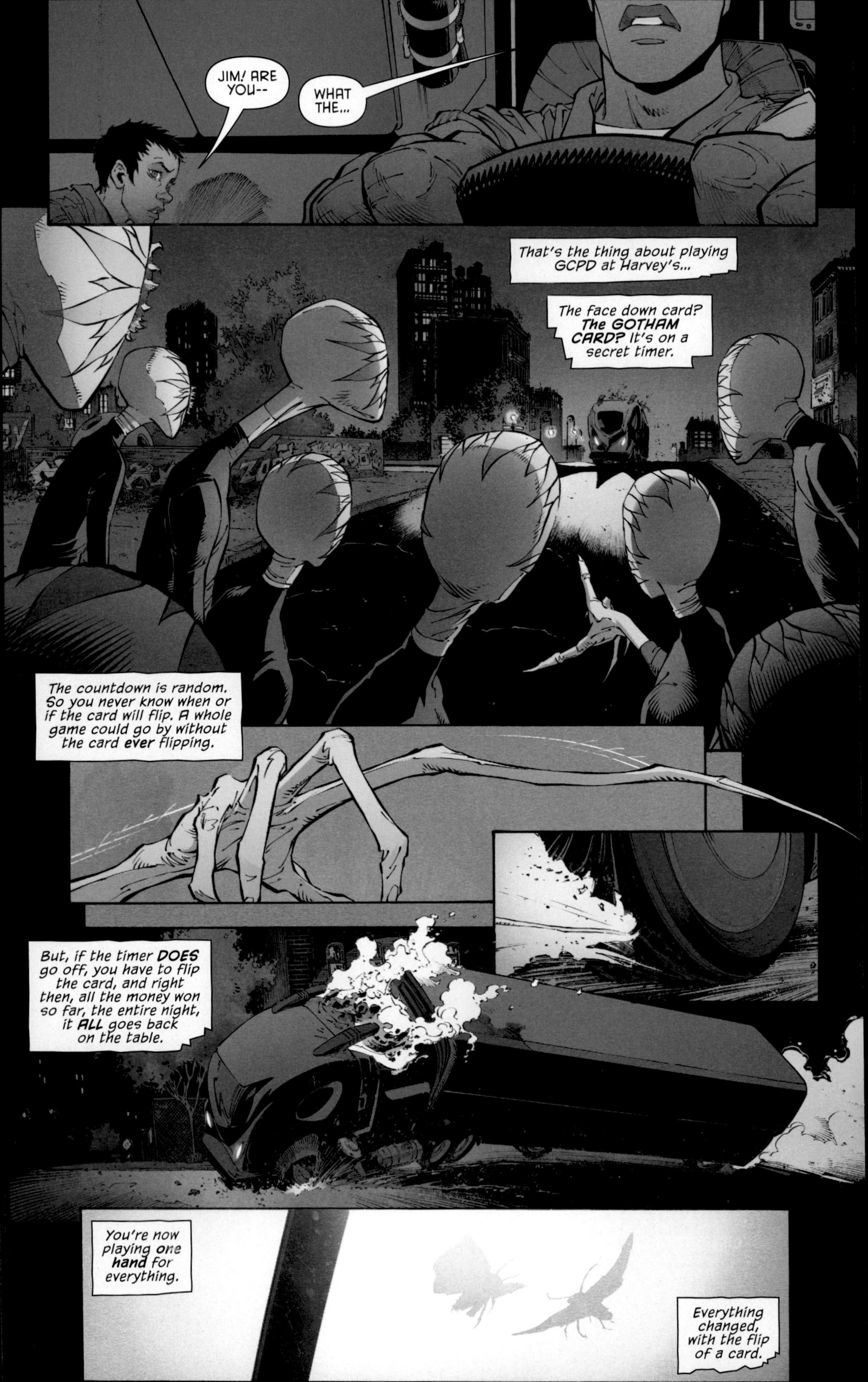
JIM! ARE YOU--
WHAT THE...
That's the thing about playing GCPD at Harvey's...
The face down card? The GOTHAM CARD? It's on a secret timer.
The countdown is random. So you never know when or if the card will flip. A whole game could go by without the card ever flipping.
But, if the timer DOES go off, you have to flip the card, and right then, all the money won so far, the entire night, it ALL goes back on the table.
You're now playing one hand for everything.
Everything changed, with the flip of a card.

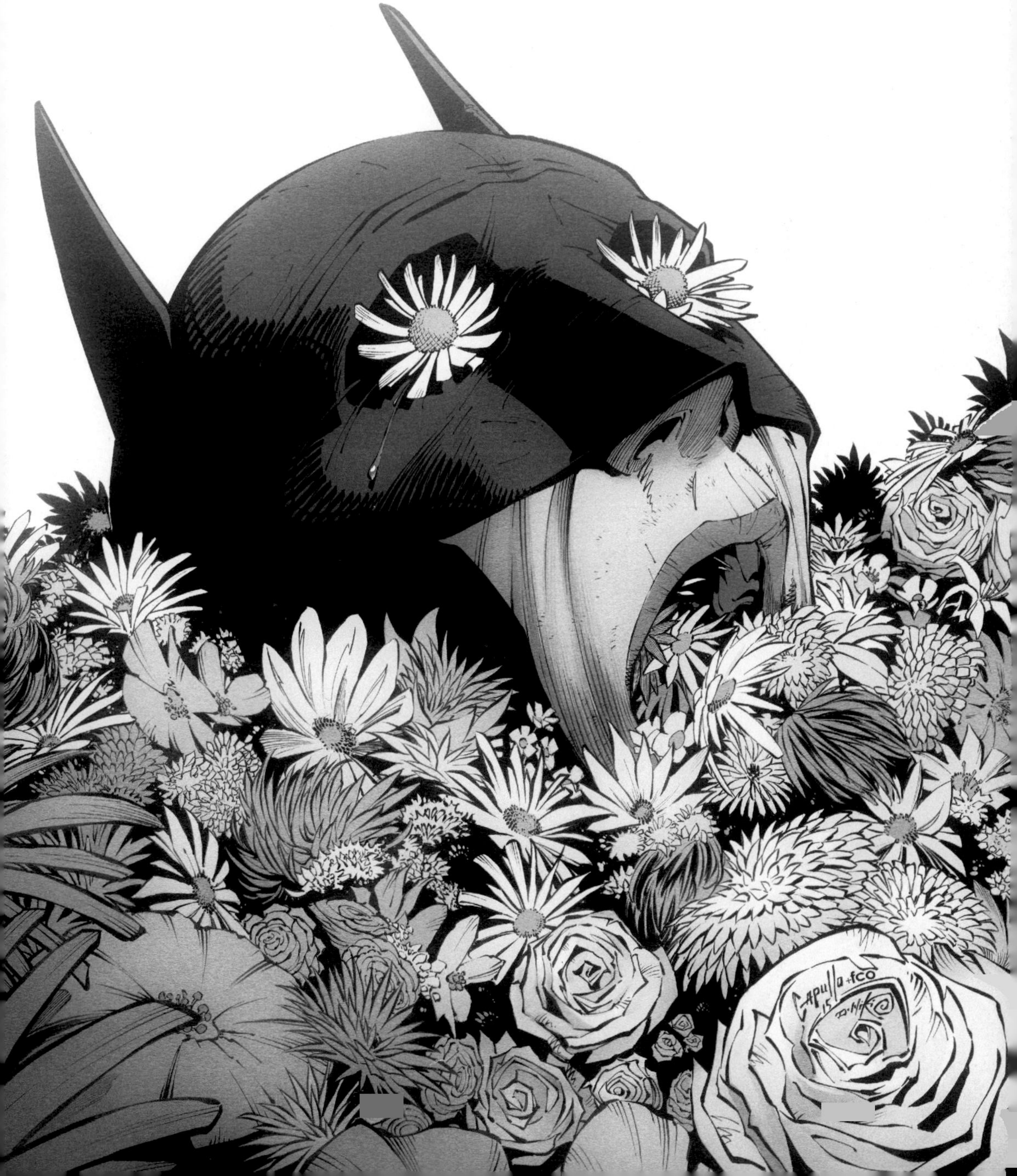

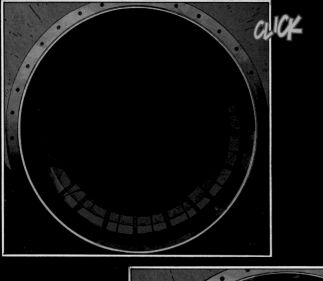

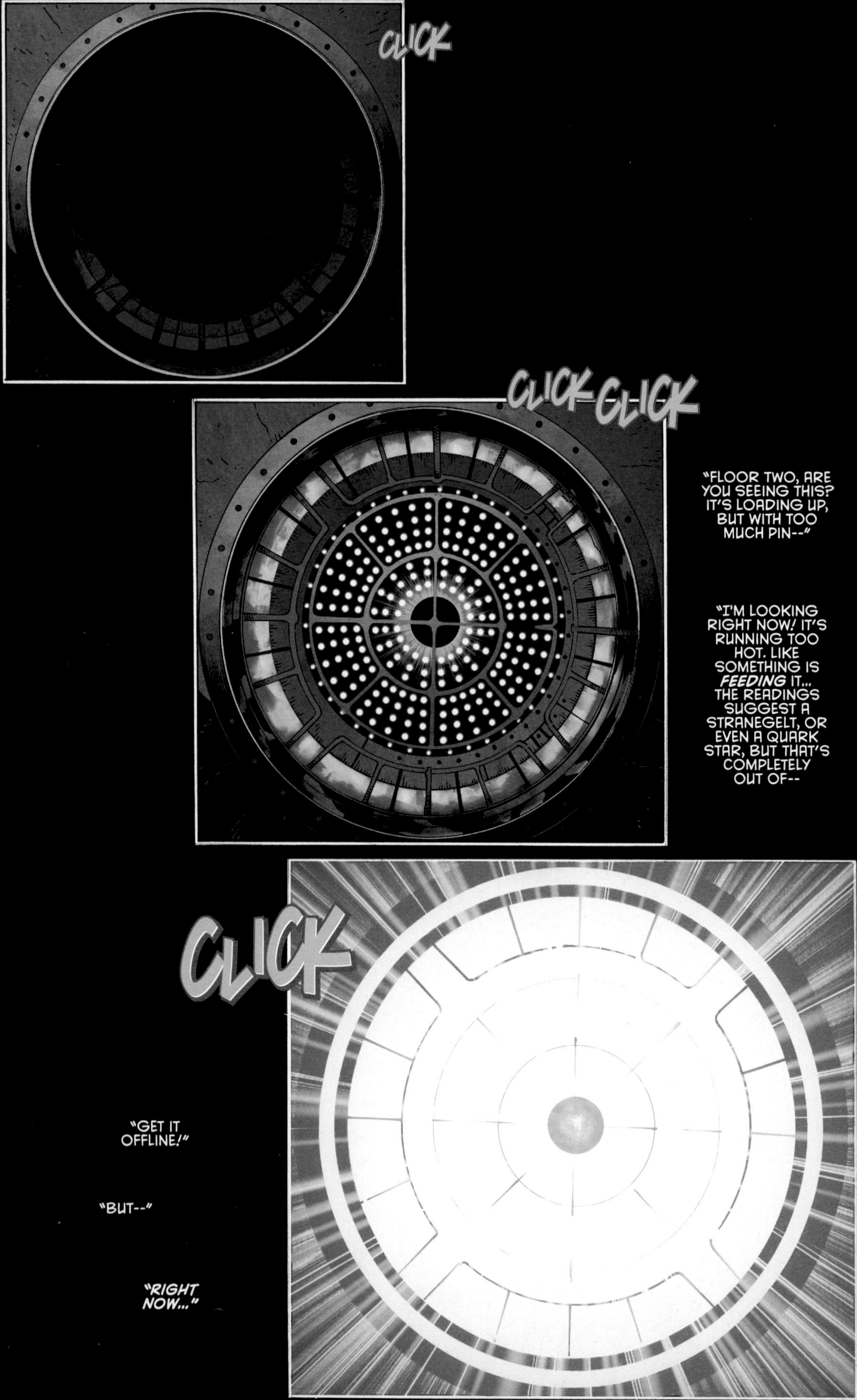

CLICK

CLICK CLICK

"FLOOR TWO, ARE YOU SEEING THIS? IT'S LOADING UP, BUT WITH TOO MUCH PIN--"

"I'M LOOKING RIGHT NOW! IT'S RUNNING TOO HOT. LIKE SOMETHING IS *FEEDING* IT... THE READINGS SUGGEST A STRANEGELT, OR EVEN A QUARK STAR, BUT THAT'S COMPLETELY OUT OF--"

CLICK

"GET IT OFFLINE!"

"BUT--"

"*RIGHT NOW...*"

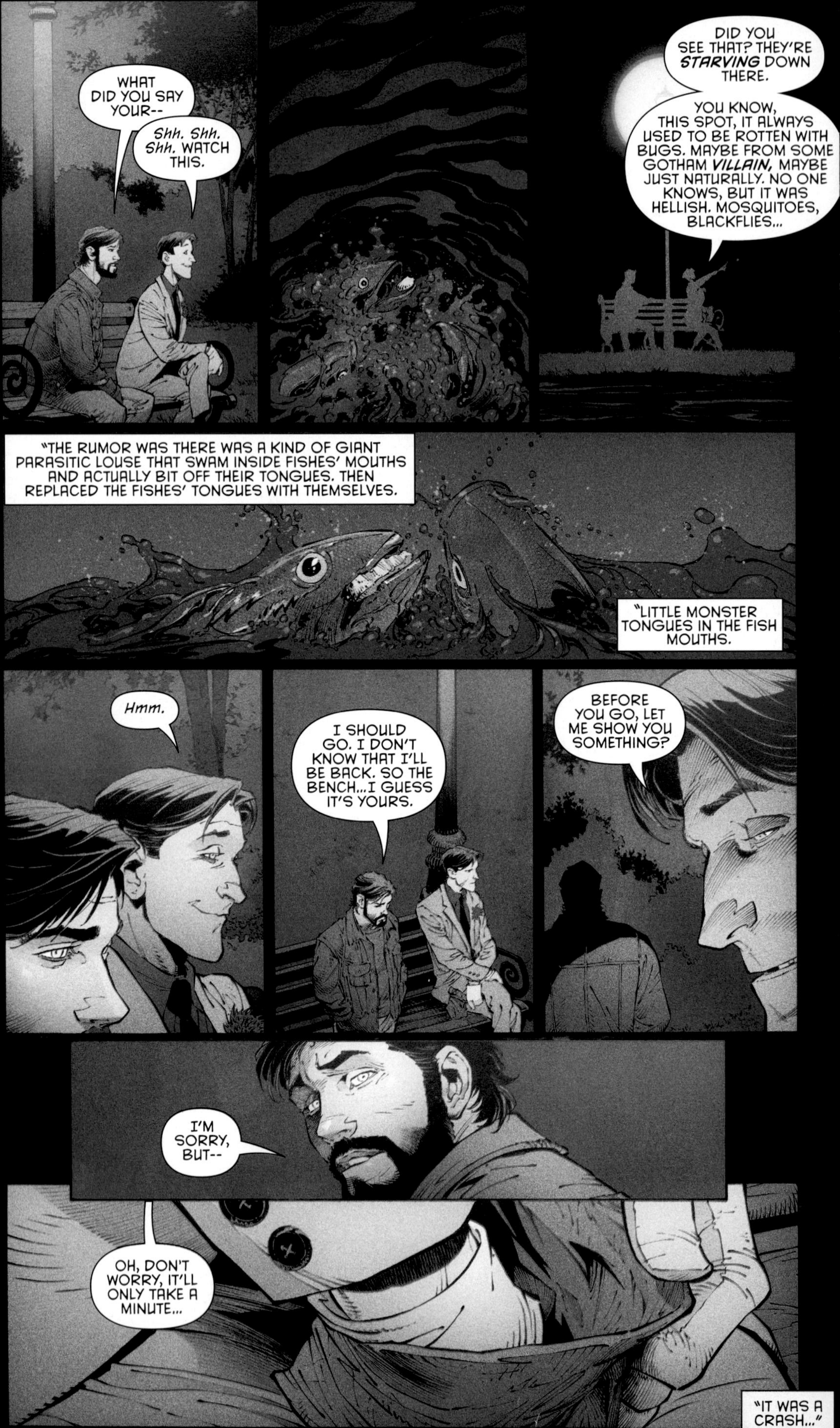

WHAT DID YOU SAY YOUR--
Shh. Shh. Shh. WATCH THIS.
DID YOU SEE THAT? THEY'RE *STARVING* DOWN THERE.
YOU KNOW, THIS SPOT, IT ALWAYS USED TO BE ROTTEN WITH BUGS. MAYBE FROM SOME GOTHAM *VILLAIN,* MAYBE JUST NATURALLY. NO ONE KNOWS, BUT IT WAS HELLISH. MOSQUITOES, BLACKFLIES...
"THE RUMOR WAS THERE WAS A KIND OF GIANT PARASITIC LOUSE THAT SWAM INSIDE FISHES' MOUTHS AND ACTUALLY BIT OFF THEIR TONGUES. THEN REPLACED THE FISHES' TONGUES WITH THEMSELVES.
"LITTLE MONSTER TONGUES IN THE FISH MOUTHS.
Hmm.
I SHOULD GO. I DON'T KNOW THAT I'LL BE BACK. SO THE BENCH...I GUESS IT'S YOURS.
BEFORE YOU GO, LET ME SHOW YOU SOMETHING?
I'M SORRY, BUT--
OH, DON'T WORRY, IT'LL ONLY TAKE A MINUTE...
"IT WAS A CRASH..."

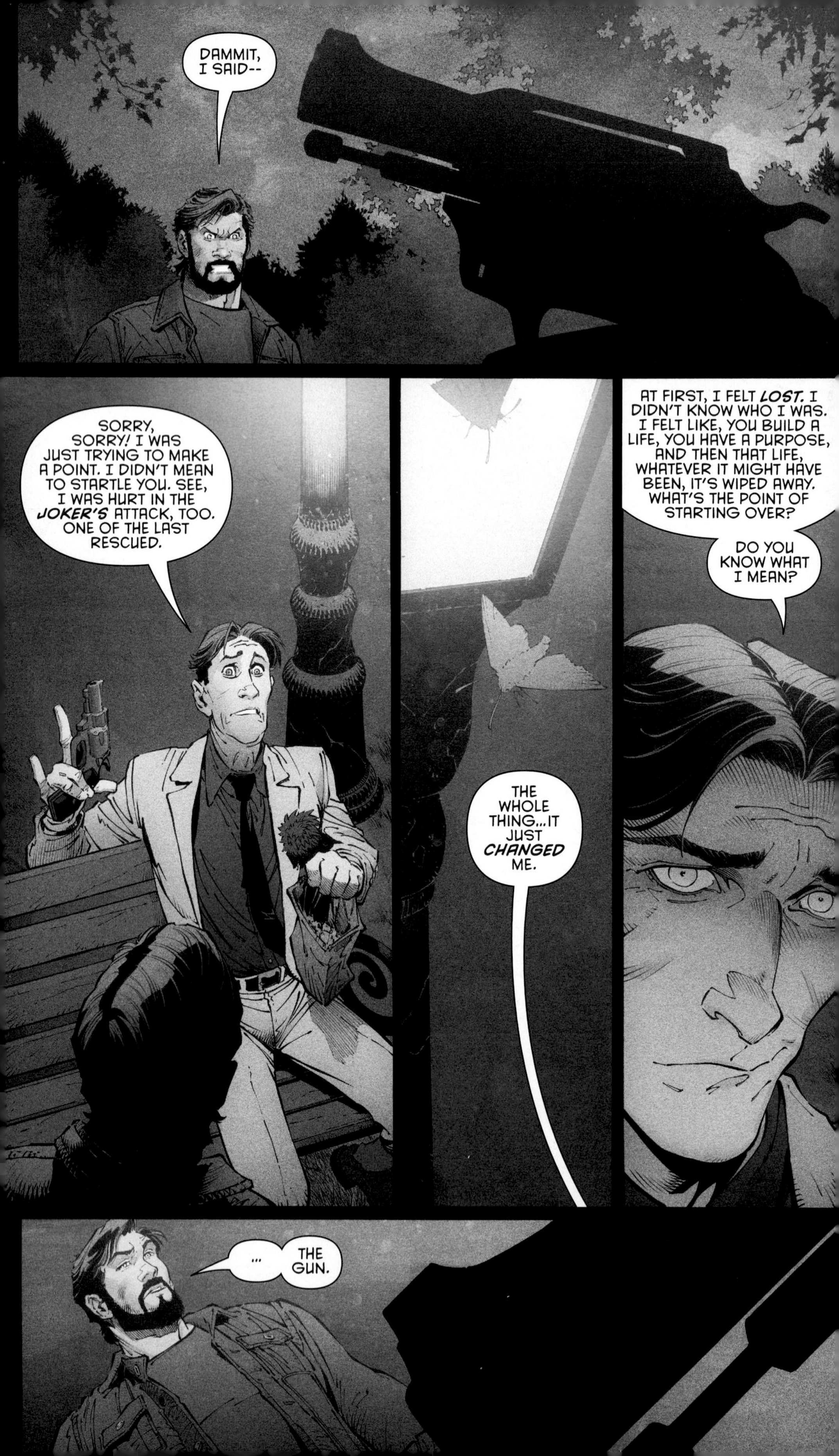
DAMMIT, I SAID--
SORRY, SORRY! I WAS JUST TRYING TO MAKE A POINT. I DIDN'T MEAN TO STARTLE YOU. SEE, I WAS HURT IN THE JOKER'S ATTACK, TOO. ONE OF THE LAST RESCUED.
THE WHOLE THING...IT JUST CHANGED ME.
AT FIRST, I FELT LOST. I DIDN'T KNOW WHO I WAS. I FELT LIKE, YOU BUILD A LIFE, YOU HAVE A PURPOSE, AND THEN THAT LIFE, WHATEVER IT MIGHT HAVE BEEN, IT'S WIPED AWAY. WHAT'S THE POINT OF STARTING OVER?
DO YOU KNOW WHAT I MEAN?
...
THE GUN.

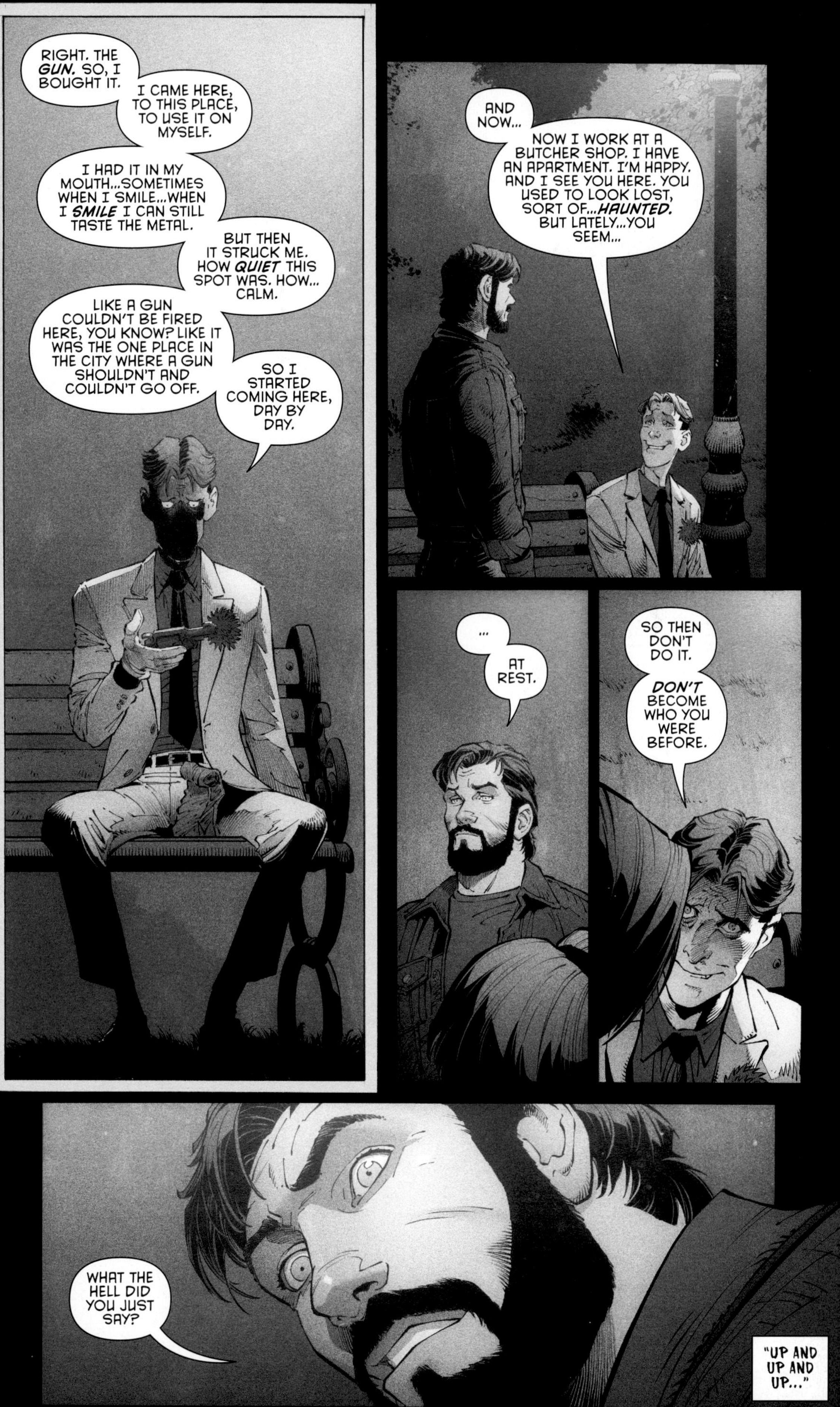
RIGHT. THE GUN. SO, I BOUGHT IT.
I CAME HERE, TO THIS PLACE, TO USE IT ON MYSELF.
I HAD IT IN MY MOUTH...SOMETIMES WHEN I SMILE...WHEN I SMILE I CAN STILL TASTE THE METAL.
BUT THEN IT STRUCK ME. HOW QUIET THIS SPOT WAS. HOW... CALM.
LIKE A GUN COULDN'T BE FIRED HERE, YOU KNOW? LIKE IT WAS THE ONE PLACE IN THE CITY WHERE A GUN SHOULDN'T AND COULDN'T GO OFF.
SO I STARTED COMING HERE, DAY BY DAY.
AND NOW...
NOW I WORK AT A BUTCHER SHOP. I HAVE AN APARTMENT. I'M HAPPY. AND I SEE YOU HERE. YOU USED TO LOOK LOST, SORT OF...HAUNTED. BUT LATELY...YOU SEEM...
...
AT REST.
SO THEN DON'T DO IT.
DON'T BECOME WHO YOU WERE BEFORE.
WHAT THE HELL DID YOU JUST SAY?
"UP AND UP AND UP..."

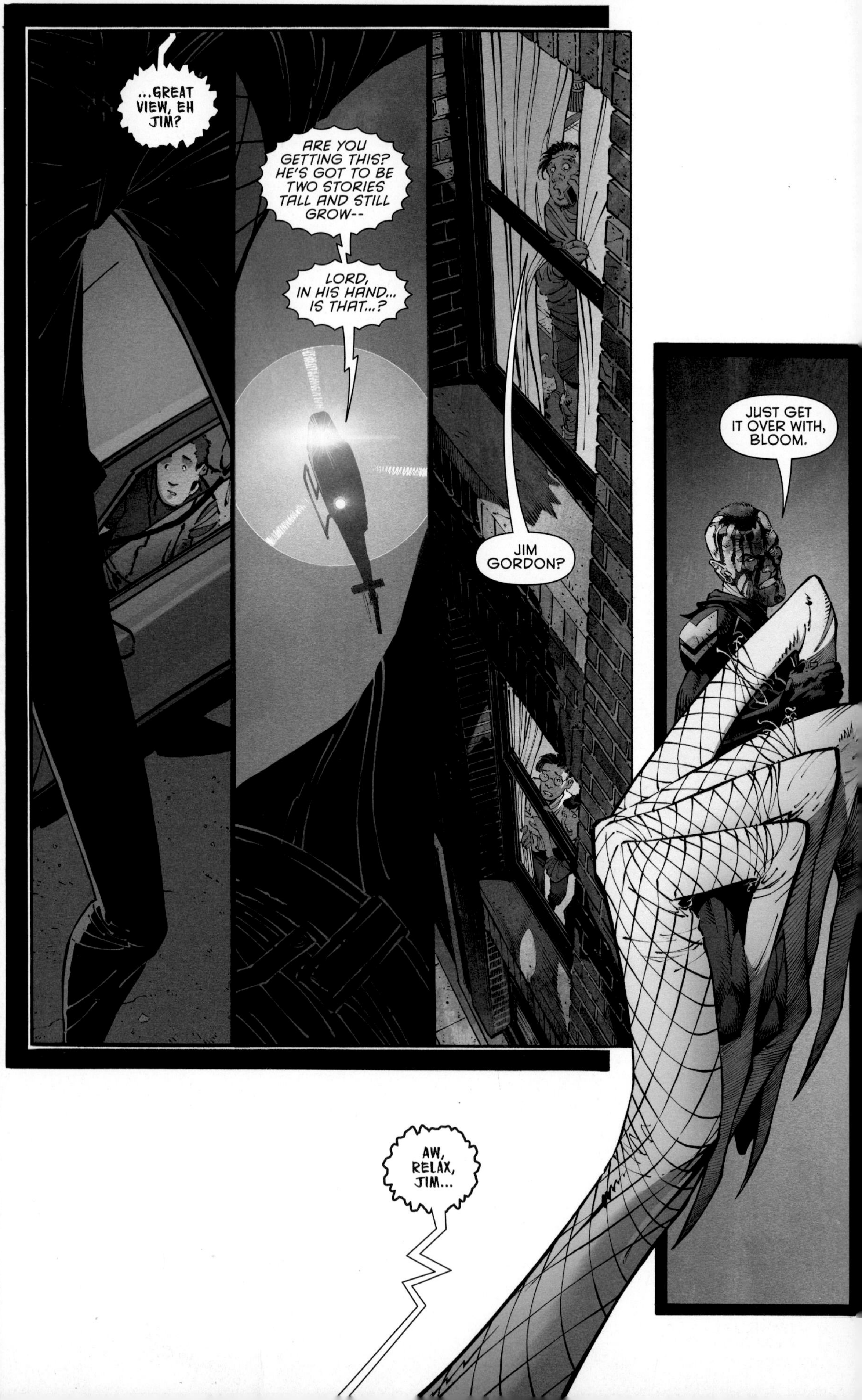
...GREAT VIEW, EH JIM?
ARE YOU GETTING THIS? HE'S GOT TO BE TWO STORIES TALL AND STILL GROW--
LORD, IN HIS HAND... IS THAT...?
JIM GORDON?
JUST GET IT OVER WITH, BLOOM.
AW, RELAX, JIM...

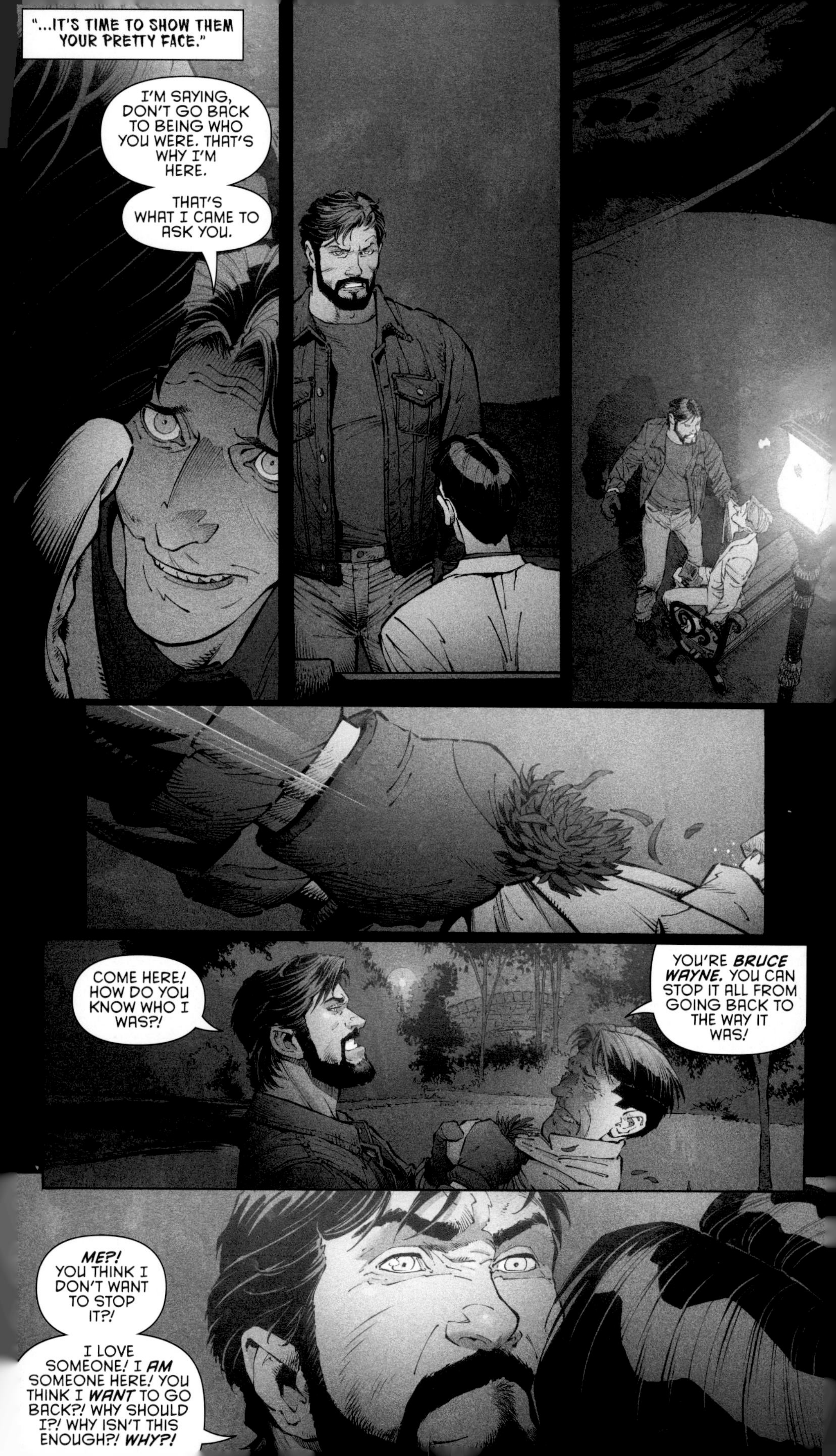
"...IT'S TIME TO SHOW THEM YOUR PRETTY FACE."
I'M SAYING, DON'T GO BACK TO BEING WHO YOU WERE. THAT'S WHY I'M HERE.
THAT'S WHAT I CAME TO ASK YOU.
COME HERE! HOW DO YOU KNOW WHO I WAS?!
YOU'RE *BRUCE WAYNE.* YOU CAN STOP IT ALL FROM GOING BACK TO THE WAY IT WAS!
ME?! YOU THINK I DON'T WANT TO STOP IT?!
I LOVE SOMEONE! I *AM* SOMEONE HERE! YOU THINK I *WANT* TO GO BACK?! WHY SHOULD I?! WHY ISN'T THIS ENOUGH?! *WHY?!*

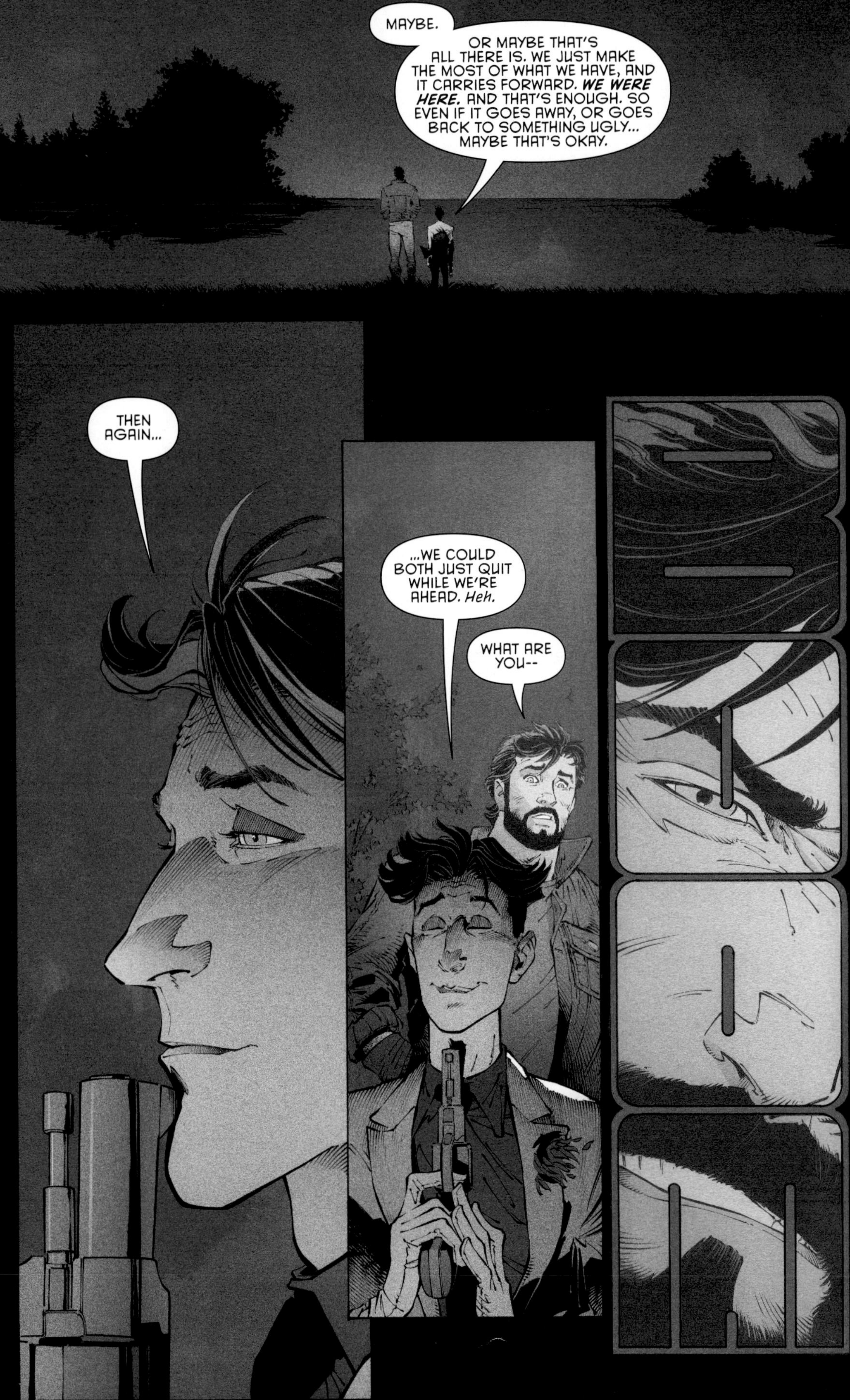
MAYBE.
OR MAYBE THAT'S ALL THERE IS. WE JUST MAKE THE MOST OF WHAT WE HAVE, AND IT CARRIES FORWARD. ***WE WERE HERE.*** AND THAT'S ENOUGH. SO EVEN IF IT GOES AWAY, OR GOES BACK TO SOMETHING UGLY... MAYBE THAT'S OKAY.
THEN AGAIN...
...WE COULD BOTH JUST QUIT WHILE WE'RE AHEAD. *Heh.*
WHAT ARE YOU--

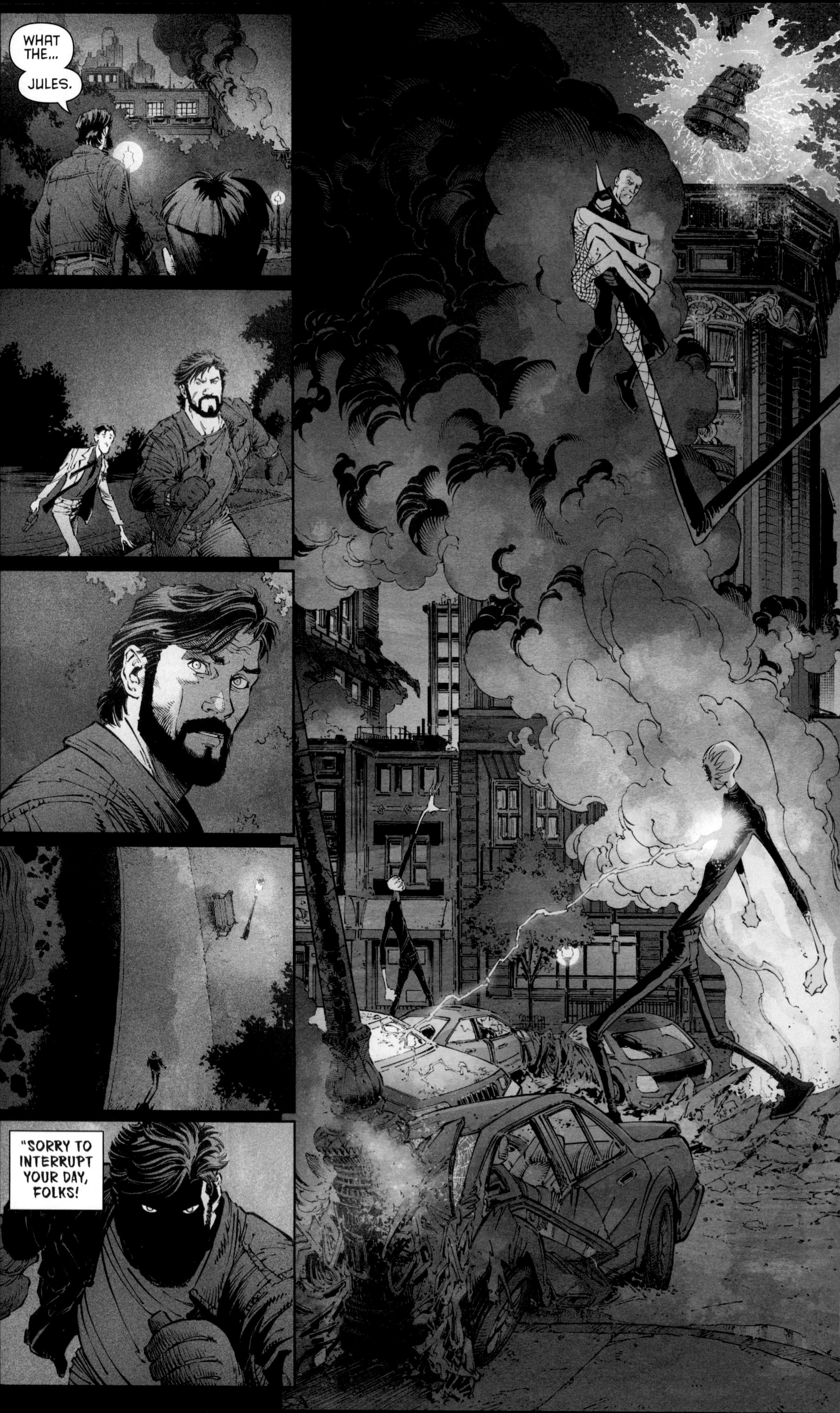
WHAT THE...
JULES.
"SORRY TO INTERRUPT YOUR DAY, FOLKS!

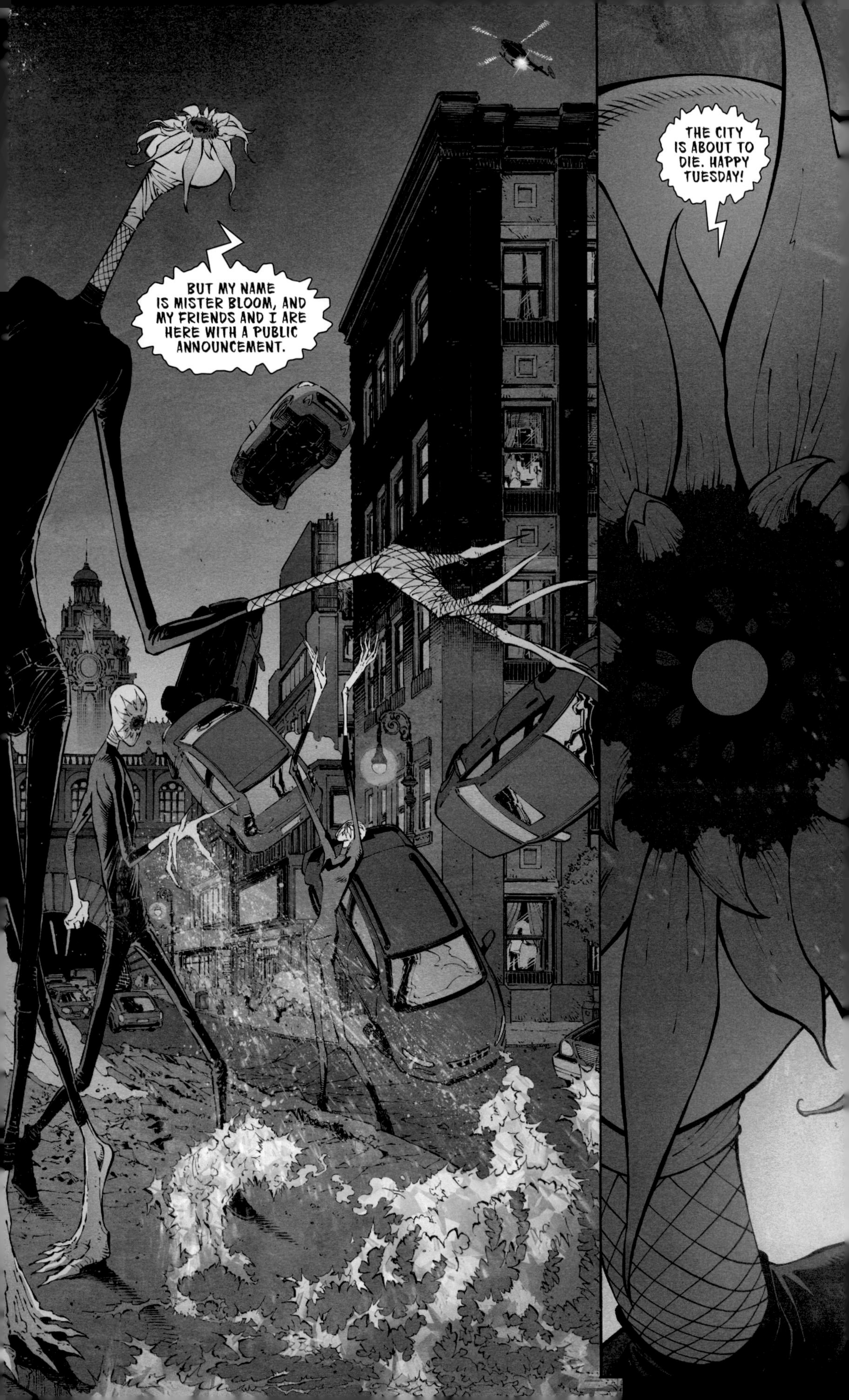
BUT MY NAME IS MISTER BLOOM, AND MY FRIENDS AND I ARE HERE WITH A PUBLIC ANNOUNCEMENT.
THE CITY IS ABOUT TO DIE. HAPPY TUESDAY!

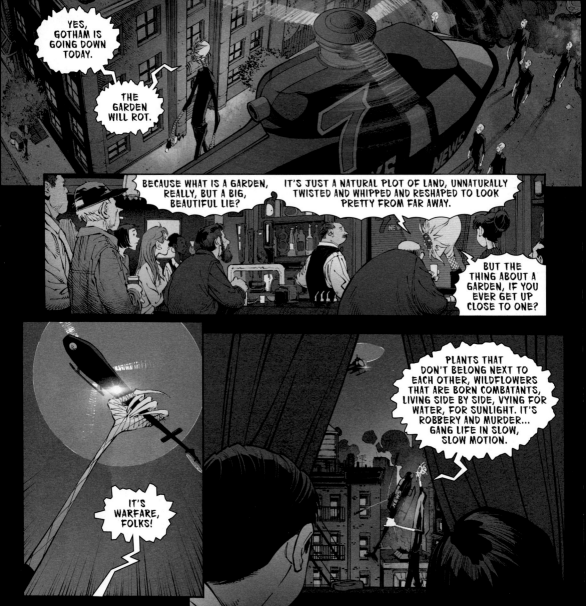

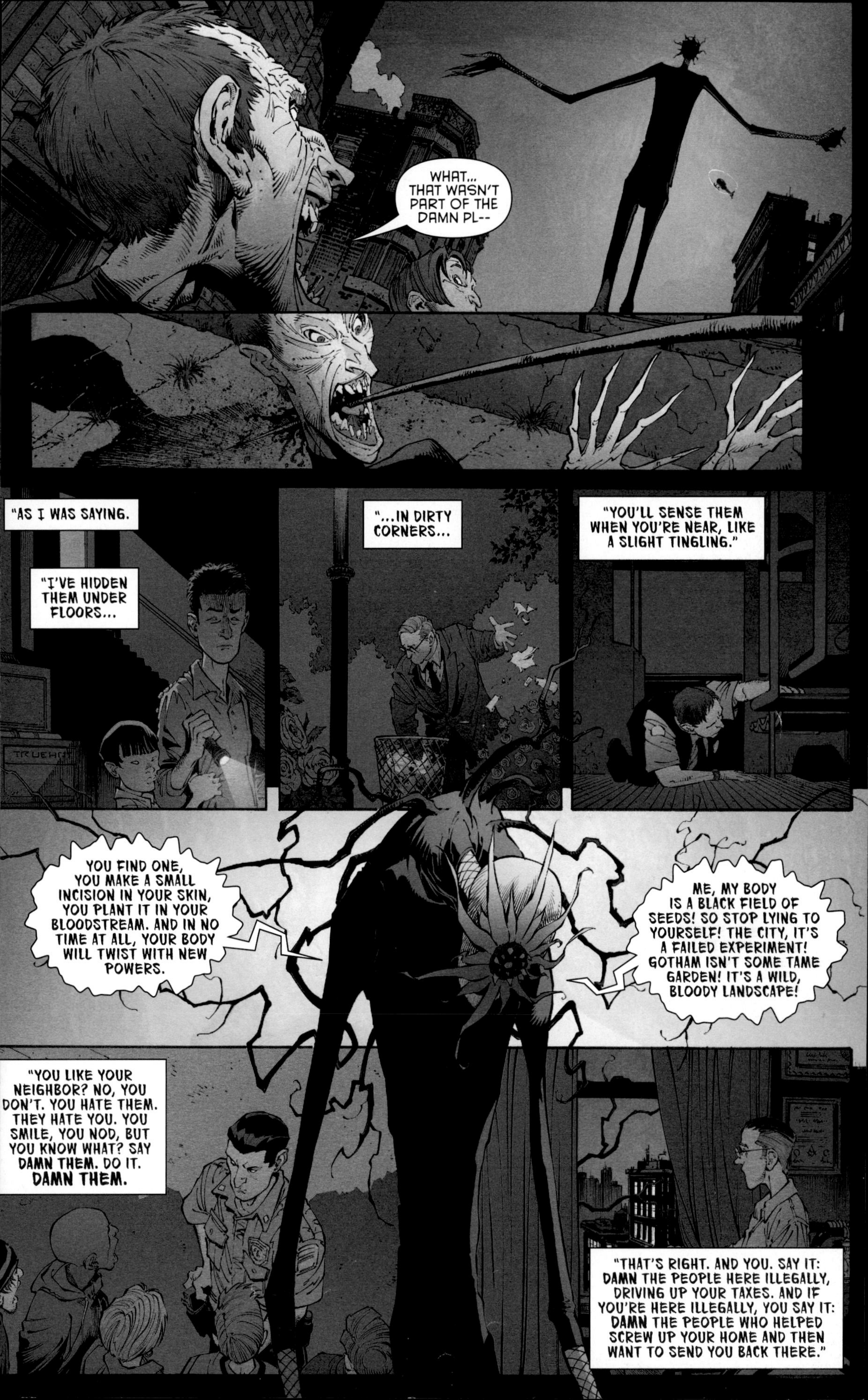

WHAT... THAT WASN'T PART OF THE DAMN PL--
"AS I WAS SAYING.
"I'VE HIDDEN THEM UNDER FLOORS...
"...IN DIRTY CORNERS...
"YOU'LL SENSE THEM WHEN YOU'RE NEAR, LIKE A SLIGHT TINGLING."
YOU FIND ONE, YOU MAKE A SMALL INCISION IN YOUR SKIN, YOU PLANT IT IN YOUR BLOODSTREAM. AND IN NO TIME AT ALL, YOUR BODY WILL TWIST WITH NEW POWERS.
ME, MY BODY IS A BLACK FIELD OF SEEDS! SO STOP LYING TO YOURSELF! THE CITY, IT'S A FAILED EXPERIMENT! GOTHAM ISN'T SOME TAME GARDEN! IT'S A WILD, BLOODY LANDSCAPE!
"YOU LIKE YOUR NEIGHBOR? NO, YOU DON'T. YOU HATE THEM. THEY HATE YOU. YOU SMILE, YOU NOD, BUT YOU KNOW WHAT? SAY DAMN THEM. DO IT. **DAMN THEM.**
"THAT'S RIGHT. AND YOU. SAY IT: DAMN THE PEOPLE HERE ILLEGALLY, DRIVING UP YOUR TAXES. AND IF YOU'RE HERE ILLEGALLY, YOU SAY IT: DAMN THE PEOPLE WHO HELPED SCREW UP YOUR HOME AND THEN WANT TO SEND YOU BACK THERE."

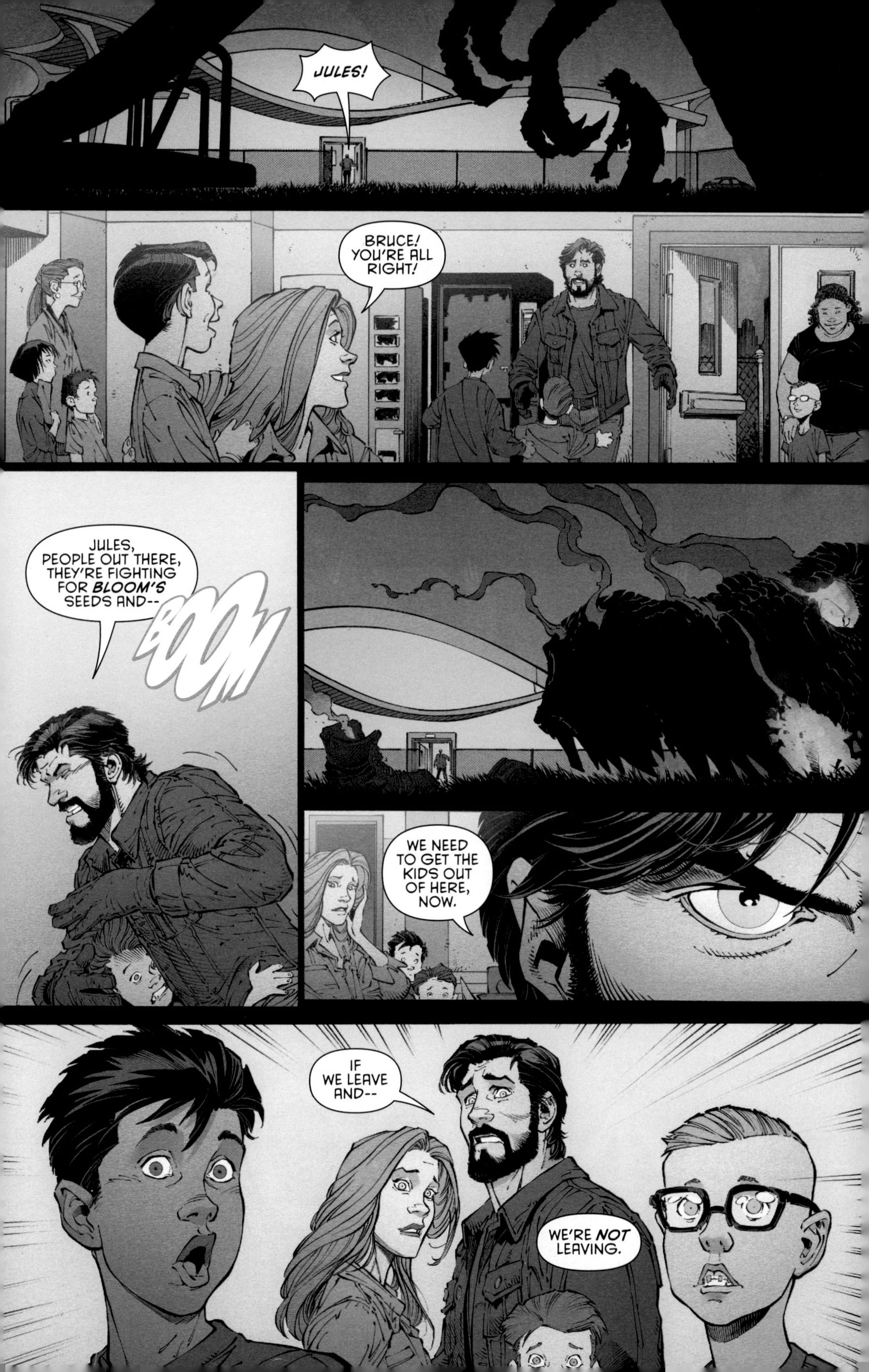
JULES!
BRUCE! YOU'RE ALL RIGHT!
JULES, PEOPLE OUT THERE, THEY'RE FIGHTING FOR *BLOOM'S* SEEDS AND--
BOOM
WE NEED TO GET THE KIDS OUT OF HERE, NOW.
IF WE LEAVE AND--
WE'RE *NOT* LEAVING.

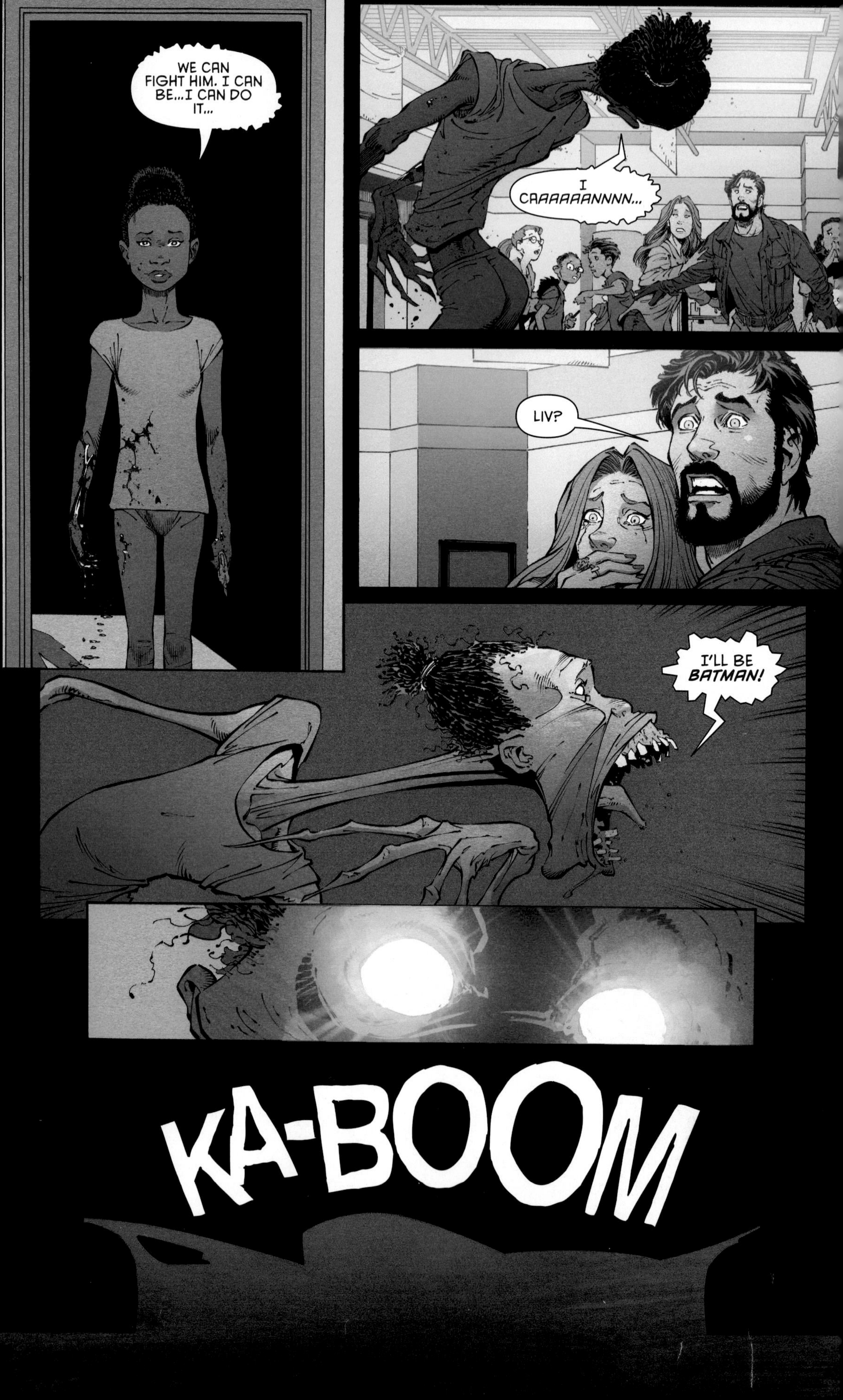
WE CAN FIGHT HIM. I CAN BE...I CAN DO IT...
I CAAAAAANNNN...
LIV?
I'LL BE BATMAN!
KA-BOOM

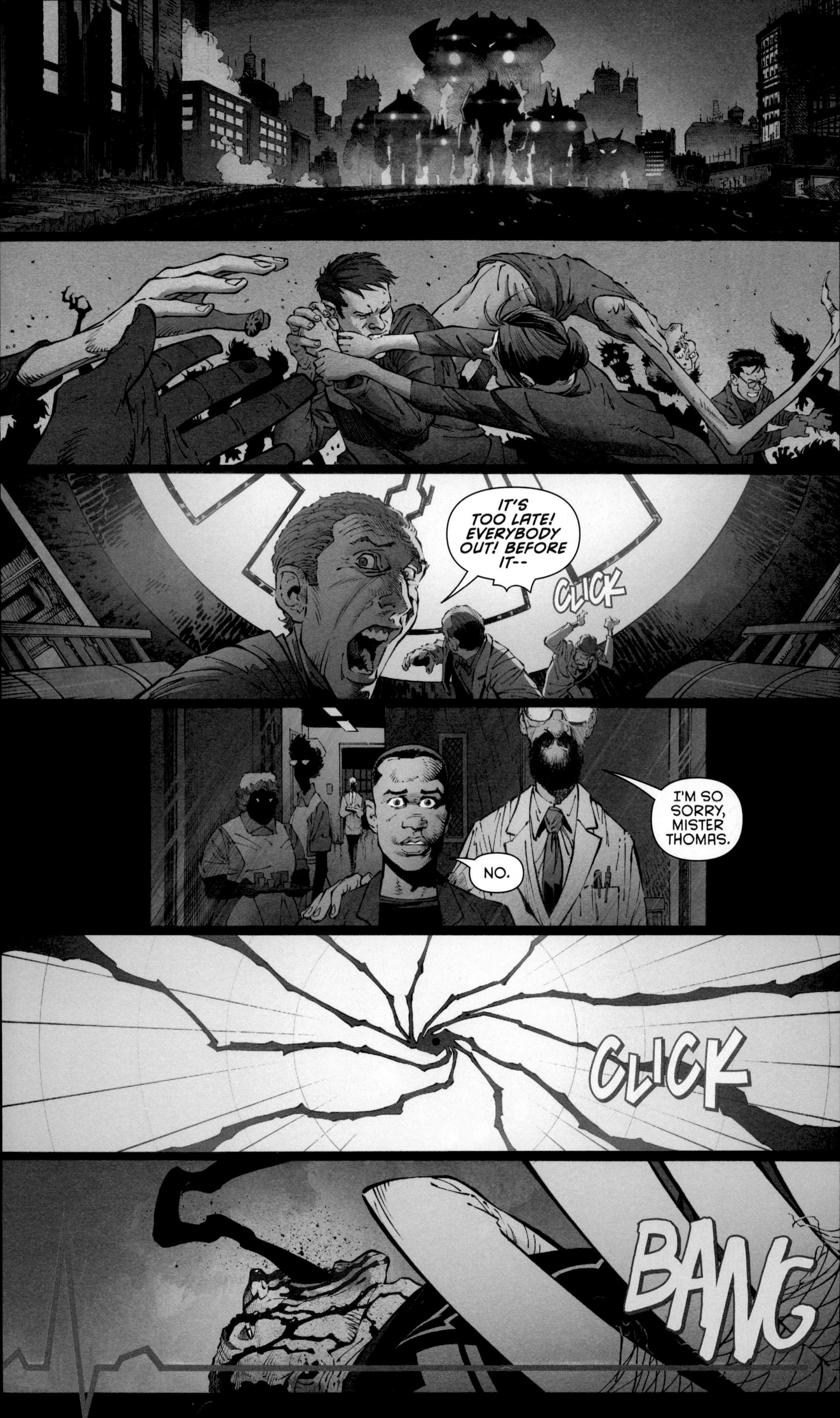
IT'S TOO LATE! EVERYBODY OUT! BEFORE IT--
CLICK
I'M SO SORRY, MISTER THOMAS.
NO.
CLICK
BANG

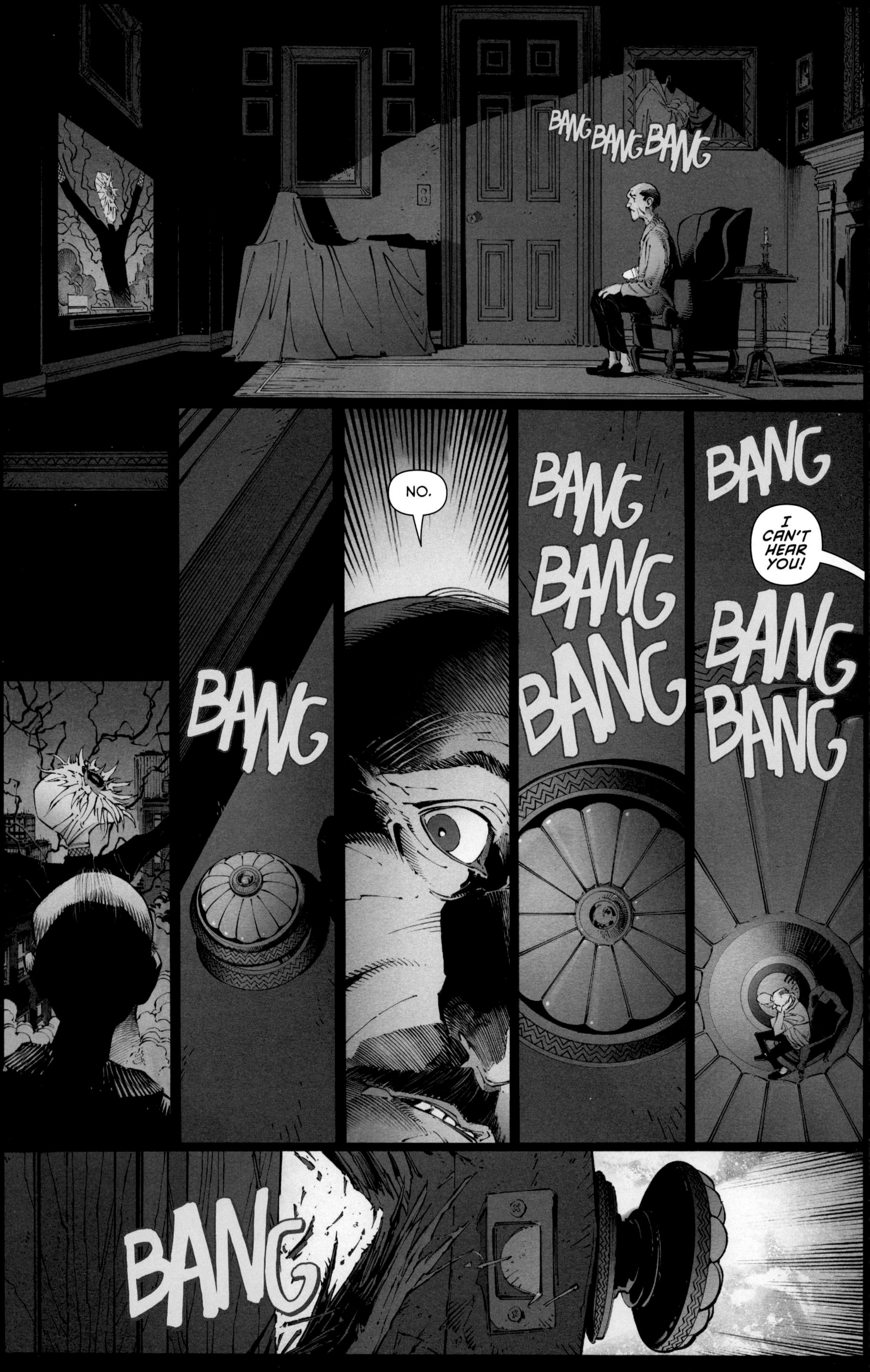
BANG BANG BANG
NO.
BANG
BANG
BANG
BANG
BANG
I CAN'T HEAR YOU!
BANG
BANG
BANG

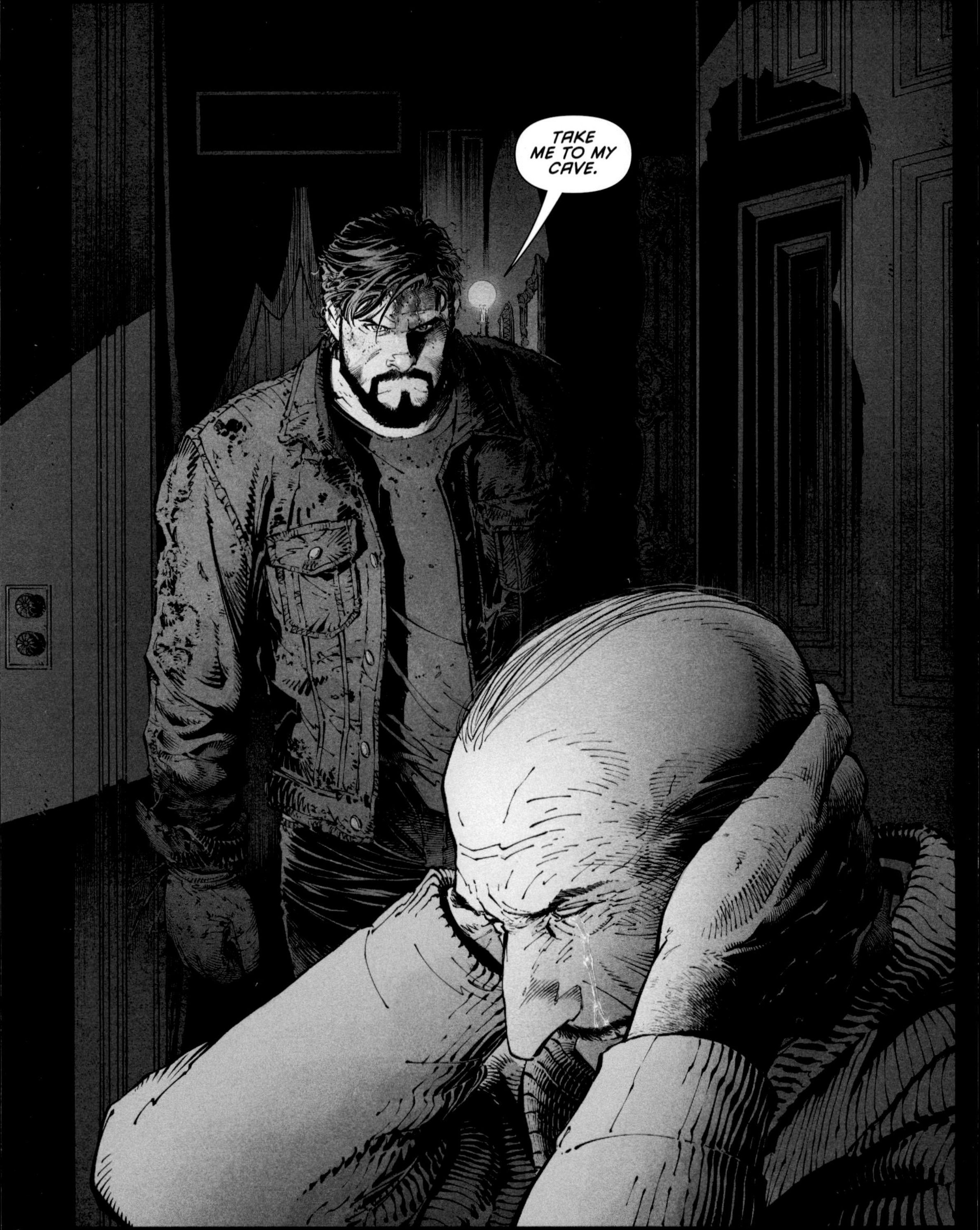
TAKE ME TO MY CAVE.

SUPERHEAVY

PART EIGHT

SCOTT SNYDER WRITER GREG CAPULLO PENCILS
DANNY MIKI INKS FCO PLASCENCIA COLORS STEVE WANDS LETTERS
CAPULLO, MIKI, PLASCENCIA COVER DAVE JOHNSON ADULT COLORING BOOK VARIANT COVER
REBECCA TAYLOR ASSOCIATE EDITOR MARK DOYLE EDITOR
BATMAN CREATED BY BOB KANE WITH BILL FINGER

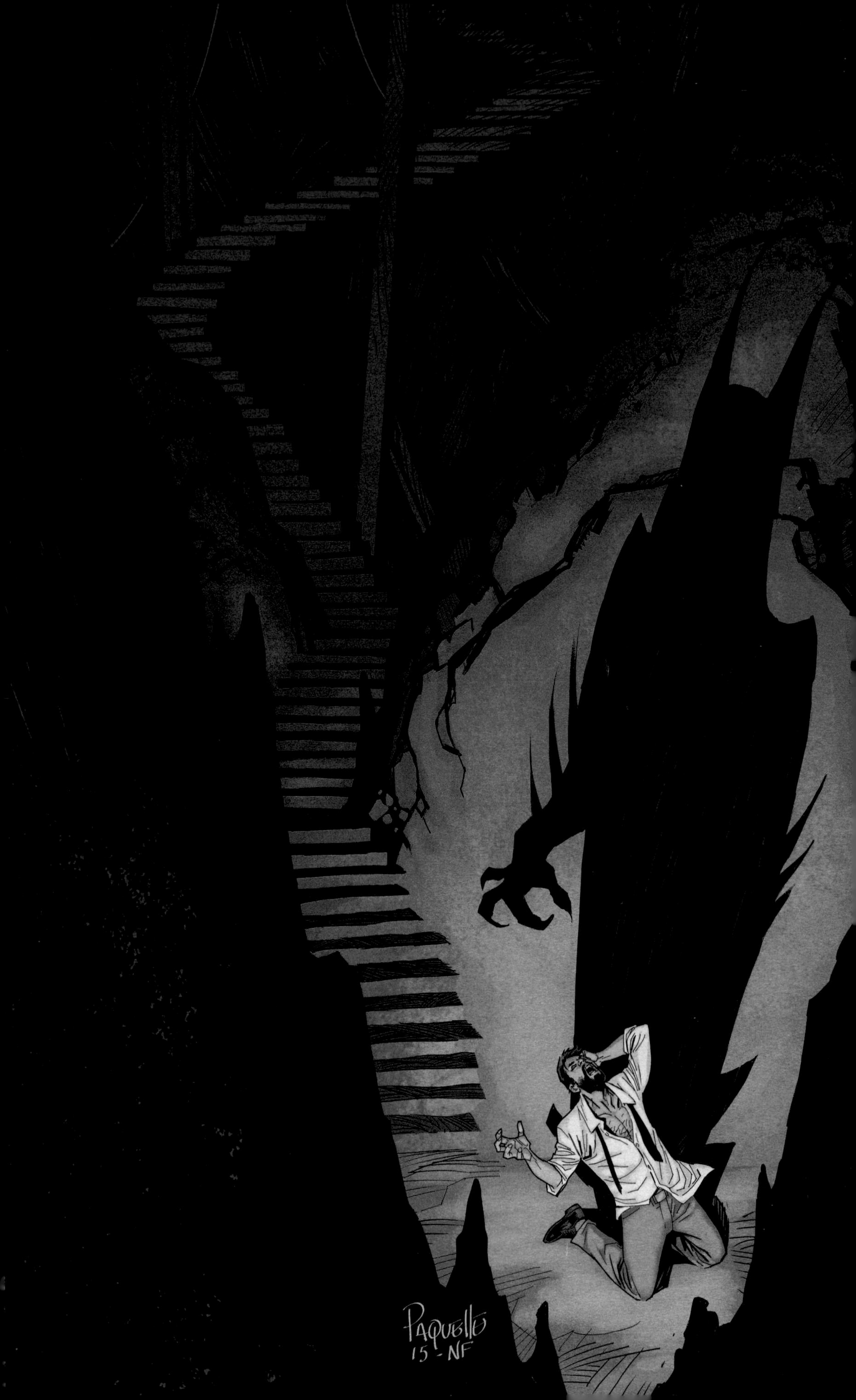

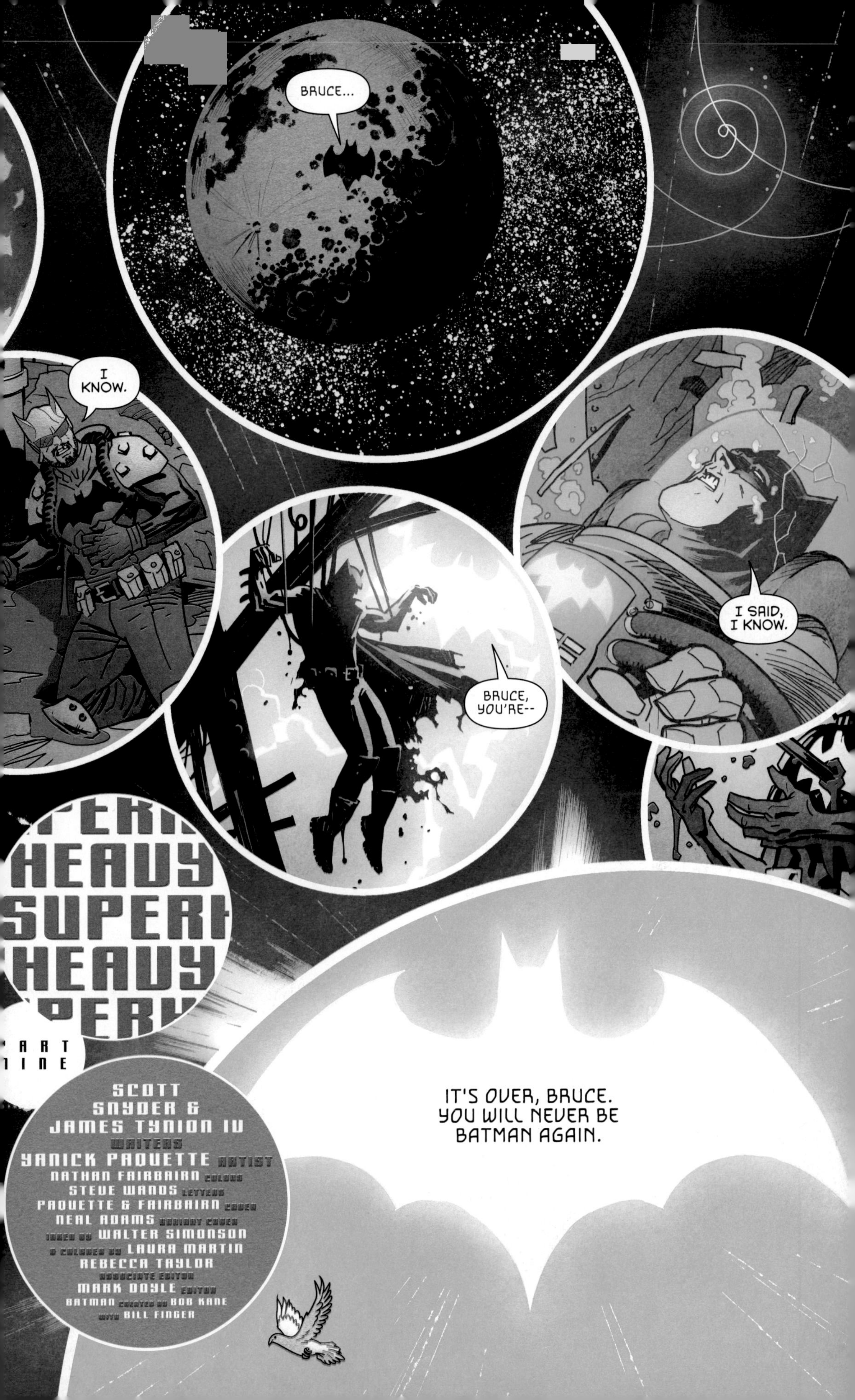
BRUCE...
I KNOW.
BRUCE, YOU'RE--
I SAID, I KNOW.
HEAVY
HEAVY
SCOTT SNYDER & JAMES TYNION IV WRITERS
YANICK PAQUETTE ARTIST
NATHAN FAIRBAIRN COLORS
STEVE WANDS LETTERS
PAQUETTE & FAIRBAIRN COVER
NEAL ADAMS VARIANT COVER
INKED BY WALTER SIMONSON
& COLORED BY LAURA MARTIN
REBECCA TAYLOR ASSOCIATE EDITOR
MARK DOYLE EDITOR
BATMAN CREATED BY BOB KANE WITH BILL FINGER
IT'S OVER, BRUCE. YOU WILL NEVER BE BATMAN AGAIN.

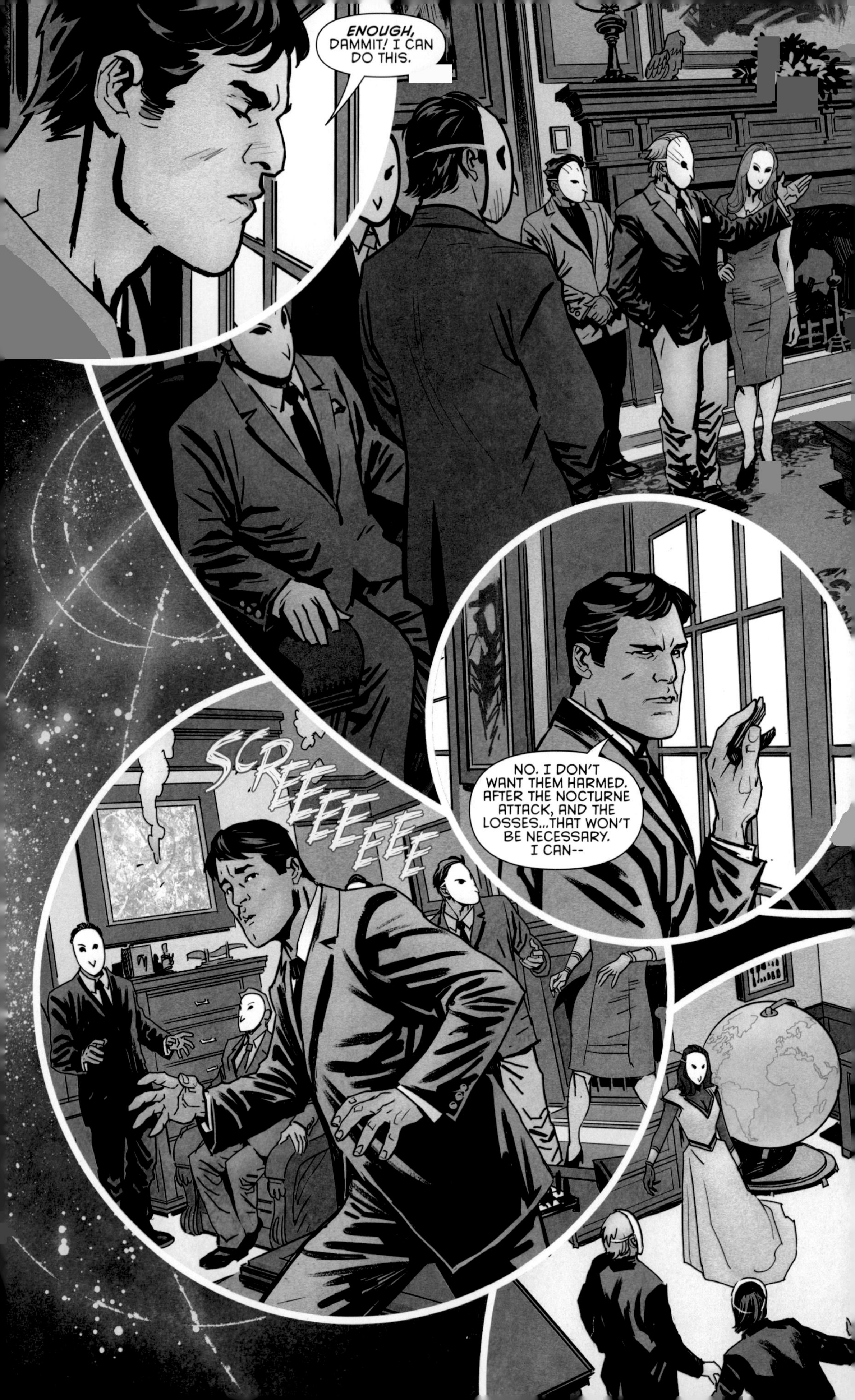
ENOUGH, DAMMIT! I CAN DO THIS.
NO. I DON'T WANT THEM HARMED. AFTER THE NOCTURNE ATTACK, AND THE LOSSES...THAT WON'T BE NECESSARY. I CAN--
SCREEEEEEEEE

WAYNE MANOR...

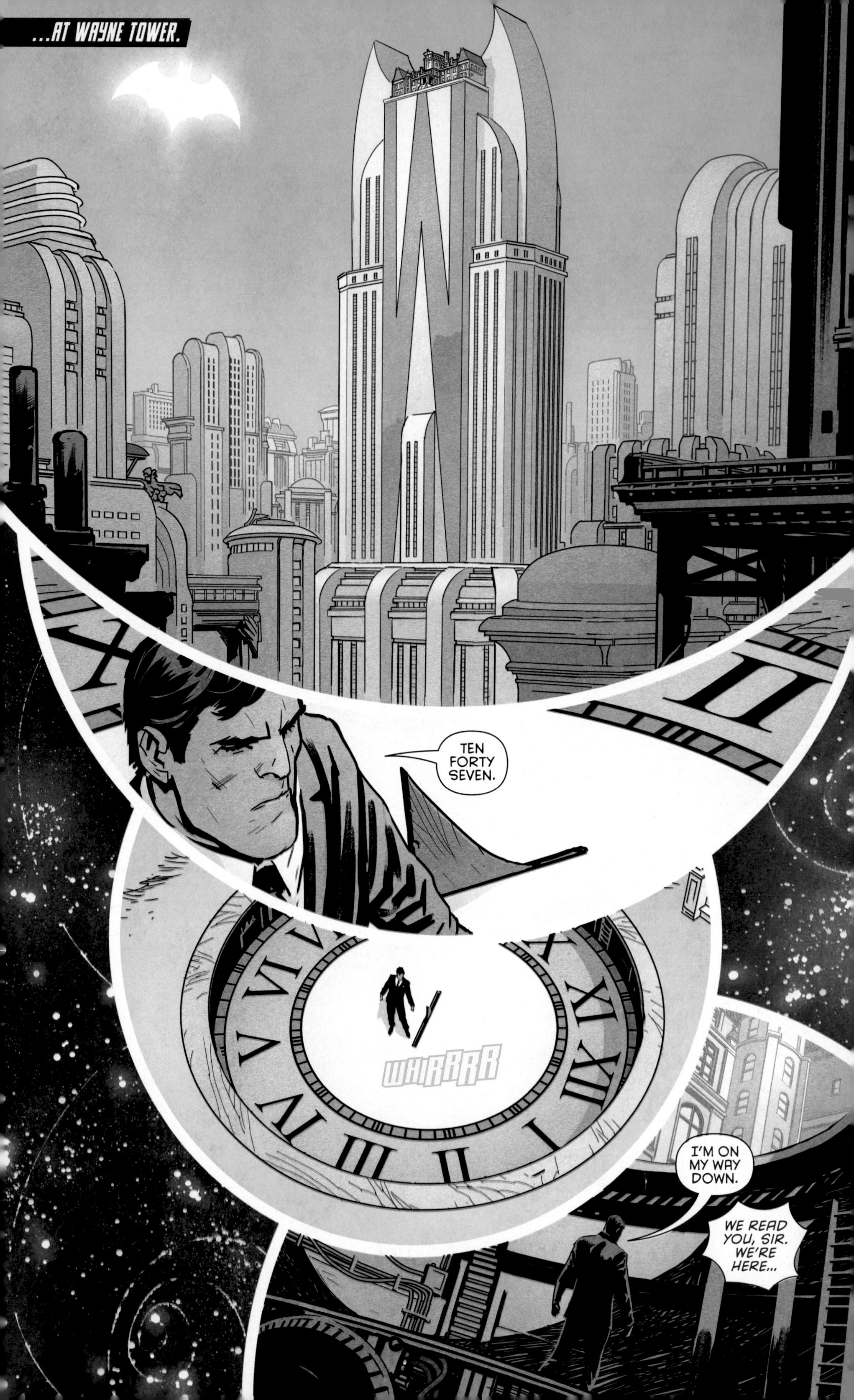
...AT WAYNE TOWER.
TEN FORTY SEVEN.
WHIRRRR
I'M ON MY WAY DOWN.
WE READ YOU, SIR. WE'RE HERE...

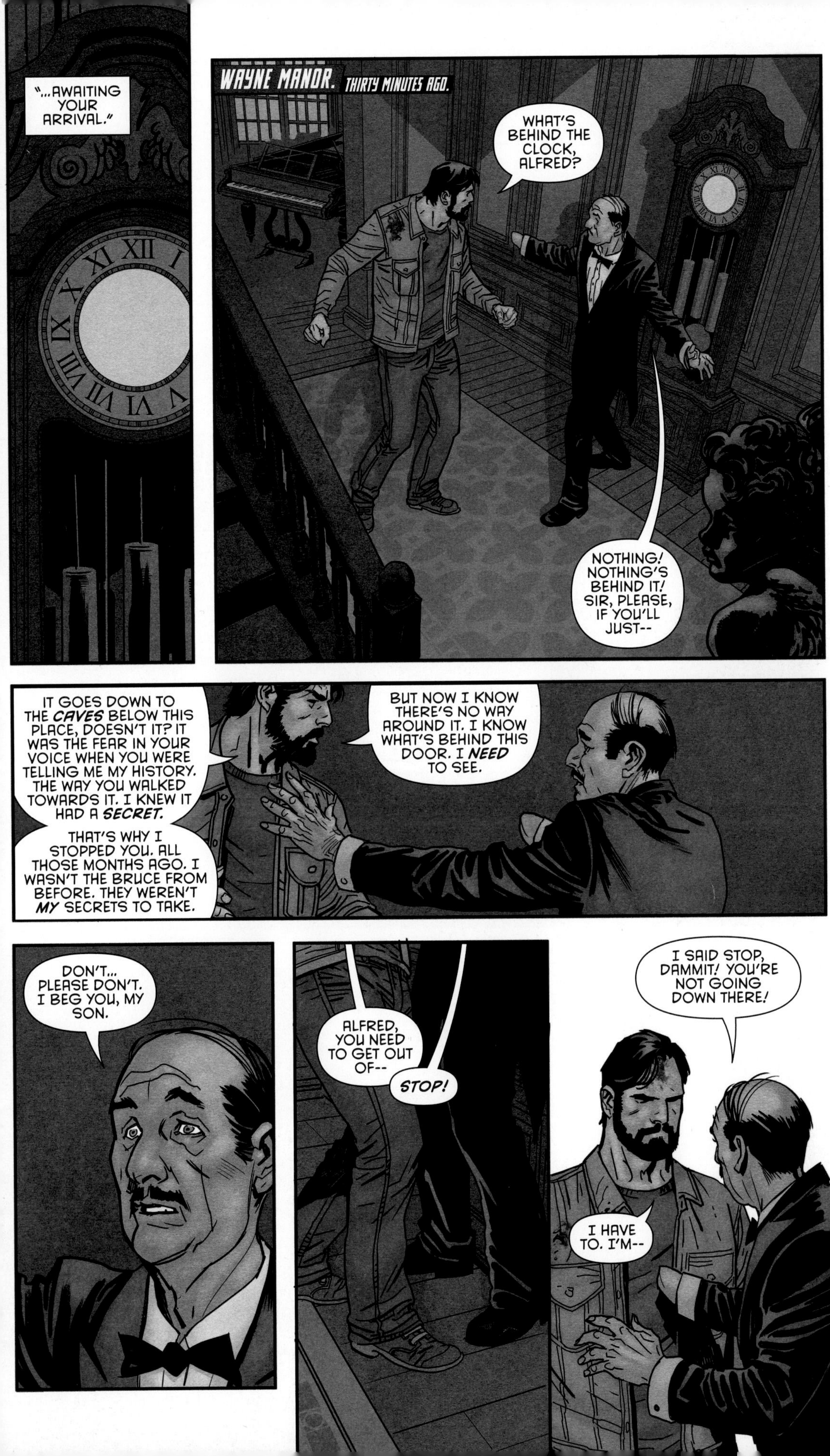
"...AWAITING YOUR ARRIVAL."
WAYNE MANOR. THIRTY MINUTES AGO.
WHAT'S BEHIND THE CLOCK, ALFRED?
NOTHING! NOTHING'S BEHIND IT! SIR, PLEASE, IF YOU'LL JUST--
IT GOES DOWN TO THE CAVES BELOW THIS PLACE, DOESN'T IT? IT WAS THE FEAR IN YOUR VOICE WHEN YOU WERE TELLING ME MY HISTORY. THE WAY YOU WALKED TOWARDS IT. I KNEW IT HAD A SECRET.
THAT'S WHY I STOPPED YOU. ALL THOSE MONTHS AGO. I WASN'T THE BRUCE FROM BEFORE. THEY WEREN'T MY SECRETS TO TAKE.
BUT NOW I KNOW THERE'S NO WAY AROUND IT. I KNOW WHAT'S BEHIND THIS DOOR. I NEED TO SEE.
DON'T... PLEASE DON'T. I BEG YOU, MY SON.
ALFRED, YOU NEED TO GET OUT OF--
STOP!
I SAID STOP, DAMMIT! YOU'RE NOT GOING DOWN THERE!
I HAVE TO. I'M--

NO! YOU'RE NOT! YOU'RE NOT HIM! HE'S *DEAD*! HE FINALLY DIED! DIED FIGHTING THAT MONSTER LIKE HE WANTED AND--

...ALFRED YOU'RE CHOK--

THE CITY GAVE YOU BACK! YOU'RE MY BOY! AND YOU *CAN'T* GO BACK!

YOU CAN'T...

THE *MACHINE*... I SMASHED IT.

WHAT MACHINE?

PLEASE, MASTER BRUCE. THERE'S NOTHING FOR YOU DOWN THERE ANYMORE. NOTHING. LET *JIM GORDON* BE THE HERO.

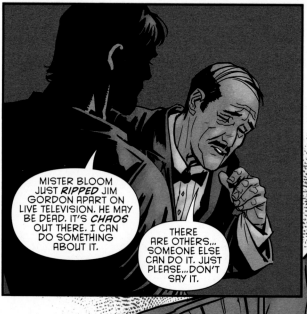

MISTER BLOOM JUST *RIPPED* JIM GORDON APART ON LIVE TELEVISION. HE MAY BE DEAD. IT'S *CHAOS* OUT THERE. I CAN DO SOMETHING ABOUT IT.

THERE ARE OTHERS... SOMEONE ELSE CAN DO IT. JUST PLEASE...DON'T SAY IT.

ALFRED.

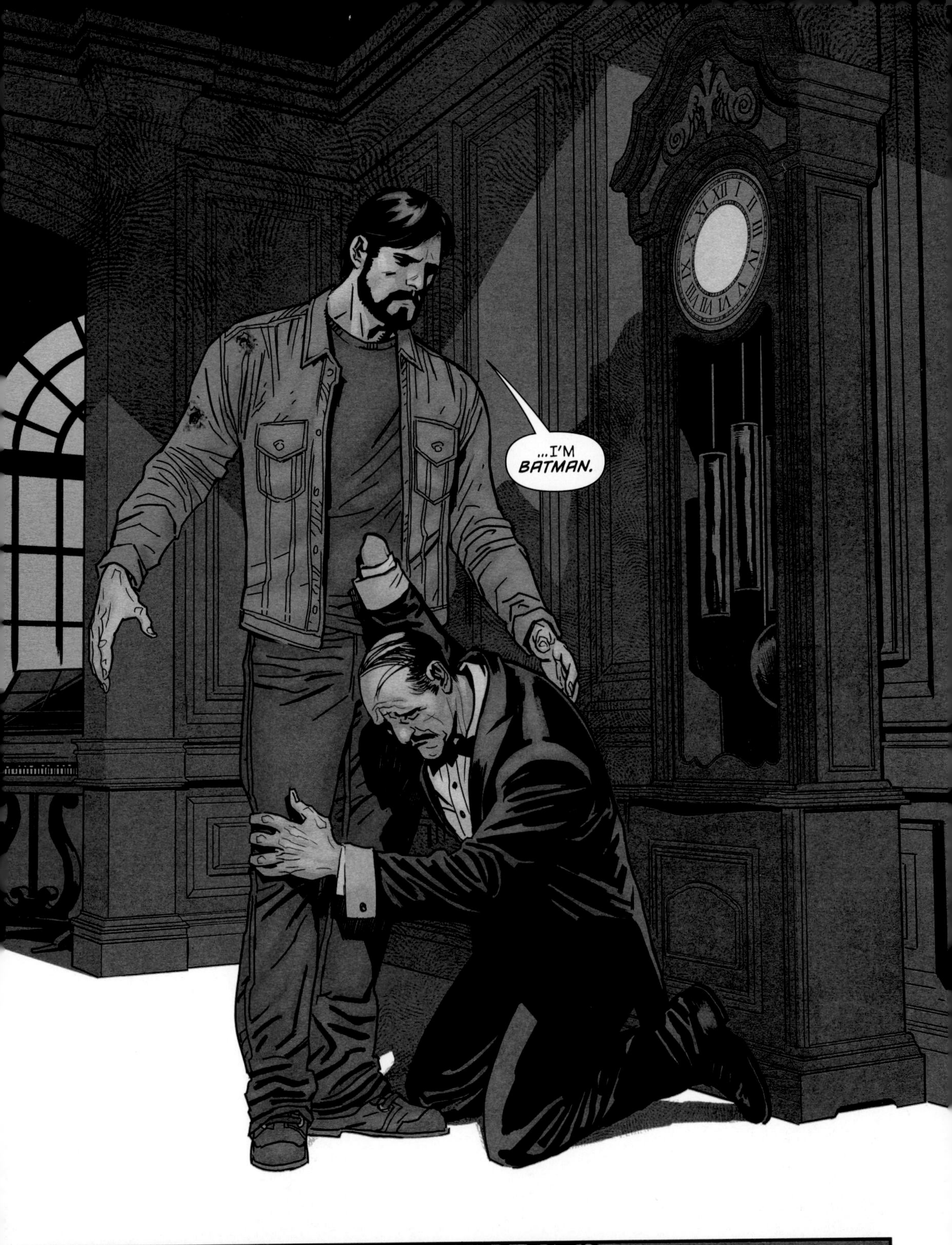
...I'M BATMAN.

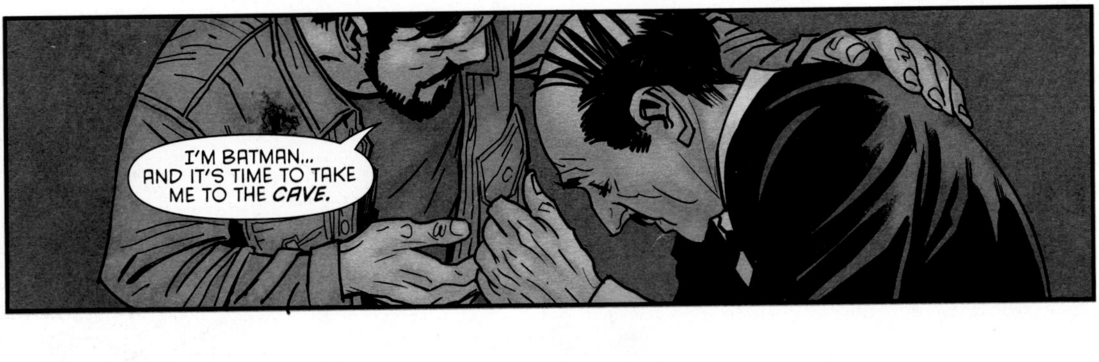
I'M BATMAN... AND IT'S TIME TO TAKE ME TO THE CAVE.

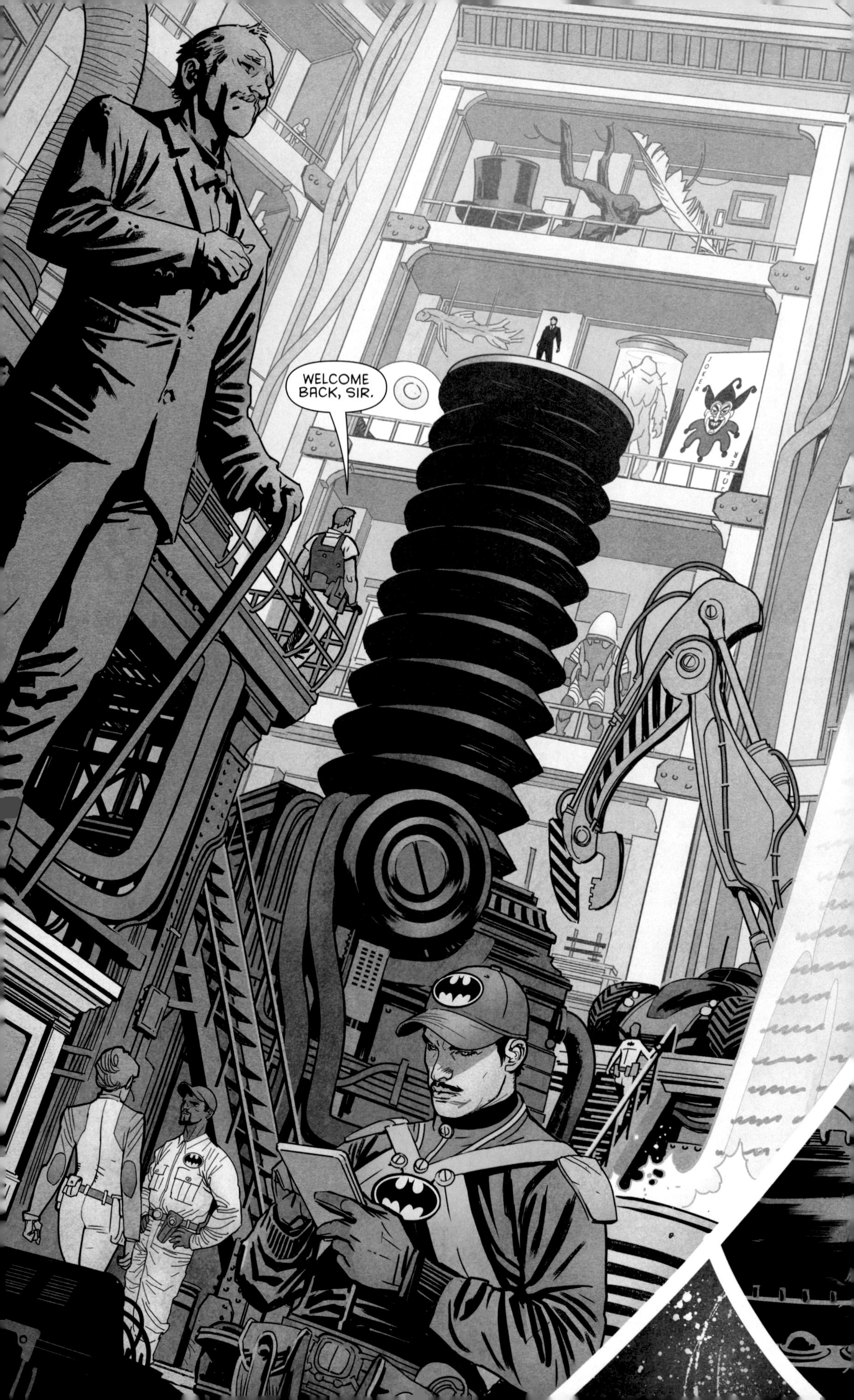
WELCOME BACK, SIR.
JOKER

MISTER CHILL.

WHERE IS IT NOW?

IT'S RIGHT ON TOP OF US, SIR. I DON'T KNOW HOW WE'RE GOING TO--

WE'LL DO IT BECAUSE WE HAVE TO.

...

DAMN RIGHT, SIR.

WHAT'S GOING ON HERE? THE MEMORIAL WATERFALL WAS SUPPOSED TO BE EXPANDED BY NOW.

IT'S JUST... WE'D HAVE TO MOVE TROPHIES, SIR. AND FRANKLY...

...I WONDERED HOW GOOD FOR MORALE--

EVERYONE WHO DIED IN GOTHAM HAS A PLACE HERE. IT'S *THEIR* CAVE, TOO. NOW LET'S HURRY...

Goo

Alex Ferr

Jeffrey V. War

arcus To Amelie

asheed Purvis   Kv

obert Greene   Ri

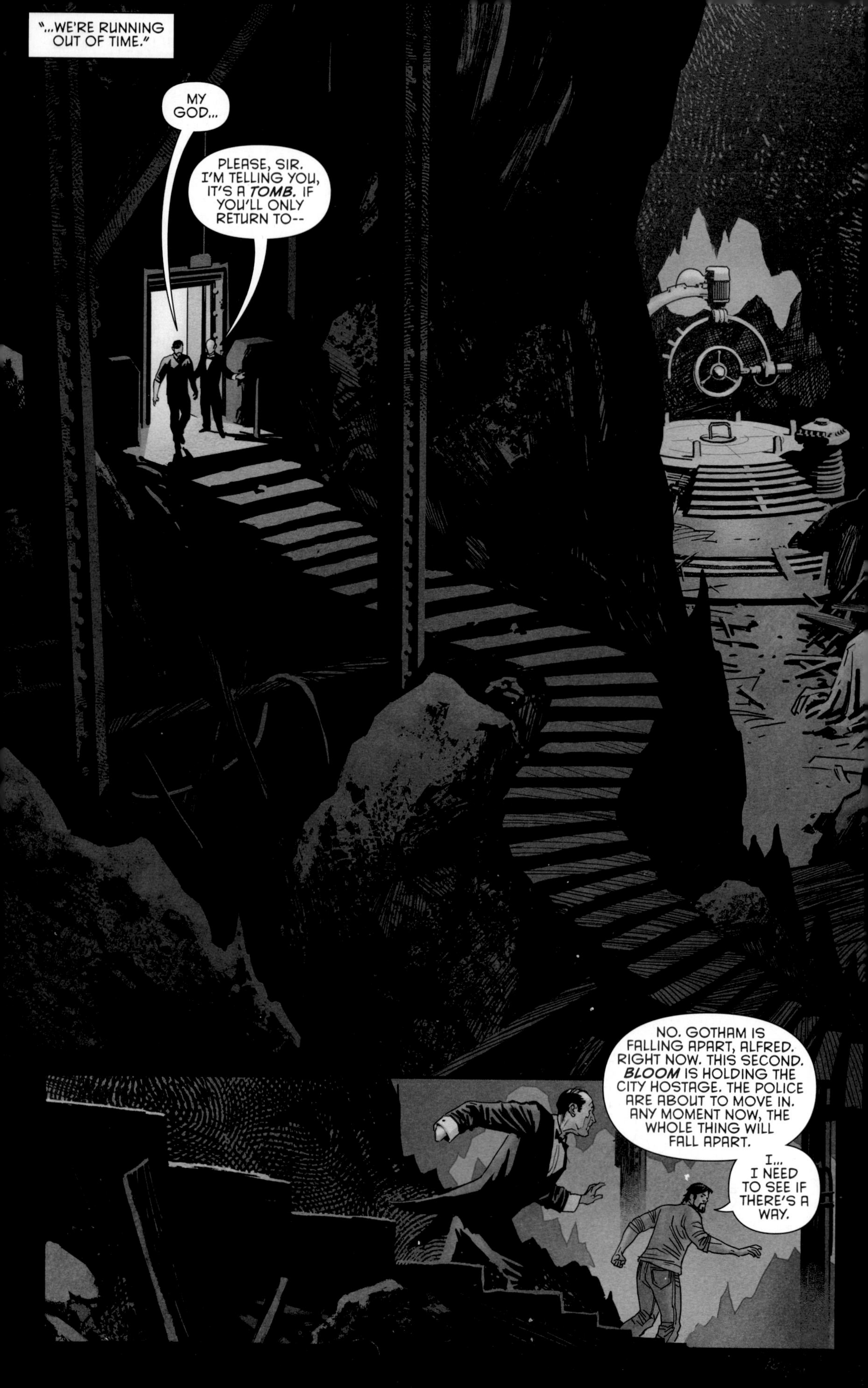
"...WE'RE RUNNING OUT OF TIME."
MY GOD...
PLEASE, SIR. I'M TELLING YOU, IT'S A *TOMB.* IF YOU'LL ONLY RETURN TO--
NO. GOTHAM IS FALLING APART, ALFRED. RIGHT NOW. THIS SECOND. *BLOOM* IS HOLDING THE CITY HOSTAGE. THE POLICE ARE ABOUT TO MOVE IN. ANY MOMENT NOW, THE WHOLE THING WILL FALL APART.
I... I NEED TO SEE IF THERE'S A WAY.

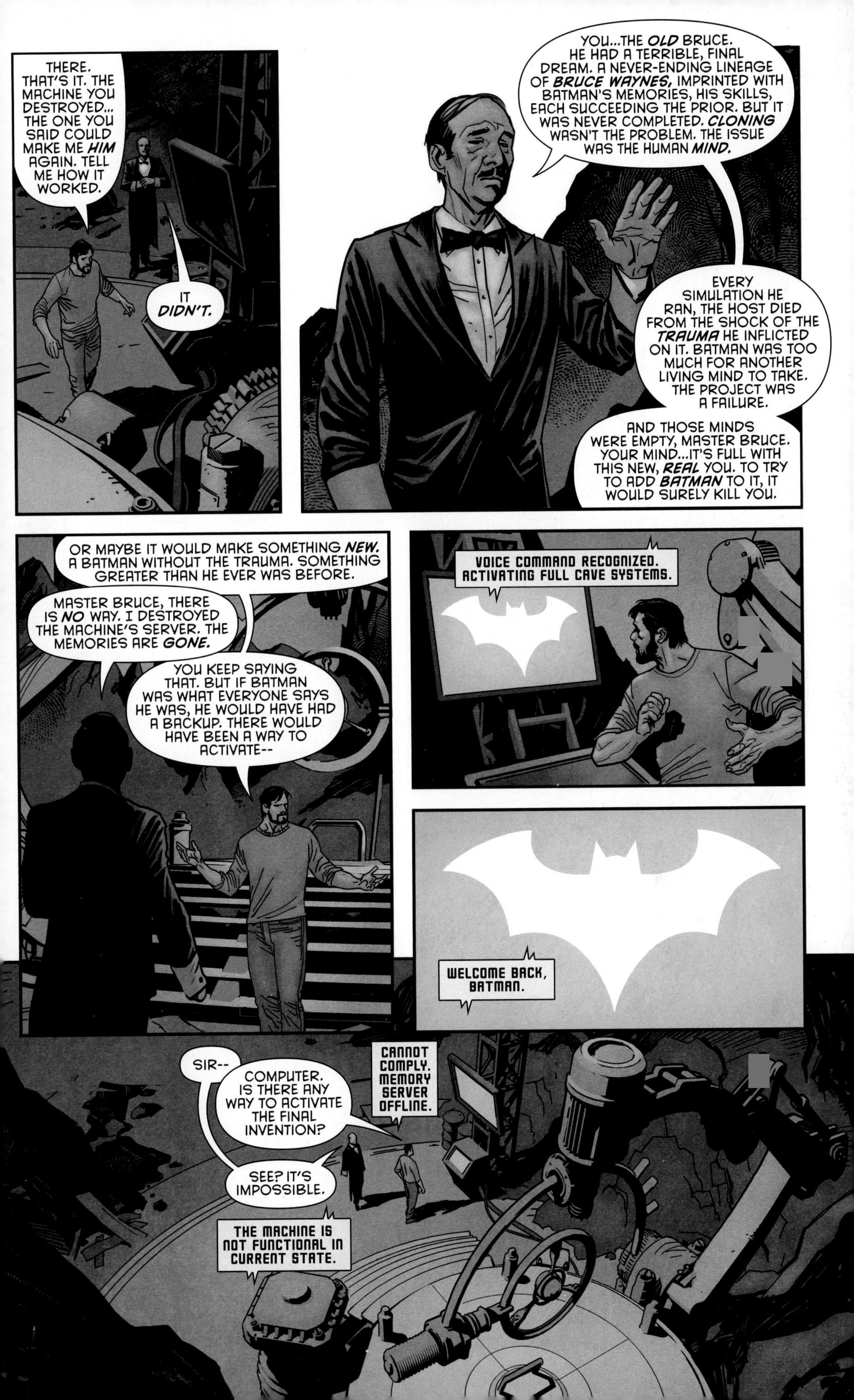
THERE. THAT'S IT. THE MACHINE YOU DESTROYED... THE ONE YOU SAID COULD MAKE ME HIM AGAIN. TELL ME HOW IT WORKED.
IT DIDN'T.
YOU...THE OLD BRUCE. HE HAD A TERRIBLE, FINAL DREAM. A NEVER-ENDING LINEAGE OF BRUCE WAYNES, IMPRINTED WITH BATMAN'S MEMORIES, HIS SKILLS, EACH SUCCEEDING THE PRIOR. BUT IT WAS NEVER COMPLETED. CLONING WASN'T THE PROBLEM. THE ISSUE WAS THE HUMAN MIND.
EVERY SIMULATION HE RAN, THE HOST DIED FROM THE SHOCK OF THE TRAUMA HE INFLICTED ON IT. BATMAN WAS TOO MUCH FOR ANOTHER LIVING MIND TO TAKE. THE PROJECT WAS A FAILURE.
AND THOSE MINDS WERE EMPTY, MASTER BRUCE. YOUR MIND...IT'S FULL WITH THIS NEW, REAL YOU. TO TRY TO ADD BATMAN TO IT, IT WOULD SURELY KILL YOU.
OR MAYBE IT WOULD MAKE SOMETHING NEW. A BATMAN WITHOUT THE TRAUMA. SOMETHING GREATER THAN HE EVER WAS BEFORE.
MASTER BRUCE, THERE IS NO WAY. I DESTROYED THE MACHINE'S SERVER. THE MEMORIES ARE GONE.
YOU KEEP SAYING THAT. BUT IF BATMAN WAS WHAT EVERYONE SAYS HE WAS, HE WOULD HAVE HAD A BACKUP. THERE WOULD HAVE BEEN A WAY TO ACTIVATE--
VOICE COMMAND RECOGNIZED. ACTIVATING FULL CAVE SYSTEMS.
WELCOME BACK, BATMAN.
SIR--
COMPUTER. IS THERE ANY WAY TO ACTIVATE THE FINAL INVENTION?
CANNOT COMPLY. MEMORY SERVER OFFLINE.
SEE? IT'S IMPOSSIBLE.
THE MACHINE IS NOT FUNCTIONAL IN CURRENT STATE.

THERE HAS TO BE A WAY...I KNOW HE WOULD HAVE HAD A WAY OUT, EVEN FROM THIS. COMPUTER...ARE ANY OTHER SERVERS COMPATIBLE WITH THE MACHINE?

ONE RESULT FOUND.

SHALL I ACTIVATE THE ALFRED PROTOCOL?

ALF

WHAT ON EARTH?

ACTIVATE IT.

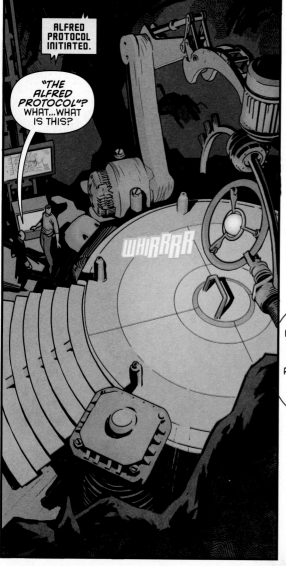

ALFRED PROTOCOL INITIATED.

"THE ALFRED PROTOCOL"? WHAT...WHAT IS THIS?

WHIRRRR

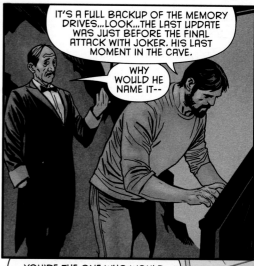

IT'S A FULL BACKUP OF THE MEMORY DRIVES...LOOK...THE LAST UPDATE WAS JUST BEFORE THE FINAL ATTACK WITH JOKER. HIS LAST MOMENT IN THE CAVE.

WHY WOULD HE NAME IT--

YOU'RE THE ONE WHO WOULD ALWAYS PATCH HIM UP AND MAKE HIM NEW WHEN HE FELL. WHO ELSE WOULD HE ENTRUST THE WHOLE OF BATMAN TO?

MAYBE THE ALFRED STANDING IN FRONT OF ME WOULDN'T DO IT, BUT I THINK THERE ARE TWO *GHOSTS* DOWN IN THIS CAVE. THE MAN I WAS, AND THE ONE PERSON HE TRUSTED MORE THAN ANYONE TO FATHER EACH GENERATION OF BATMAN.

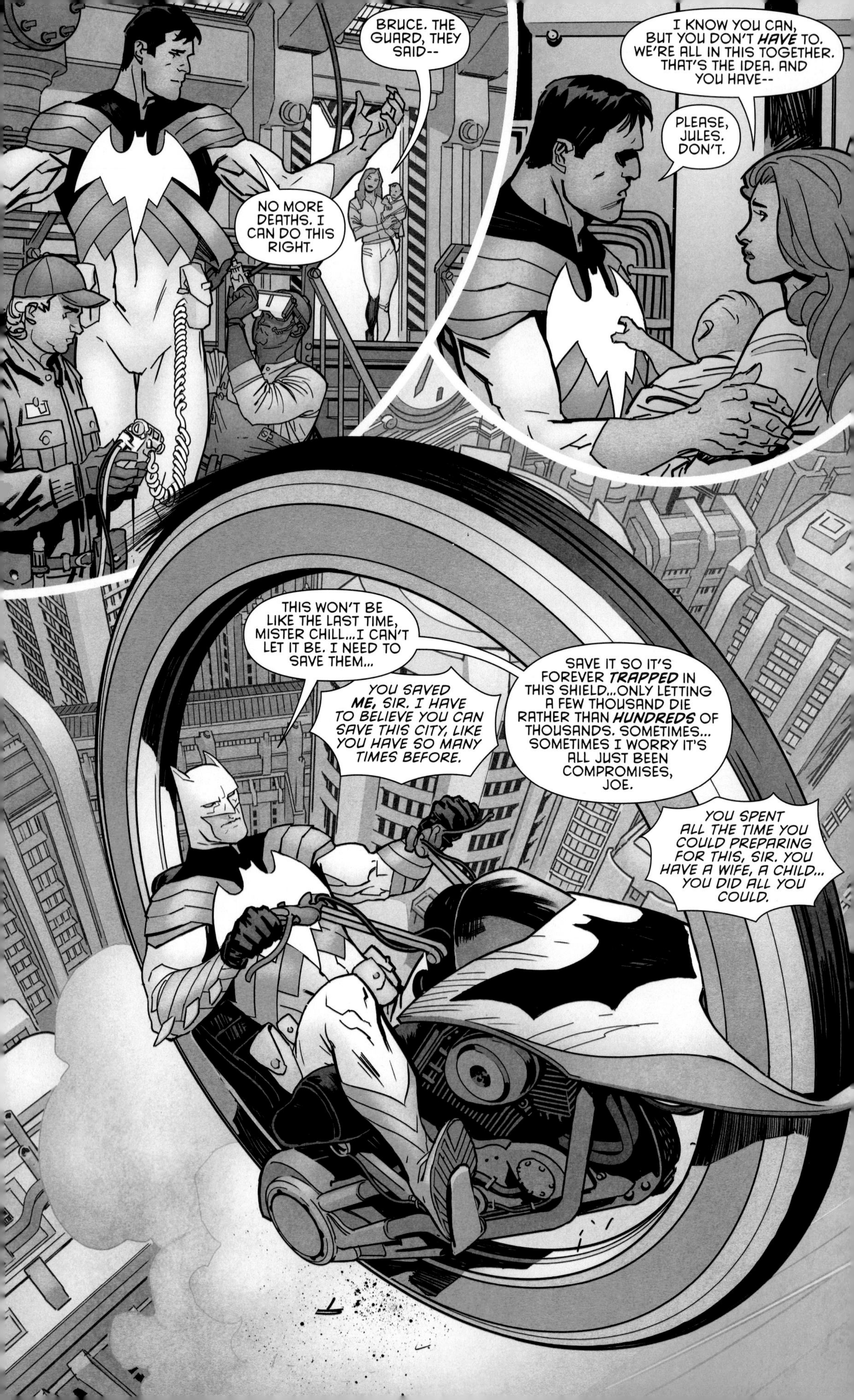
BRUCE. THE GUARD, THEY SAID--
NO MORE DEATHS. I CAN DO THIS RIGHT.
I KNOW YOU CAN, BUT YOU DON'T *HAVE* TO. WE'RE ALL IN THIS TOGETHER. THAT'S THE IDEA. AND YOU HAVE--
PLEASE, JULES. DON'T.
THIS WON'T BE LIKE THE LAST TIME, MISTER CHILL...I CAN'T LET IT BE. I NEED TO SAVE THEM...
YOU SAVED ***ME,*** *SIR. I HAVE TO BELIEVE YOU CAN SAVE THIS CITY, LIKE YOU HAVE SO MANY TIMES BEFORE.*
SAVE IT SO IT'S FOREVER ***TRAPPED*** IN THIS SHIELD...ONLY LETTING A FEW THOUSAND DIE RATHER THAN ***HUNDREDS*** OF THOUSANDS. SOMETIMES... SOMETIMES I WORRY IT'S ALL JUST BEEN COMPROMISES, JOE.
YOU SPENT ALL THE TIME YOU COULD PREPARING FOR THIS, SIR. YOU HAVE A WIFE, A CHILD... YOU DID ALL YOU COULD.

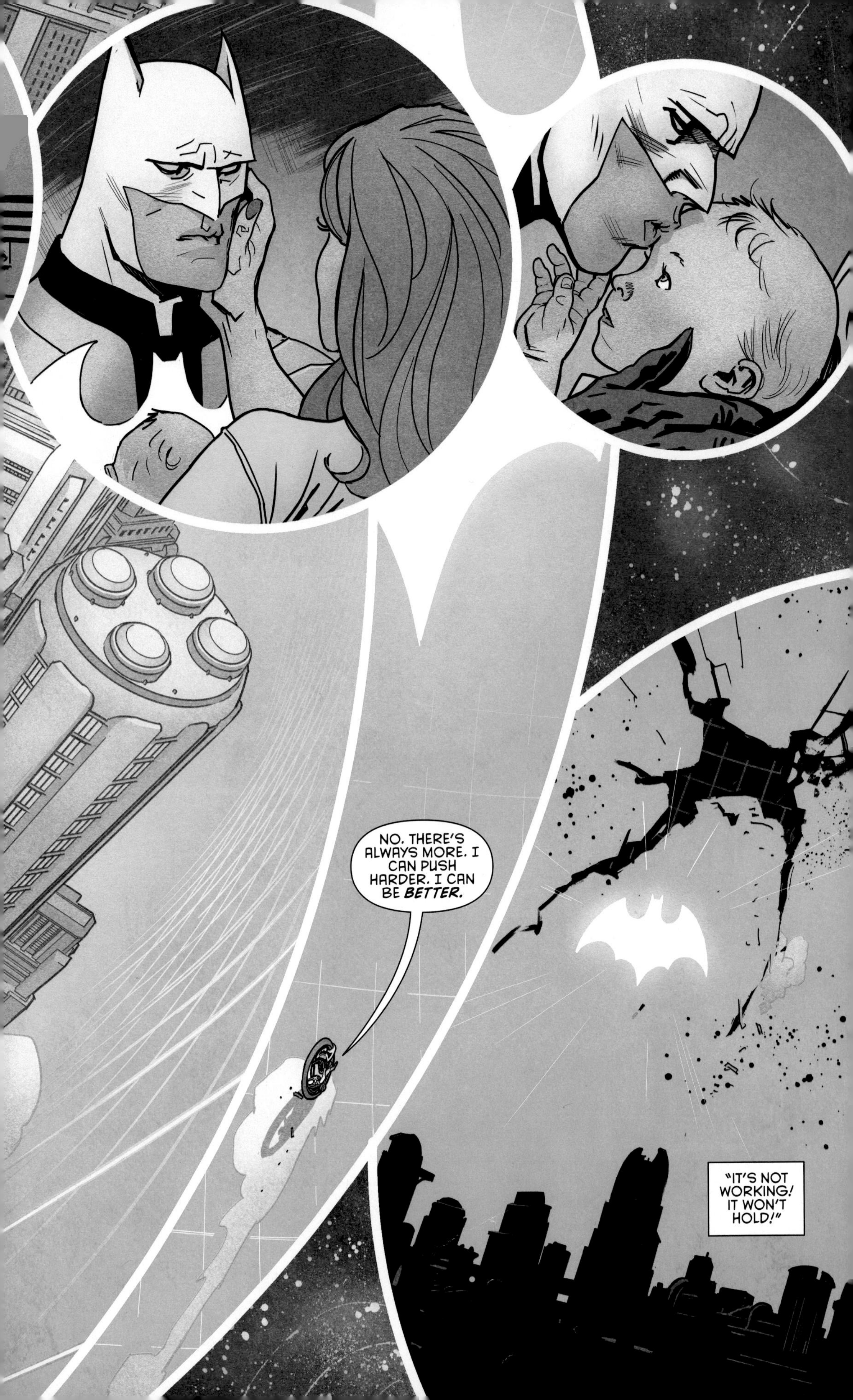
NO. THERE'S ALWAYS MORE. I CAN PUSH HARDER. I CAN BE *BETTER.*
"IT'S NOT WORKING! IT WON'T HOLD!"

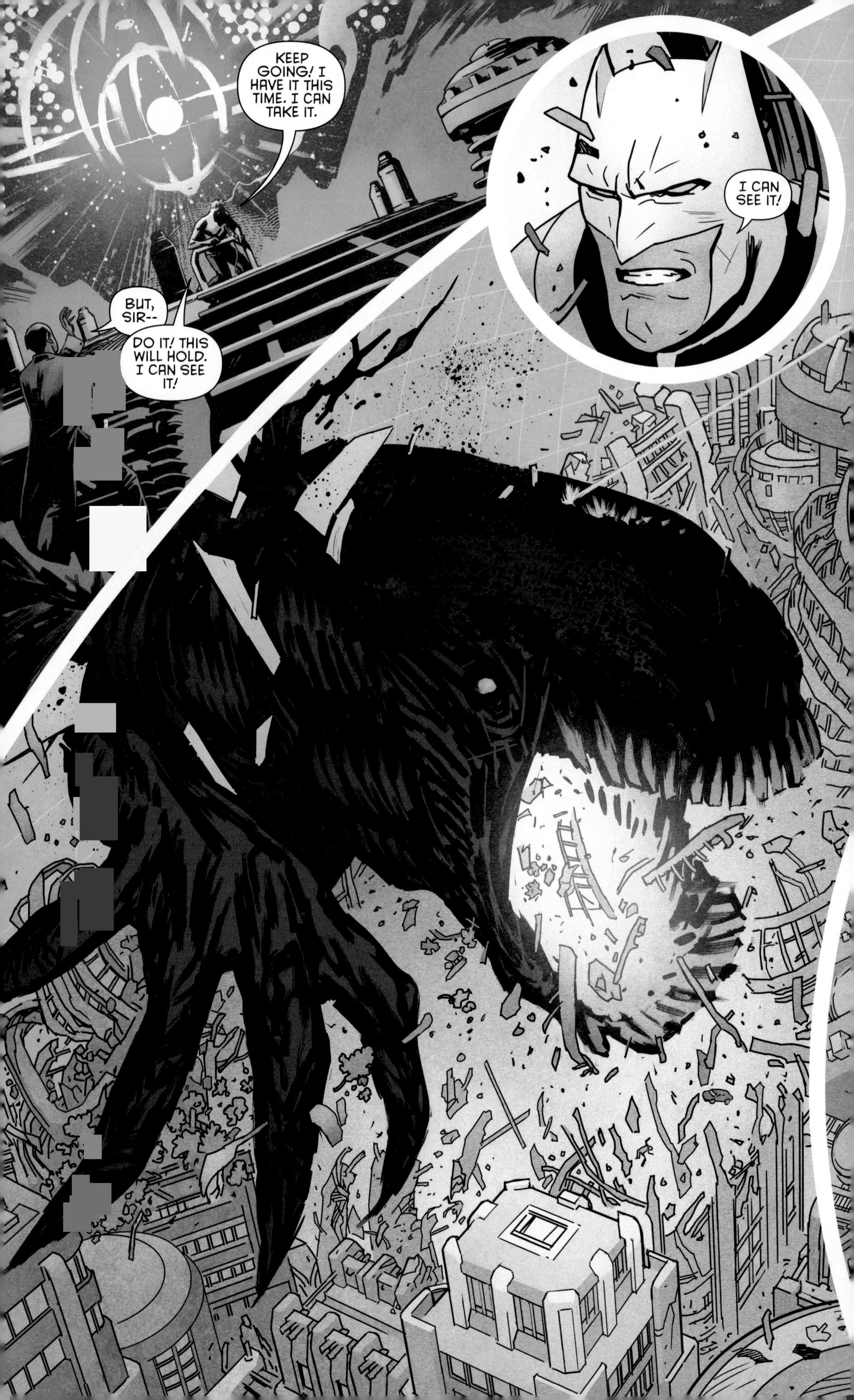
KEEP GOING! I HAVE IT THIS TIME. I CAN TAKE IT.
BUT, SIR--
DO IT! THIS WILL HOLD. I CAN SEE IT!
I CAN SEE IT!

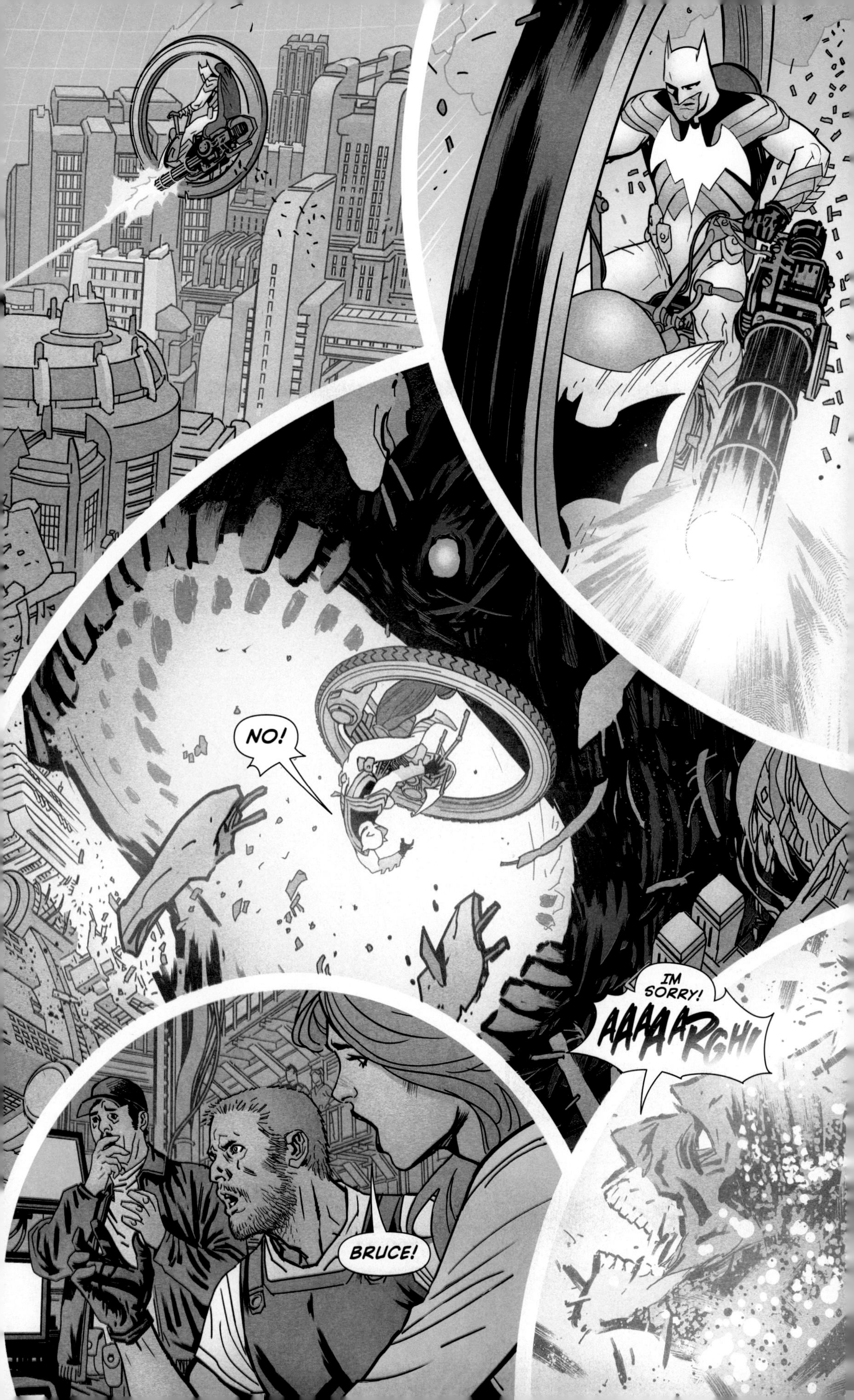
NO!
IM SORRY!
AAAAARGH!
BRUCE!

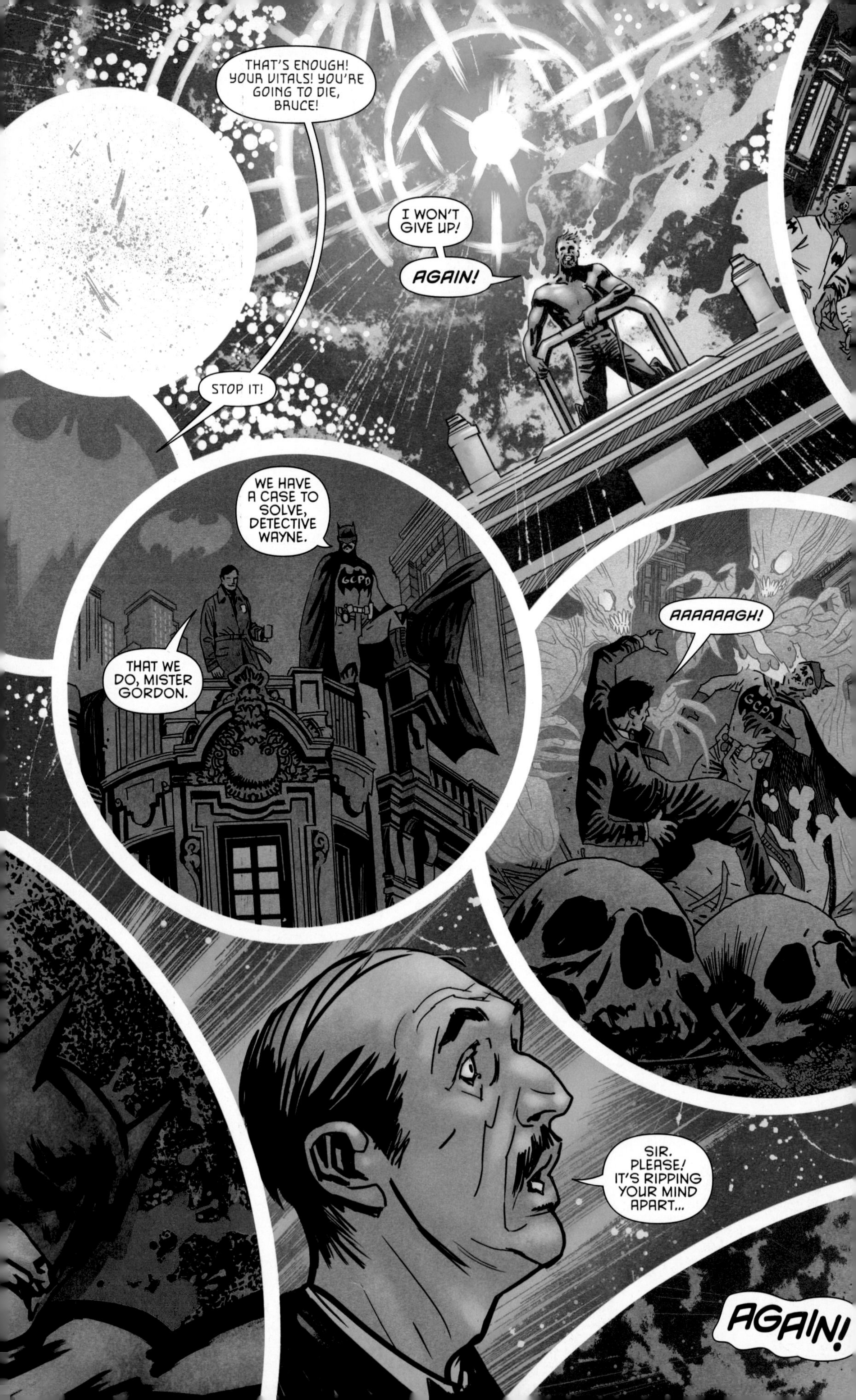

THAT'S ENOUGH! YOUR VITALS! YOU'RE GOING TO DIE, BRUCE!
STOP IT!
I WON'T GIVE UP!
AGAIN!
WE HAVE A CASE TO SOLVE, DETECTIVE WAYNE.
THAT WE DO, MISTER GORDON.
AAAAAAGH!
SIR. PLEASE! IT'S RIPPING YOUR MIND APART...
AGAIN!

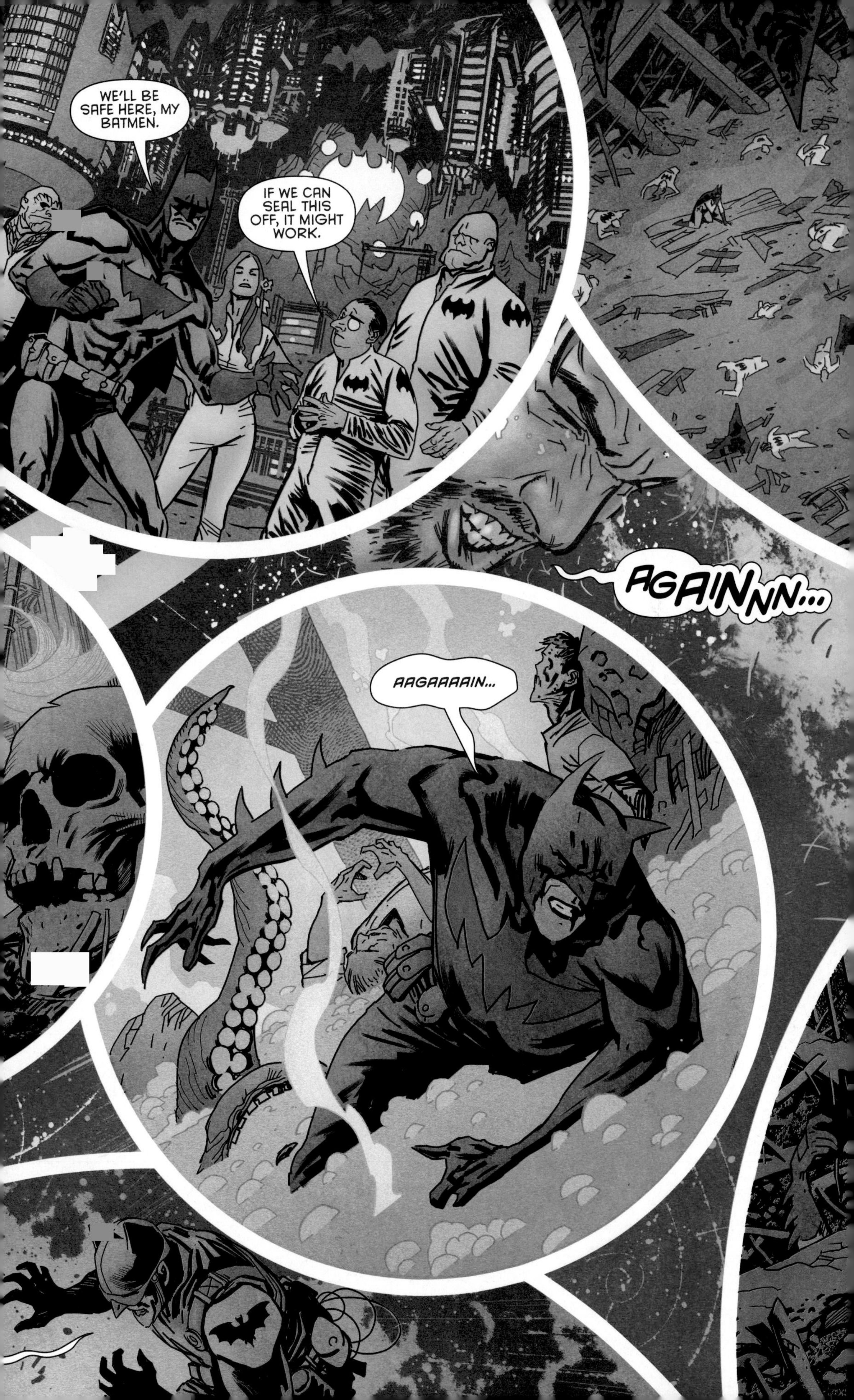
WE'LL BE SAFE HERE, MY BATMEN.
IF WE CAN SEAL THIS OFF, IT MIGHT WORK.
AGAINNNN...
AAGAAAAIN...

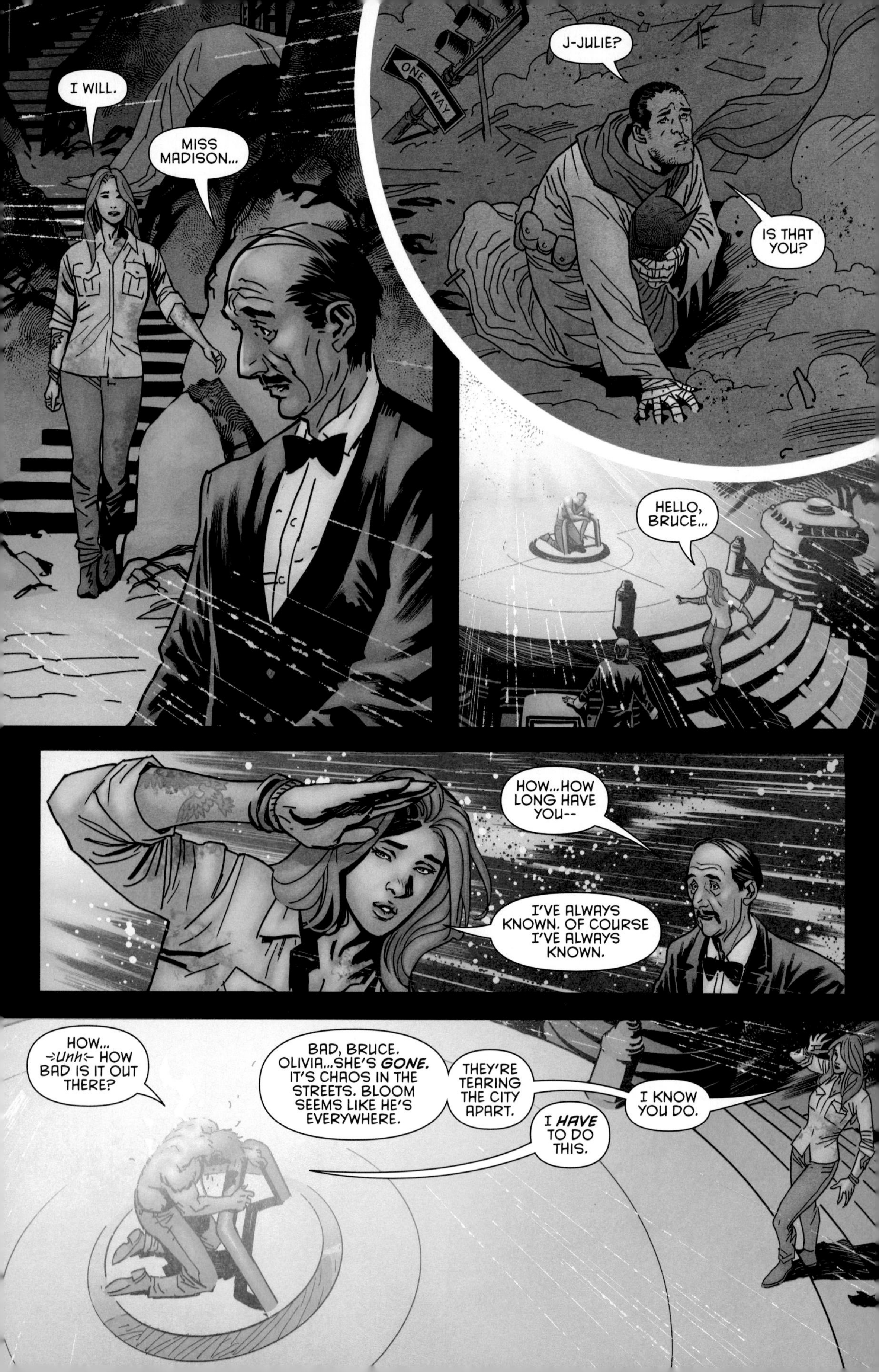
I WILL.
MISS MADISON...
J-JULIE?
IS THAT YOU?
ONE WAY
HELLO, BRUCE...
HOW...HOW LONG HAVE YOU--
I'VE ALWAYS KNOWN. OF COURSE I'VE ALWAYS KNOWN.
HOW... *Unh* HOW BAD IS IT OUT THERE?
BAD, BRUCE. OLIVIA...SHE'S *GONE.* IT'S CHAOS IN THE STREETS. BLOOM SEEMS LIKE HE'S EVERYWHERE.
THEY'RE TEARING THE CITY APART.
I KNOW YOU DO.
I *HAVE* TO DO THIS.

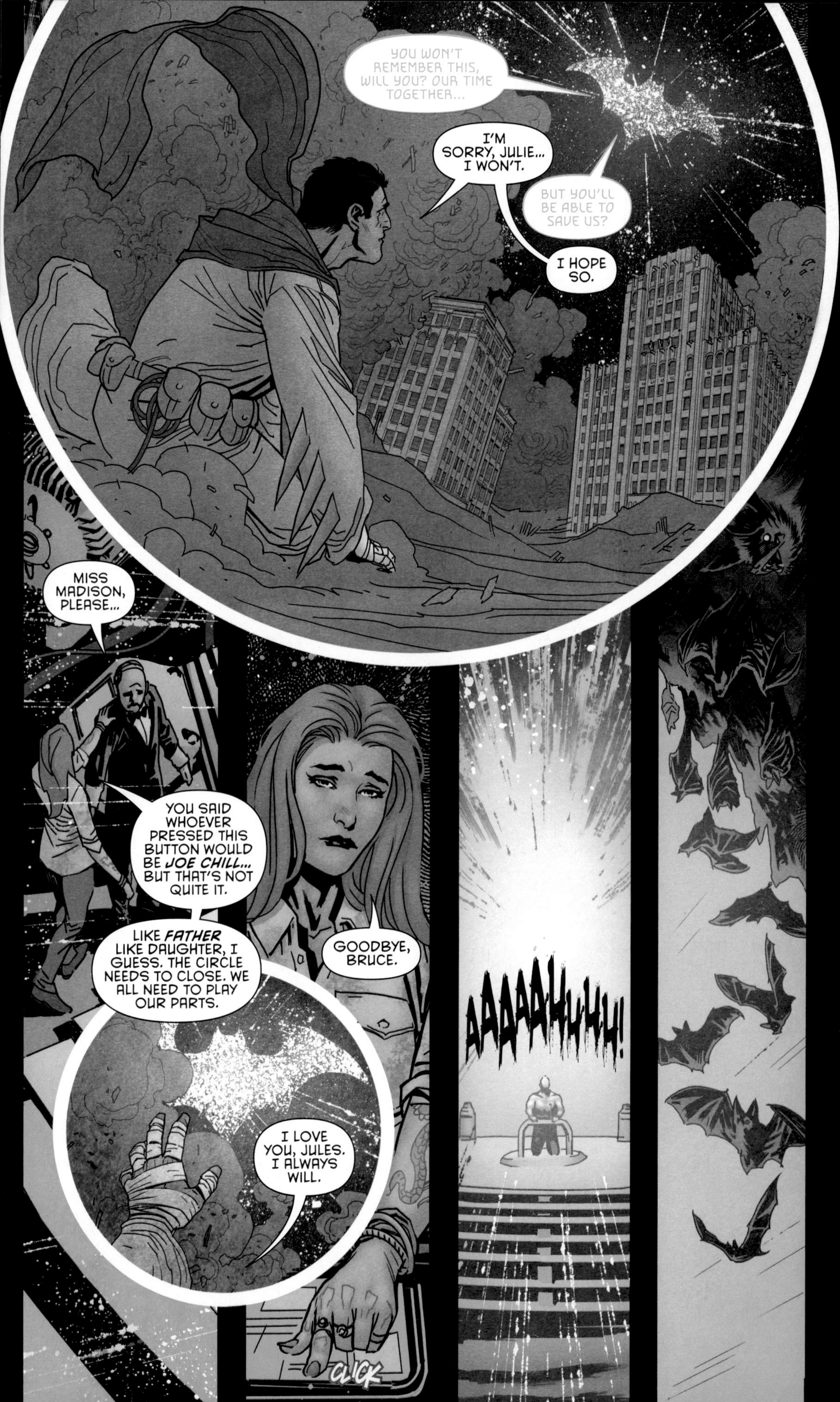
YOU WON'T REMEMBER THIS, WILL YOU? OUR TIME TOGETHER...
I'M SORRY, JULIE... I WON'T.
BUT YOU'LL BE ABLE TO SAVE US?
I HOPE SO.
MISS MADISON, PLEASE...
YOU SAID WHOEVER PRESSED THIS BUTTON WOULD BE JOE CHILL... BUT THAT'S NOT QUITE IT.
LIKE FATHER LIKE DAUGHTER, I GUESS. THE CIRCLE NEEDS TO CLOSE. WE ALL NEED TO PLAY OUR PARTS.
GOODBYE, BRUCE.
I LOVE YOU, JULES. I ALWAYS WILL.
CLICK
AAAAAHHHH!

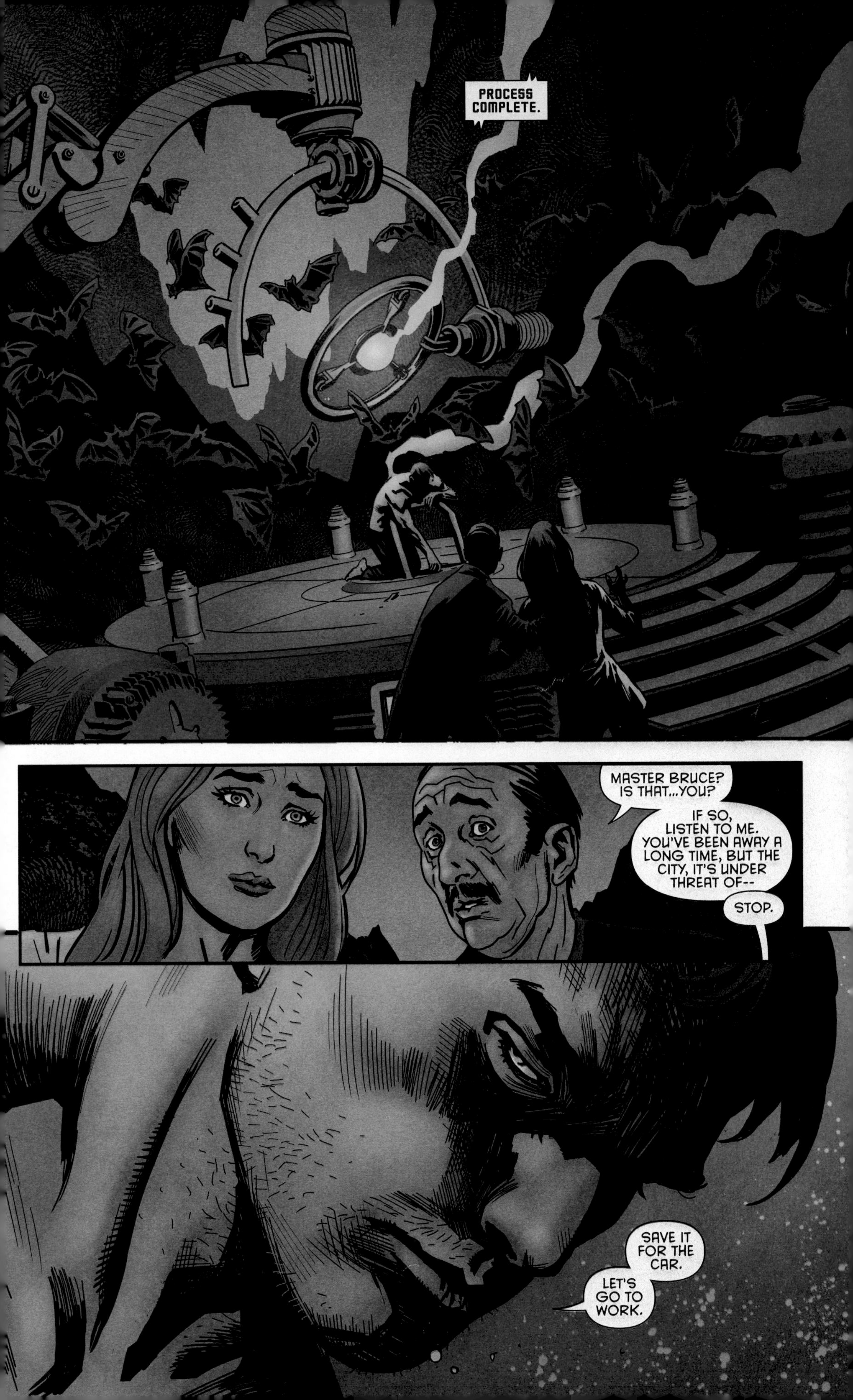
PROCESS COMPLETE.
MASTER BRUCE? IS THAT...YOU?
IF SO, LISTEN TO ME. YOU'VE BEEN AWAY A LONG TIME, BUT THE CITY, IT'S UNDER THREAT OF--
STOP.
SAVE IT FOR THE CAR.
LET'S GO TO WORK.

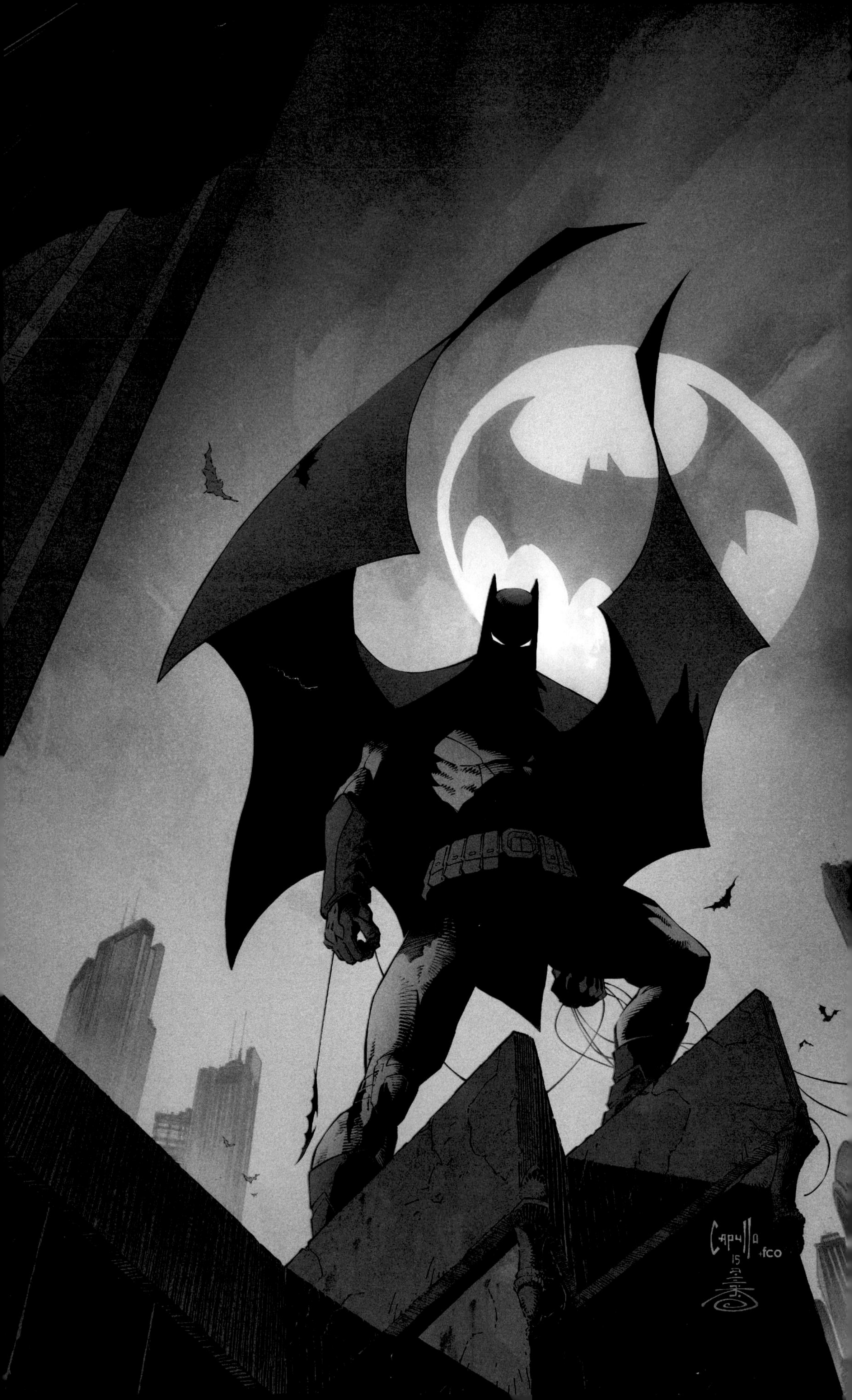
Capullo
15
+fco

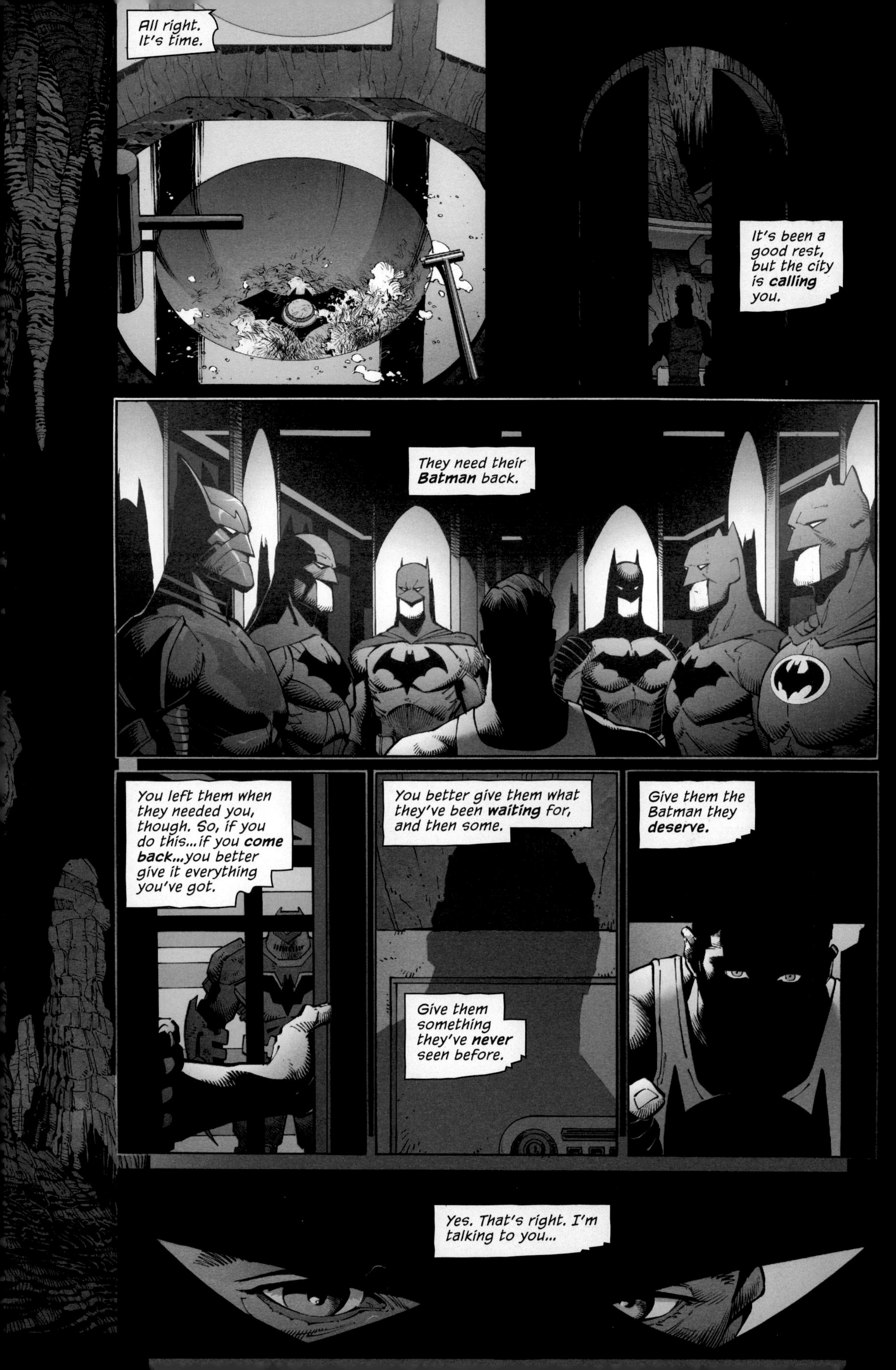
All right. It's time.
It's been a good rest, but the city is **calling** you.
They need their **Batman** back.
You left them when they needed you, though. So, if you do this...if you **come back...**you better give it everything you've got.
You better give them what they've been **waiting** for, and then some.
Give them something they've **never** seen before.
Give them the Batman they **deserve.**
Yes. That's right. I'm talking to you...

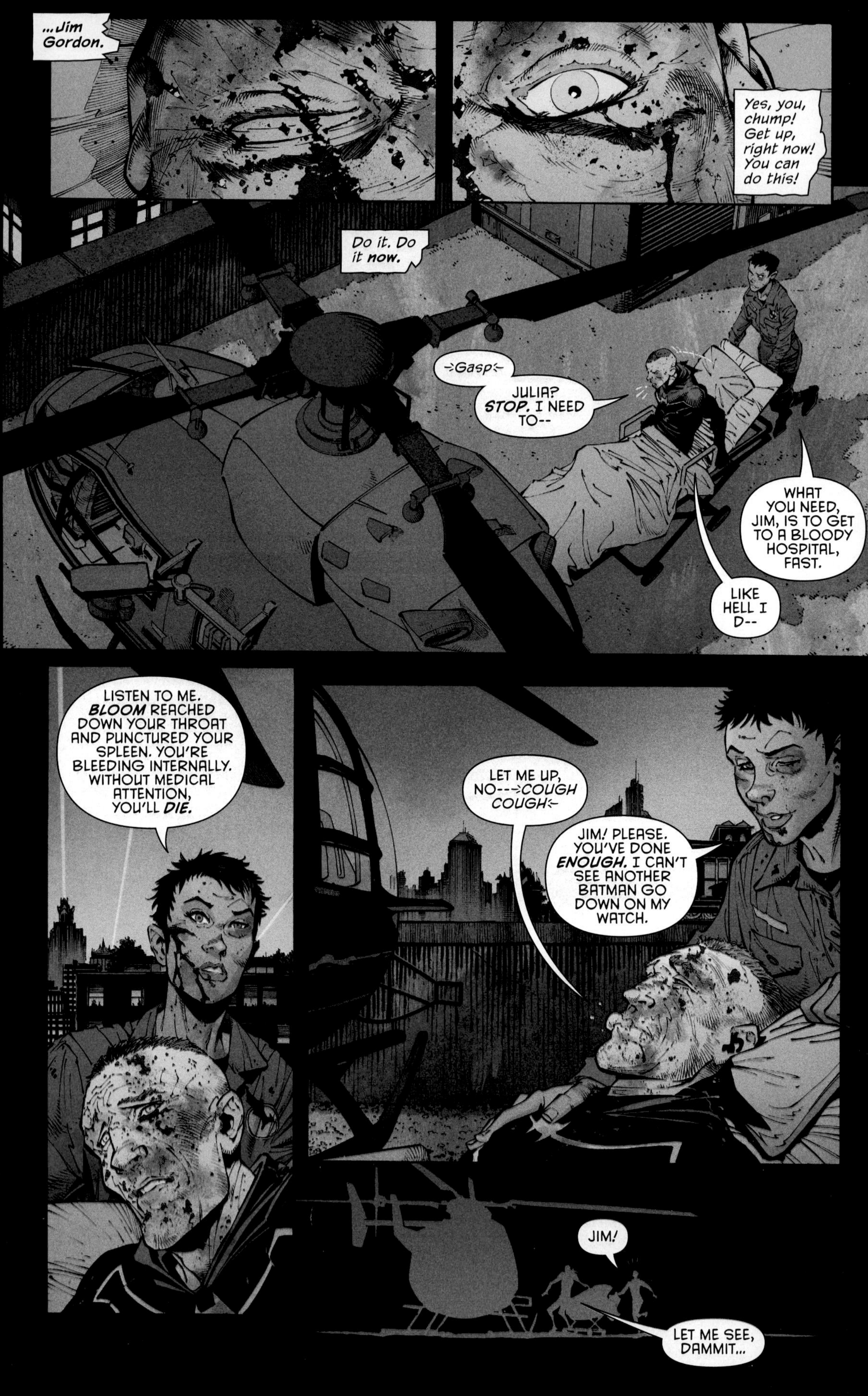

...Jim Gordon.
Yes, you, chump! Get up, right now! You can do this!
Do it. Do it **now.**
-›Gasp‹-
JULIA? **STOP.** I NEED TO--
WHAT YOU NEED, JIM, IS TO GET TO A BLOODY HOSPITAL, FAST.
LIKE HELL I D--
LISTEN TO ME. **BLOOM** REACHED DOWN YOUR THROAT AND PUNCTURED YOUR SPLEEN. YOU'RE BLEEDING INTERNALLY. WITHOUT MEDICAL ATTENTION, YOU'LL **DIE.**
LET ME UP, NO---›*COUGH COUGH*‹-
JIM! PLEASE. YOU'VE DONE **ENOUGH.** I CAN'T SEE ANOTHER BATMAN GO DOWN ON MY WATCH.
JIM!
LET ME SEE, DAMMIT...

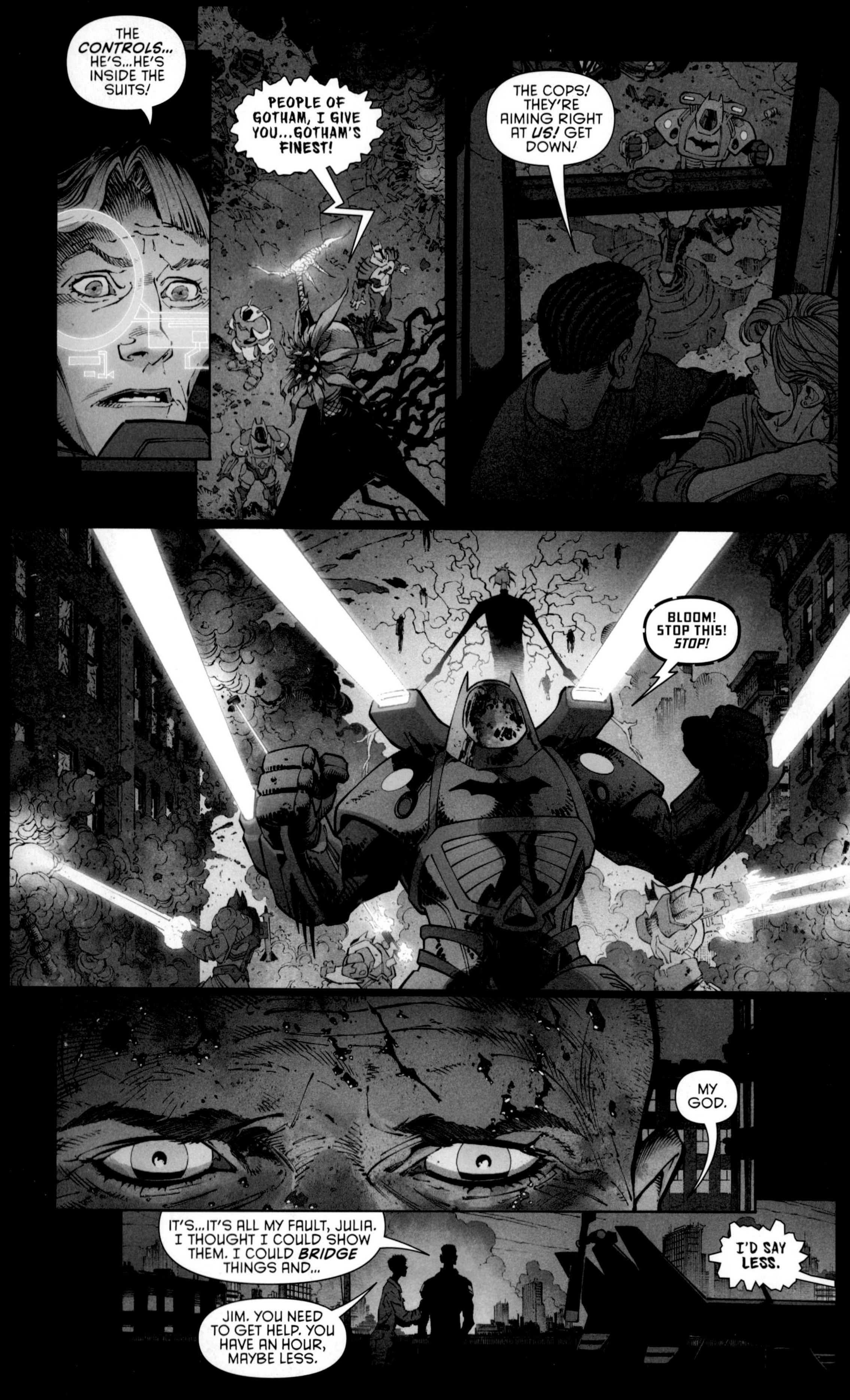
THE CONTROLS... HE'S...HE'S INSIDE THE SUITS!
PEOPLE OF GOTHAM, I GIVE YOU...GOTHAM'S FINEST!
THE COPS! THEY'RE AIMING RIGHT AT US! GET DOWN!
BLOOM! STOP THIS! STOP!
MY GOD.
IT'S...IT'S ALL MY FAULT, JULIA. I THOUGHT I COULD SHOW THEM. I COULD BRIDGE THINGS AND...
JIM. YOU NEED TO GET HELP. YOU HAVE AN HOUR, MAYBE LESS.
I'D SAY LESS.

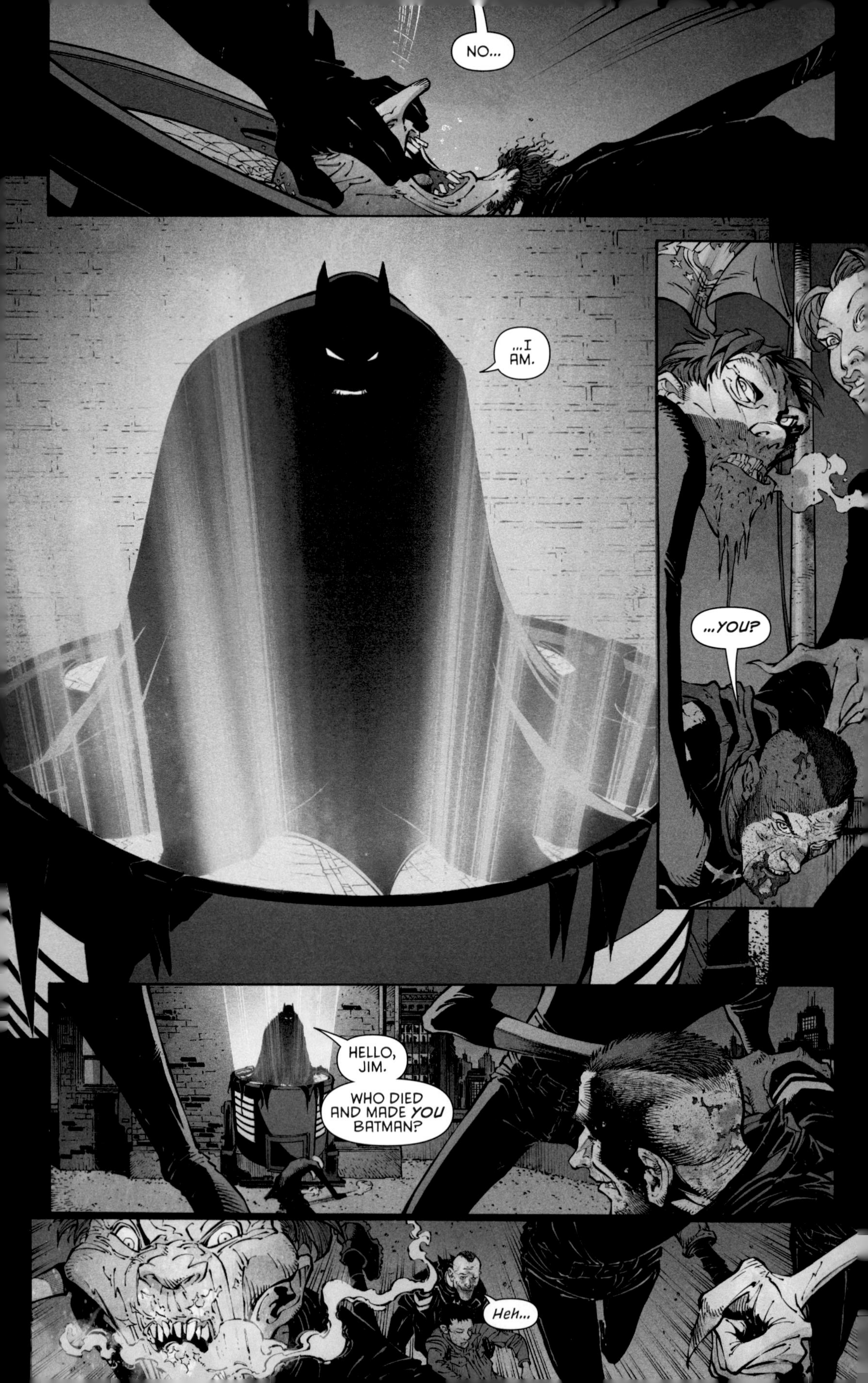
NO...
...I AM.
...YOU?
HELLO, JIM.
WHO DIED AND MADE *YOU* BATMAN?
Heh...

SUPERHEAVY

PART TEN

SCOTT SNYDER WRITER **GREG CAPULLO** PENCILS
DANNY MIKI INKS **FCO PLASCENCIA** COLORS
YANICK PAQUETTE EPILOGUE ART **NATHAN FAIRBAIRN** EPILOGUE COLORS
STEVE WANDS LETTERS **CAPULLO, MIKI, PLASCENCIA** COVER

BATMAN & SUPERMAN VARIANT COVERS BY
CHRIS DAUGHTRY, JIM LEE & ALEX SINCLAIR; DAVE JOHNSON & DAVE McCAIG
REBECCA TAYLOR ASSOCIATE EDITOR **MARK DOYLE** EDITOR
BATMAN CREATED BY BOB KANE WITH BILL FINGER

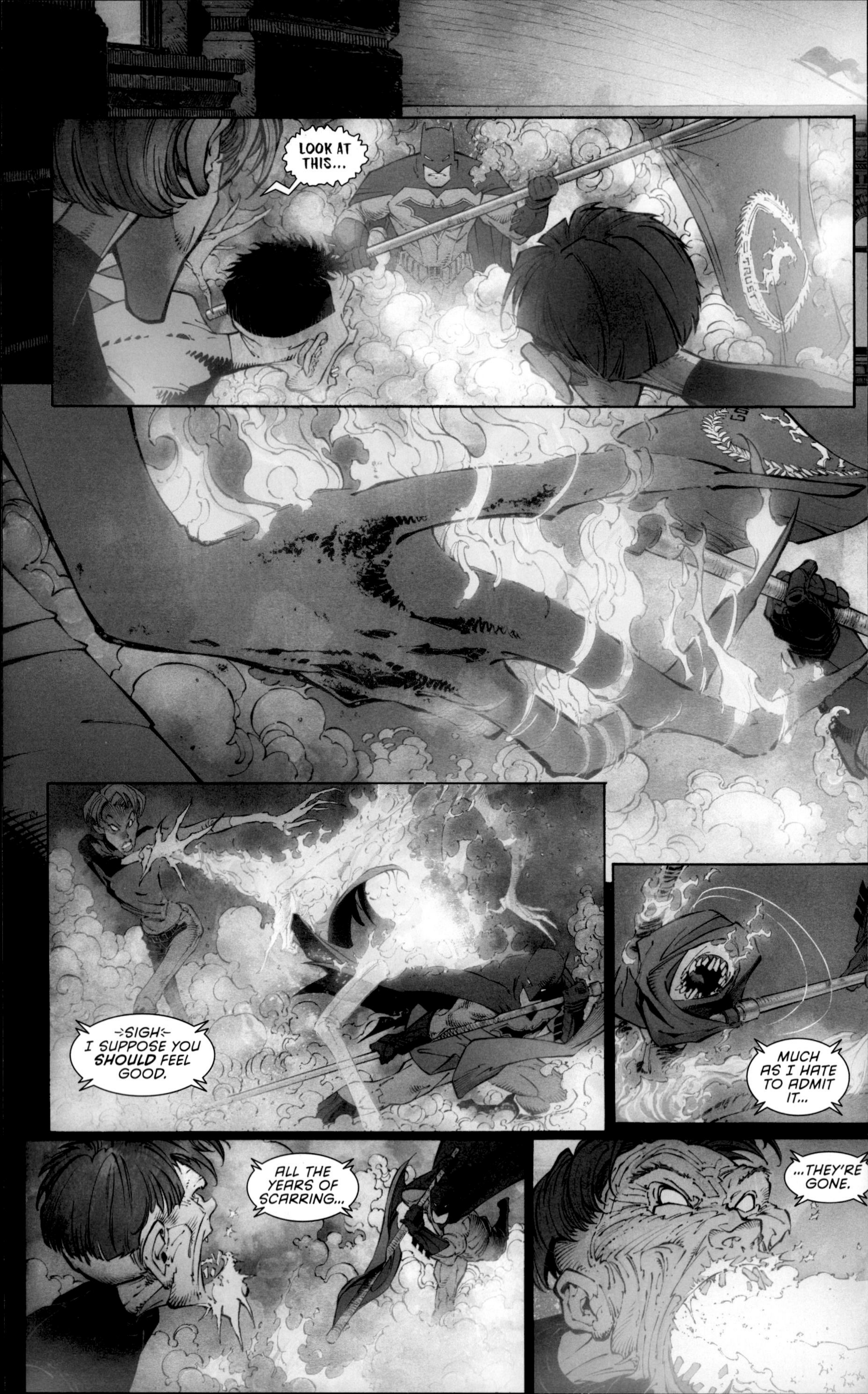
LOOK AT THIS...
TRUST
-SIGH- I SUPPOSE YOU SHOULD FEEL GOOD.
MUCH AS I HATE TO ADMIT IT...
ALL THE YEARS OF SCARRING...
...THEY'RE GONE.

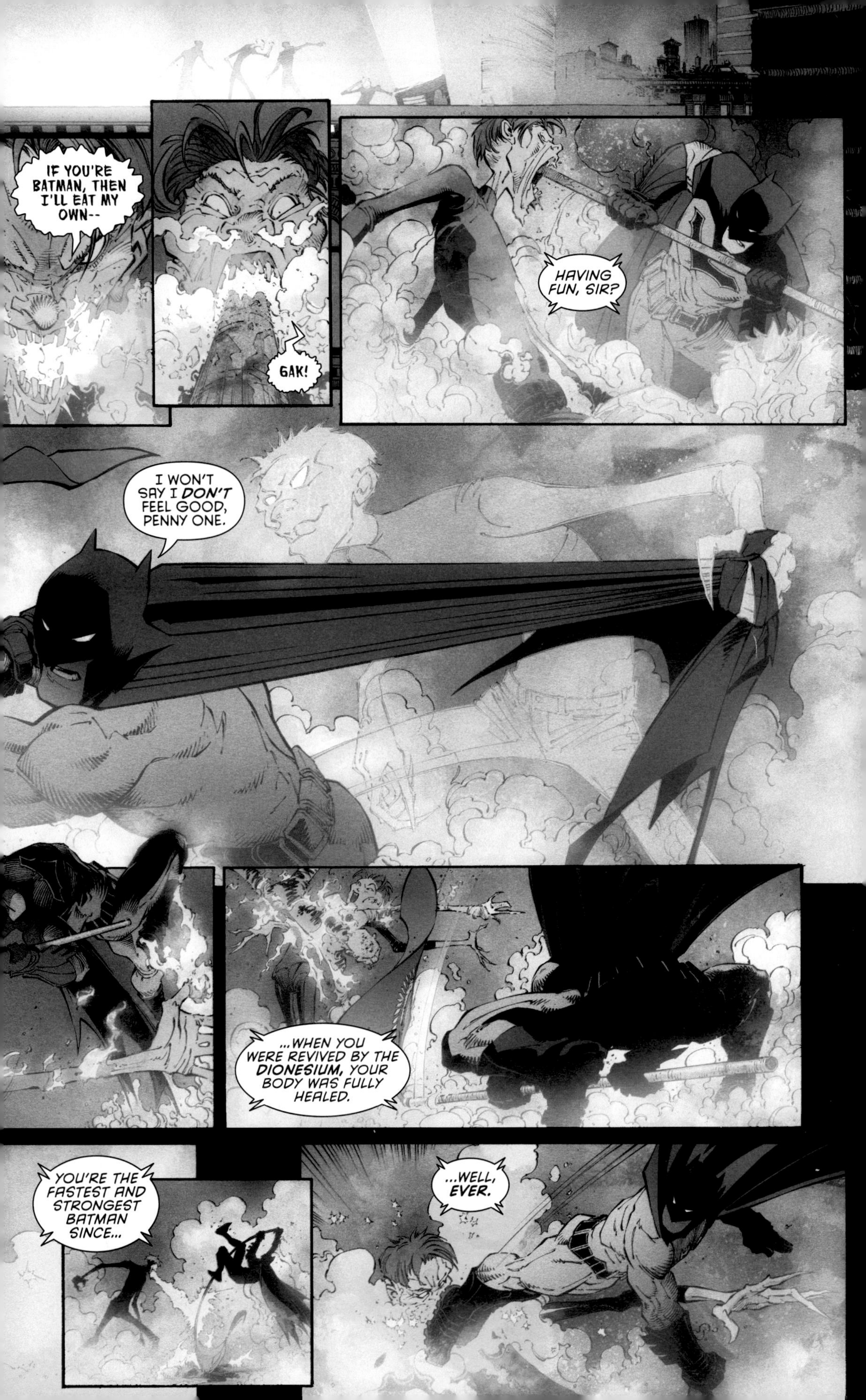
IF YOU'RE BATMAN, THEN I'LL EAT MY OWN--
GAK!
HAVING FUN, SIR?
I WON'T SAY I DON'T FEEL GOOD, PENNY ONE.
...WHEN YOU WERE REVIVED BY THE DIONESIUM, YOUR BODY WAS FULLY HEALED.
YOU'RE THE FASTEST AND STRONGEST BATMAN SINCE...
...WELL, EVER.

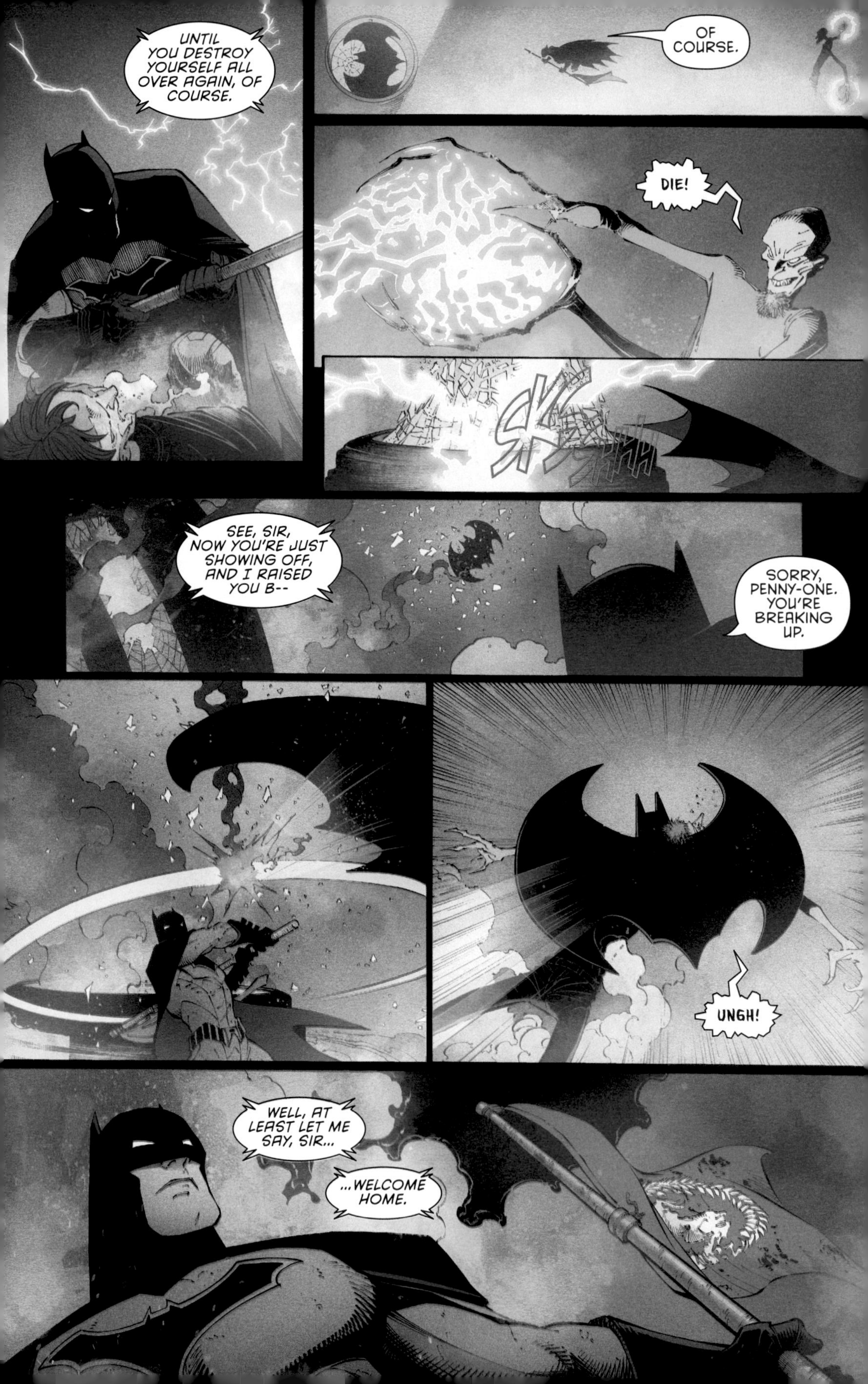
UNTIL YOU DESTROY YOURSELF ALL OVER AGAIN, OF COURSE.
OF COURSE.
DIE!
SEE, SIR, NOW YOU'RE JUST SHOWING OFF, AND I RAISED YOU B--
SORRY, PENNY-ONE. YOU'RE BREAKING UP.
UNGH!
WELL, AT LEAST LET ME SAY, SIR...
...WELCOME HOME.

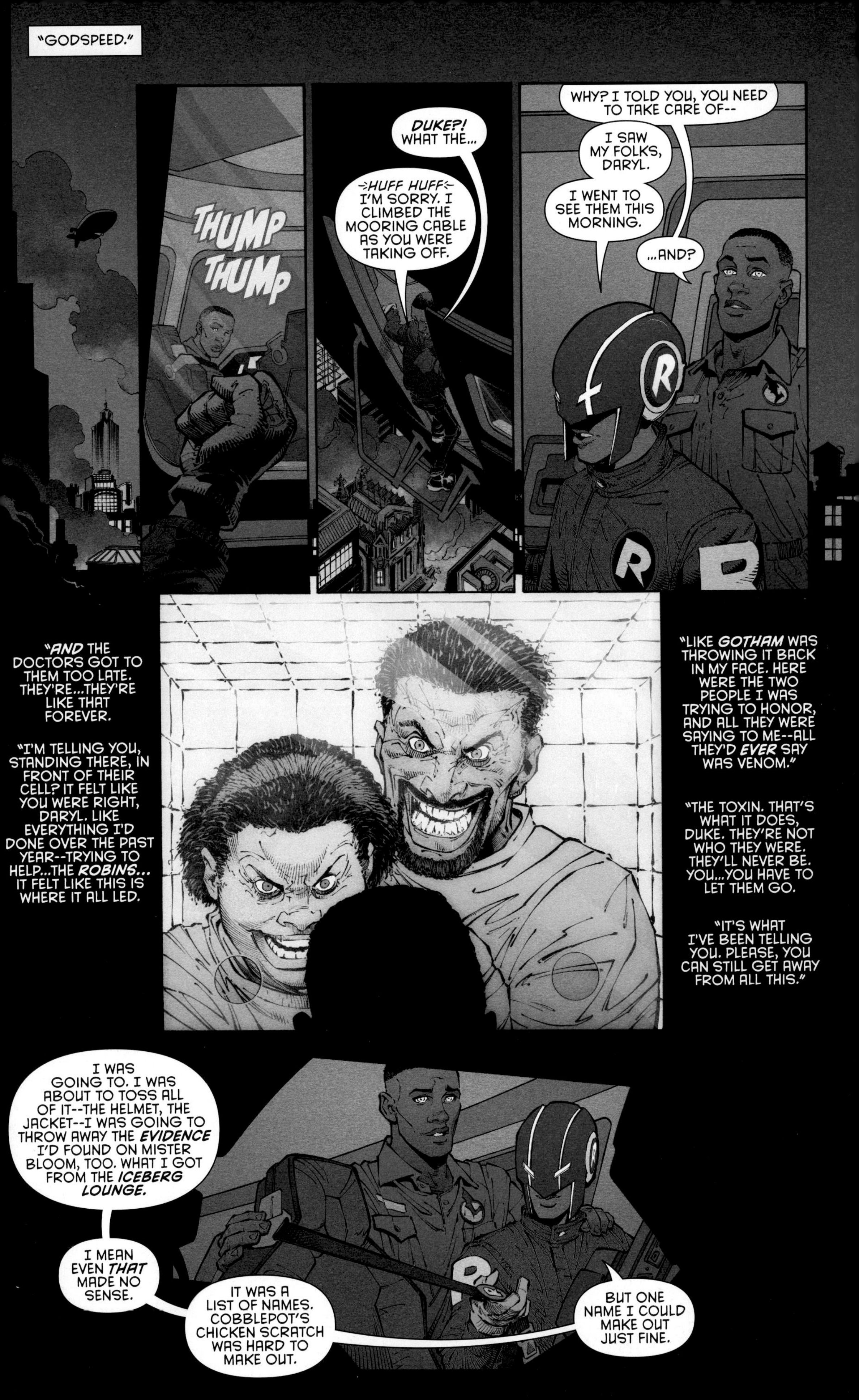
"GODSPEED."
THUMP THUMP
DUKE?! WHAT THE...
-HUFF HUFF- I'M SORRY. I CLIMBED THE MOORING CABLE AS YOU WERE TAKING OFF.
WHY? I TOLD YOU, YOU NEED TO TAKE CARE OF--
I SAW MY FOLKS, DARYL.
I WENT TO SEE THEM THIS MORNING.
...AND?
"AND THE DOCTORS GOT TO THEM TOO LATE. THEY'RE...THEY'RE LIKE THAT FOREVER.
"I'M TELLING YOU, STANDING THERE, IN FRONT OF THEIR CELL? IT FELT LIKE YOU WERE RIGHT, DARYL. LIKE EVERYTHING I'D DONE OVER THE PAST YEAR--TRYING TO HELP...THE ROBINS... IT FELT LIKE THIS IS WHERE IT ALL LED.
"LIKE GOTHAM WAS THROWING IT BACK IN MY FACE. HERE WERE THE TWO PEOPLE I WAS TRYING TO HONOR, AND ALL THEY WERE SAYING TO ME--ALL THEY'D EVER SAY WAS VENOM."
"THE TOXIN. THAT'S WHAT IT DOES, DUKE. THEY'RE NOT WHO THEY WERE. THEY'LL NEVER BE. YOU...YOU HAVE TO LET THEM GO.
"IT'S WHAT I'VE BEEN TELLING YOU. PLEASE, YOU CAN STILL GET AWAY FROM ALL THIS."
I WAS GOING TO. I WAS ABOUT TO TOSS ALL OF IT--THE HELMET, THE JACKET--I WAS GOING TO THROW AWAY THE EVIDENCE I'D FOUND ON MISTER BLOOM, TOO. WHAT I GOT FROM THE ICEBERG LOUNGE.
I MEAN EVEN THAT MADE NO SENSE.
IT WAS A LIST OF NAMES. COBBLEPOT'S CHICKEN SCRATCH WAS HARD TO MAKE OUT.
BUT ONE NAME I COULD MAKE OUT JUST FINE.

MINE.

YOU? BUT THAT'S *INSANE*.

I KNOW. THEN I GOT A CLEARER RES ON SOME OF THE OTHER NAMES, AND I SAW *THIS*.

DUKE THOMAS

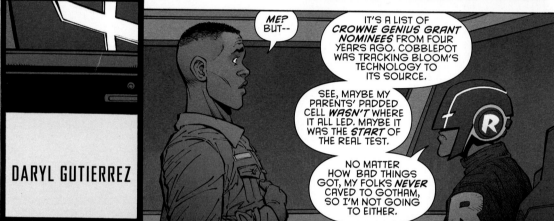

ME? BUT--

IT'S A LIST OF *CROWNE GENIUS GRANT NOMINEES* FROM FOUR YEARS AGO. COBBLEPOT WAS TRACKING BLOOM'S TECHNOLOGY TO ITS SOURCE.

SEE, MAYBE MY PARENTS' PADDED CELL *WASN'T* WHERE IT ALL LED. MAYBE IT WAS THE *START* OF THE REAL TEST.

NO MATTER HOW BAD THINGS GOT, MY FOLKS *NEVER* CAVED TO GOTHAM, SO I'M NOT GOING TO EITHER.

DARYL GUTIERREZ

WHAT ARE YOU SAYING?

I'M SAYING YOU NEED TO TELL ME WHAT'S GOING ON. RIGHT NOW.

NO!

"AND HERE WE GO..."

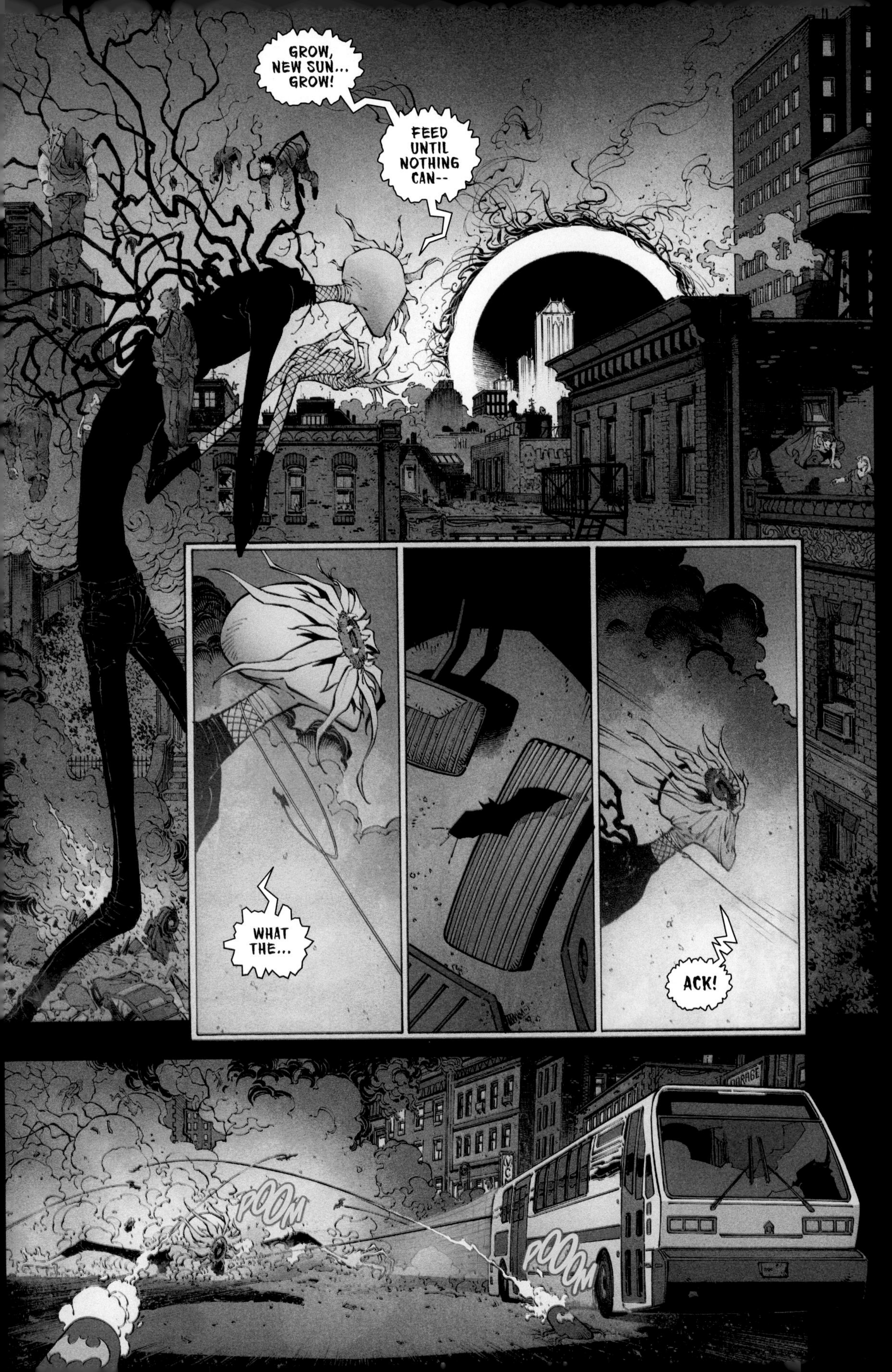
GROW, NEW SUN... GROW!
FEED UNTIL NOTHING CAN--
WHAT THE...
ACK!
POOM
POOOM

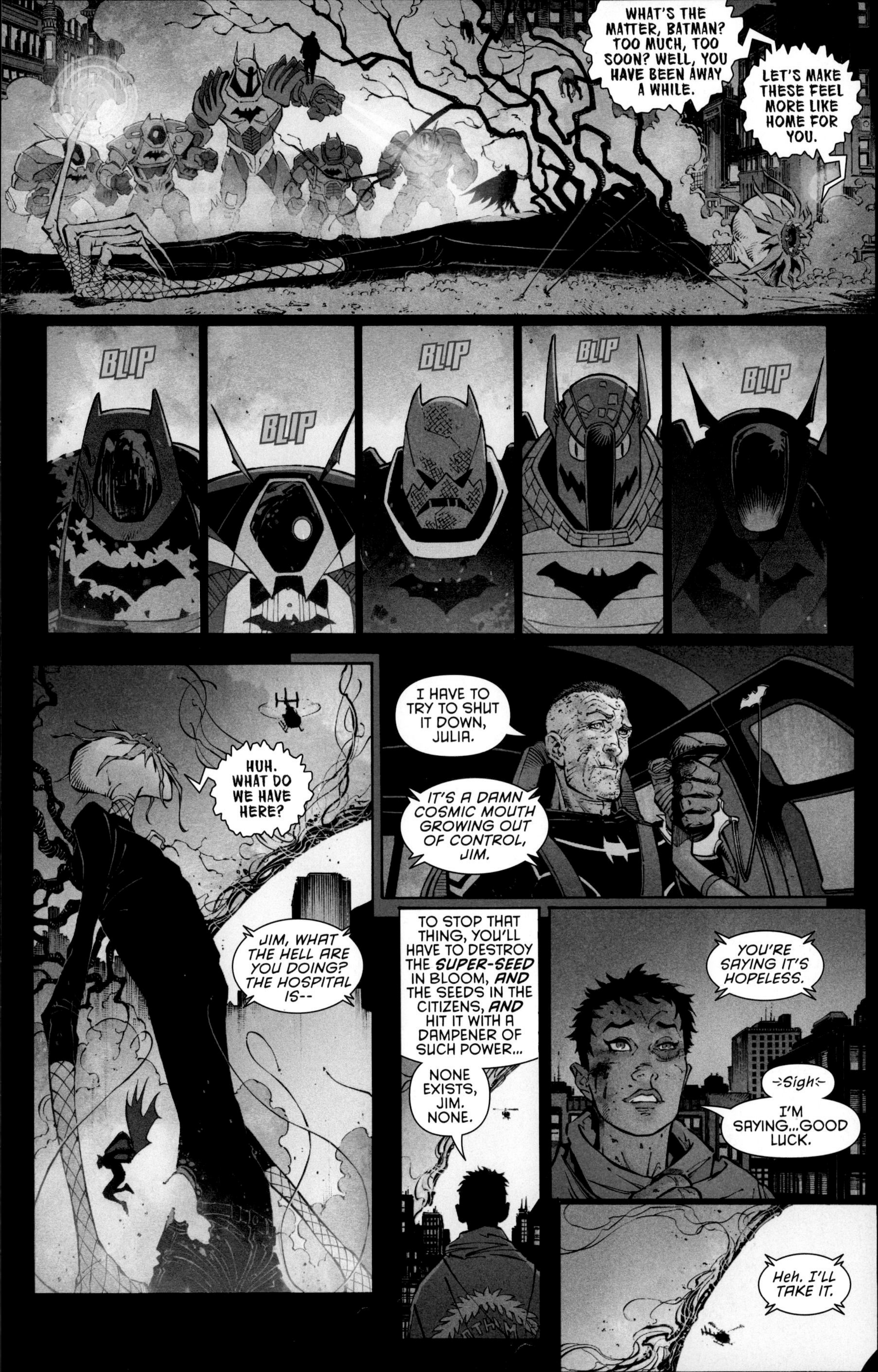
WHAT'S THE MATTER, BATMAN? TOO MUCH, TOO SOON? WELL, YOU HAVE BEEN AWAY A WHILE.
LET'S MAKE THESE FEEL MORE LIKE HOME FOR YOU.
BLIP
BLIP
BLIP
BLIP
BLIP
HUH. WHAT DO WE HAVE HERE?
JIM, WHAT THE HELL ARE YOU DOING? THE HOSPITAL IS--
I HAVE TO TRY TO SHUT IT DOWN, JULIA.
IT'S A DAMN COSMIC MOUTH GROWING OUT OF CONTROL, JIM.
TO STOP THAT THING, YOU'LL HAVE TO DESTROY THE SUPER-SEED IN BLOOM, AND THE SEEDS IN THE CITIZENS, AND HIT IT WITH A DAMPENER OF SUCH POWER...
NONE EXISTS, JIM. NONE.
YOU'RE SAYING IT'S HOPELESS.
~Sigh~
I'M SAYING...GOOD LUCK.
Heh. I'LL TAKE IT.

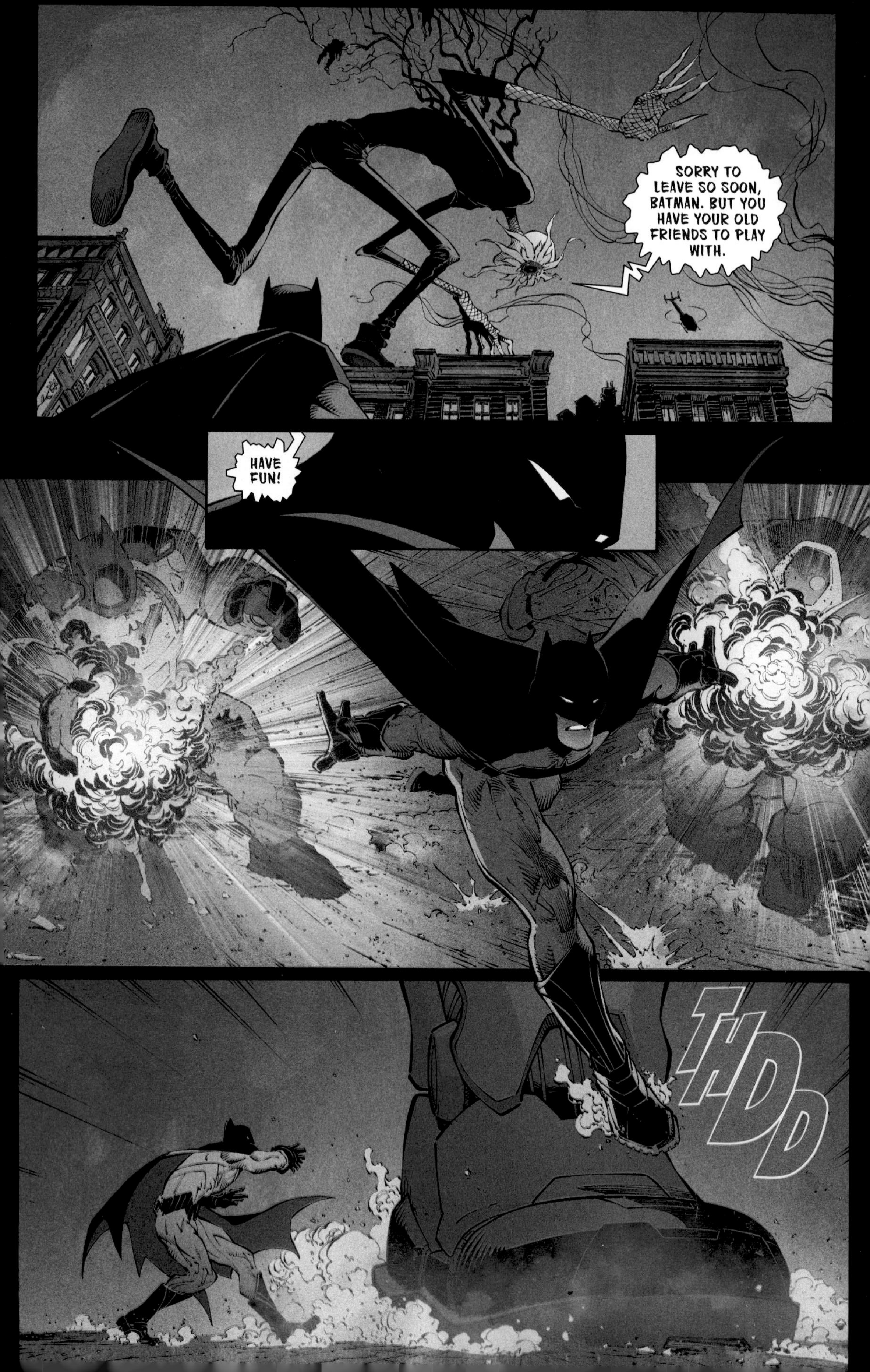
SORRY TO LEAVE SO SOON, BATMAN. BUT YOU HAVE YOUR OLD FRIENDS TO PLAY WITH.
HAVE FUN!
THDD

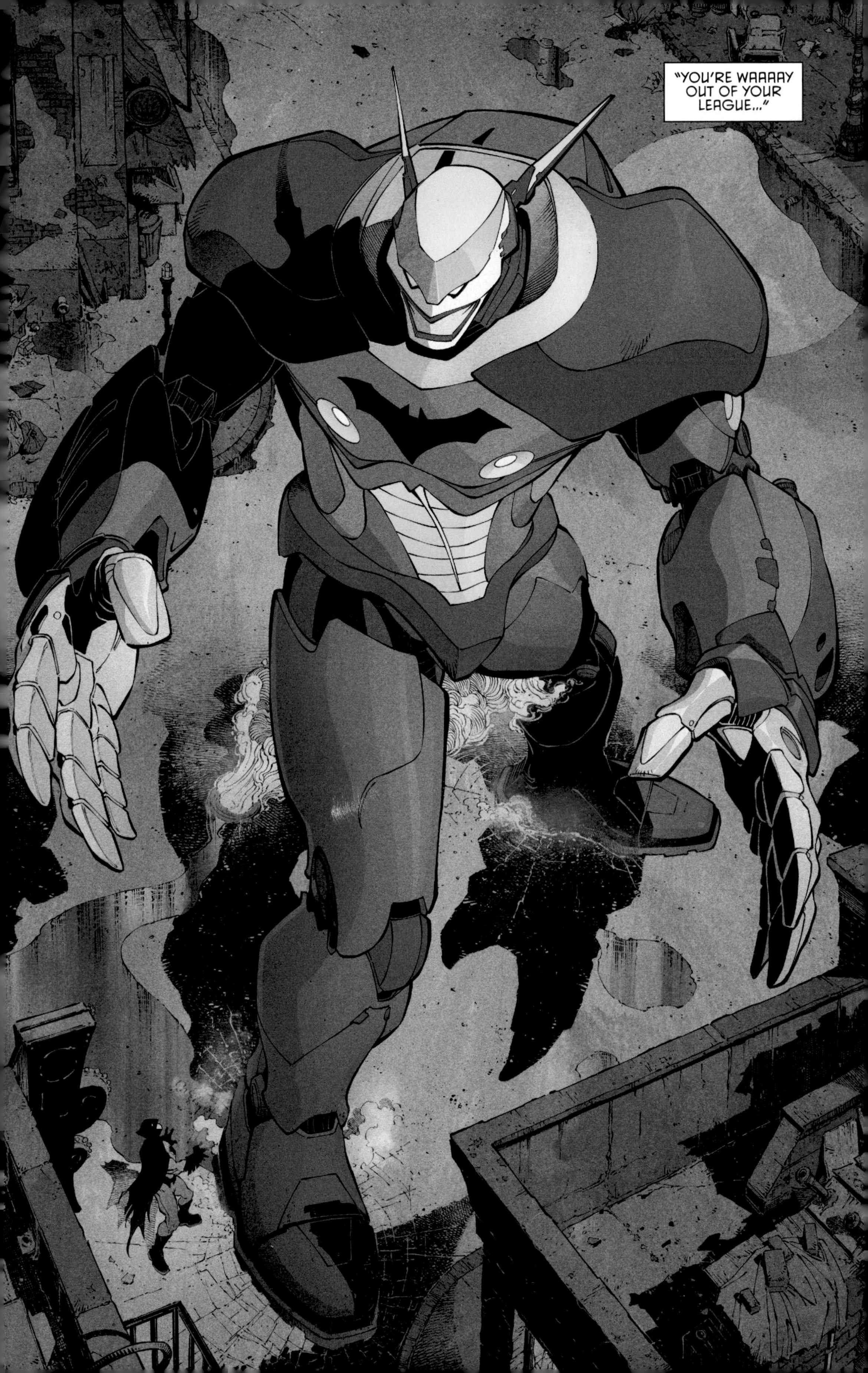
"YOU'RE WAAAAY OUT OF YOUR LEAGUE..."

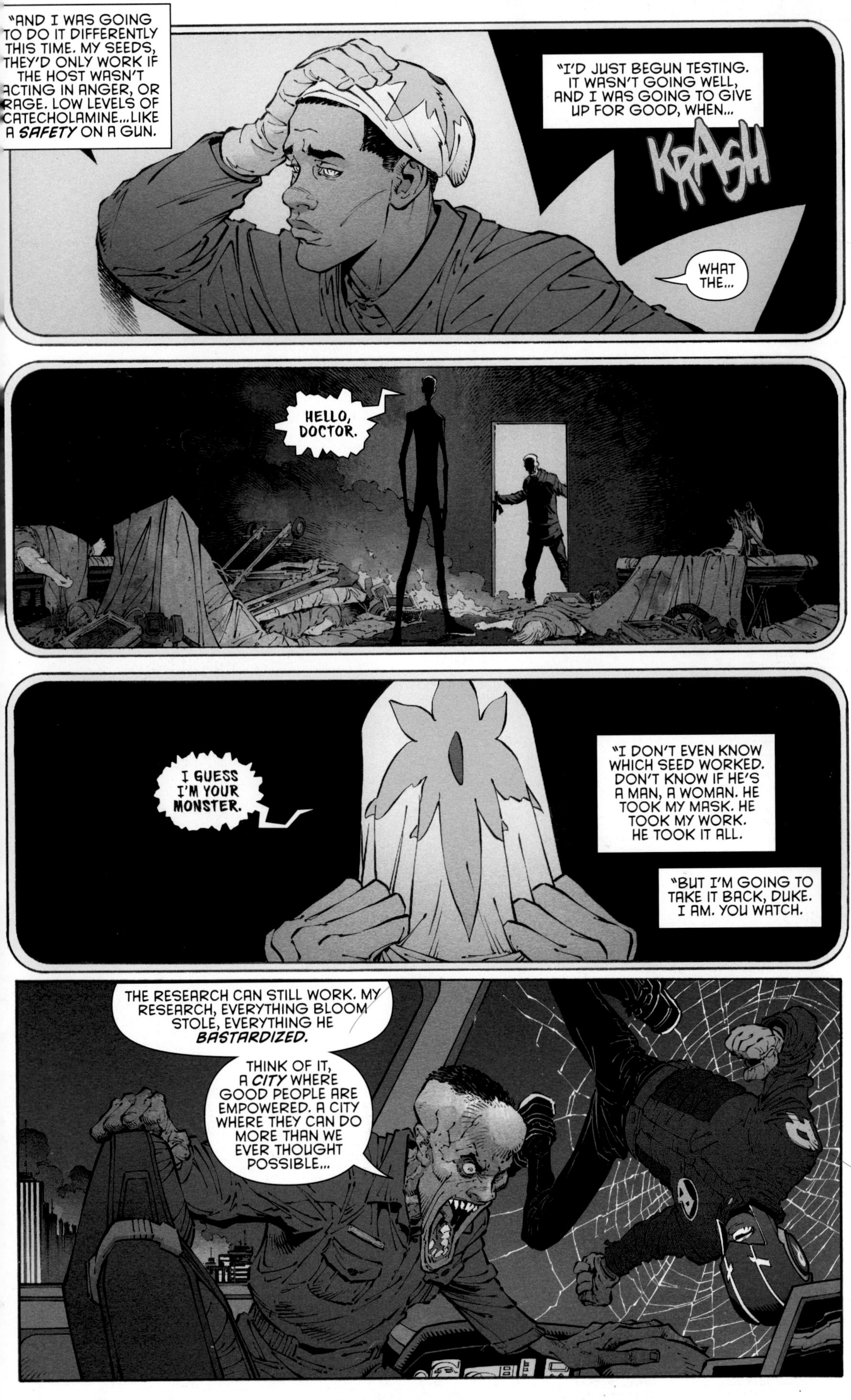
"AND I WAS GOING TO DO IT DIFFERENTLY THIS TIME. MY SEEDS, THEY'D ONLY WORK IF THE HOST WASN'T ACTING IN ANGER, OR RAGE. LOW LEVELS OF CATECHOLAMINE...LIKE A SAFETY ON A GUN.
"I'D JUST BEGUN TESTING. IT WASN'T GOING WELL, AND I WAS GOING TO GIVE UP FOR GOOD, WHEN...
KRASH
WHAT THE...
HELLO, DOCTOR.
I GUESS I'M YOUR MONSTER.
"I DON'T EVEN KNOW WHICH SEED WORKED. DON'T KNOW IF HE'S A MAN, A WOMAN. HE TOOK MY MASK. HE TOOK MY WORK. HE TOOK IT ALL.
"BUT I'M GOING TO TAKE IT BACK, DUKE. I AM. YOU WATCH.
THE RESEARCH CAN STILL WORK. MY RESEARCH, EVERYTHING BLOOM STOLE, EVERYTHING HE BASTARDIZED.
THINK OF IT, A CITY WHERE GOOD PEOPLE ARE EMPOWERED. A CITY WHERE THEY CAN DO MORE THAN WE EVER THOUGHT POSSIBLE...

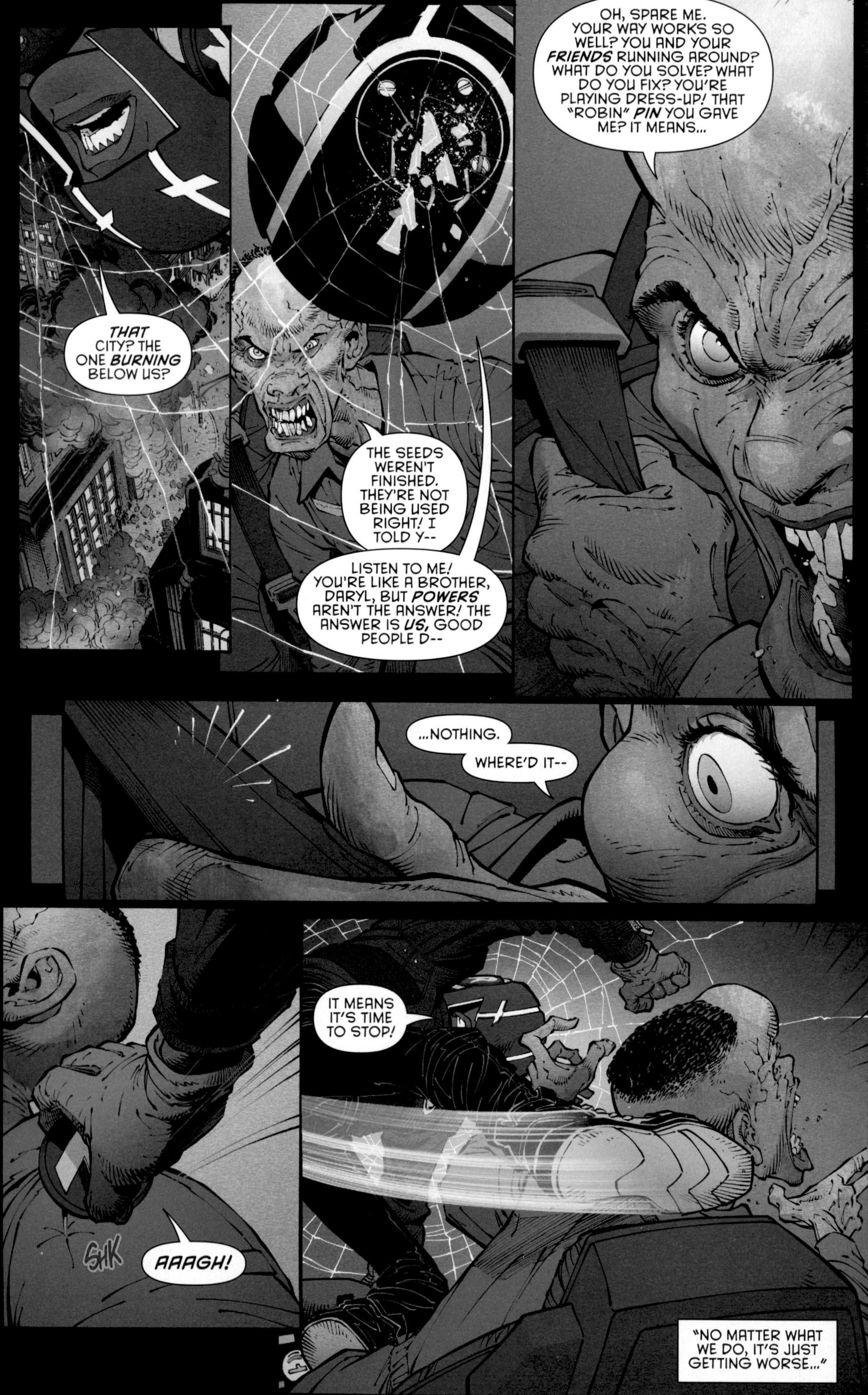
THAT CITY? THE ONE BURNING BELOW US?
THE SEEDS WEREN'T FINISHED. THEY'RE NOT BEING USED RIGHT! I TOLD Y--
LISTEN TO ME! YOU'RE LIKE A BROTHER, DARYL, BUT POWERS AREN'T THE ANSWER! THE ANSWER IS US, GOOD PEOPLE D--
OH, SPARE ME. YOUR WAY WORKS SO WELL? YOU AND YOUR FRIENDS RUNNING AROUND? WHAT DO YOU SOLVE? WHAT DO YOU FIX? YOU'RE PLAYING DRESS-UP! THAT "ROBIN" PIN YOU GAVE ME? IT MEANS...
...NOTHING.
WHERE'D IT--
SHK
AAAGH!
IT MEANS IT'S TIME TO STOP!
"NO MATTER WHAT WE DO, IT'S JUST GETTING WORSE..."

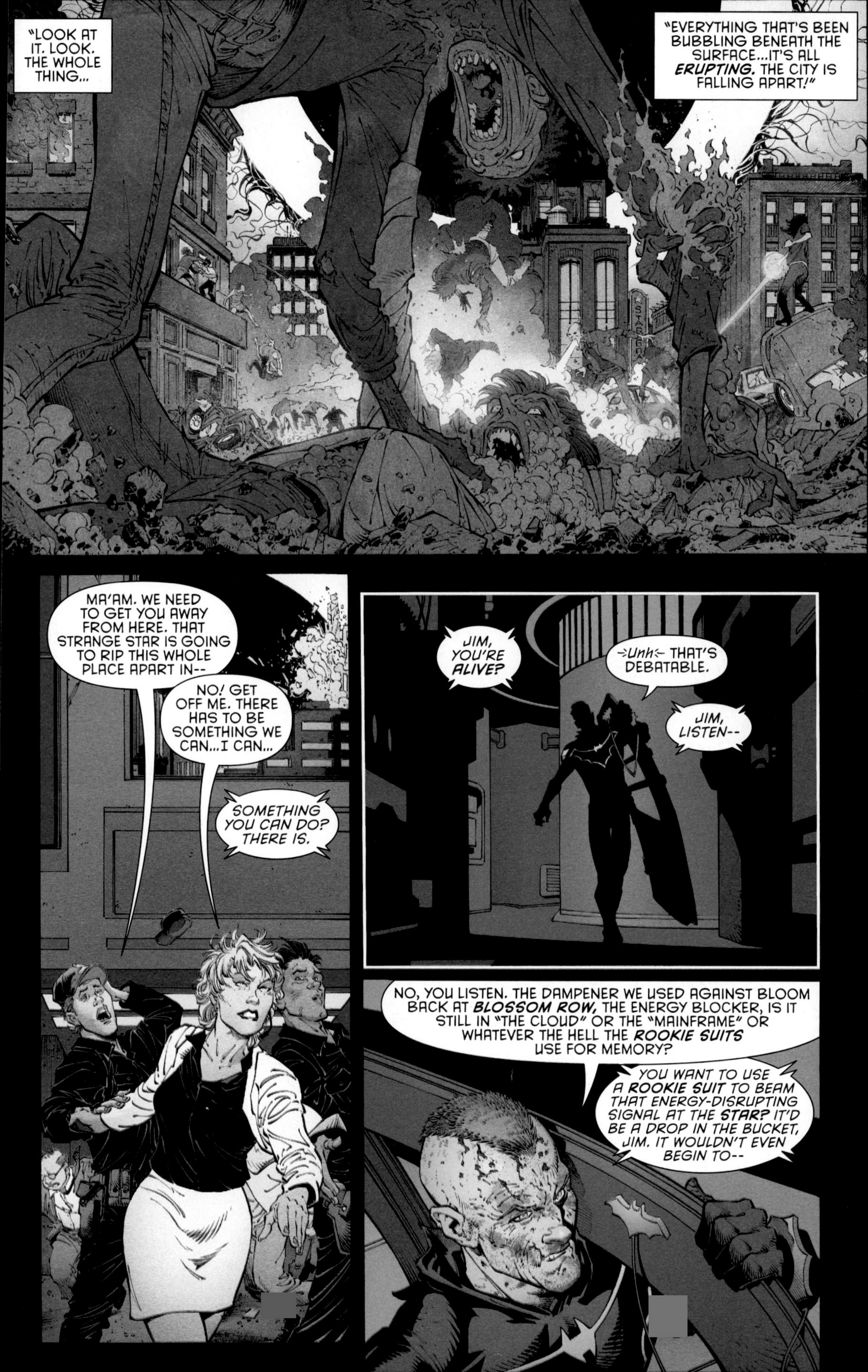
"LOOK AT IT. LOOK. THE WHOLE THING...
"EVERYTHING THAT'S BEEN BUBBLING BENEATH THE SURFACE...IT'S ALL ERUPTING. THE CITY IS FALLING APART!"
MA'AM. WE NEED TO GET YOU AWAY FROM HERE. THAT STRANGE STAR IS GOING TO RIP THIS WHOLE PLACE APART IN--
NO! GET OFF ME. THERE HAS TO BE SOMETHING WE CAN...I CAN...
SOMETHING YOU CAN DO? THERE IS.
JIM, YOU'RE ALIVE?
-Unh- THAT'S DEBATABLE.
JIM, LISTEN--
NO, YOU LISTEN. THE DAMPENER WE USED AGAINST BLOOM BACK AT BLOSSOM ROW, THE ENERGY BLOCKER, IS IT STILL IN "THE CLOUD" OR THE "MAINFRAME" OR WHATEVER THE HELL THE ROOKIE SUITS USE FOR MEMORY?
YOU WANT TO USE A ROOKIE SUIT TO BEAM THAT ENERGY-DISRUPTING SIGNAL AT THE STAR? IT'D BE A DROP IN THE BUCKET, JIM. IT WOULDN'T EVEN BEGIN TO--

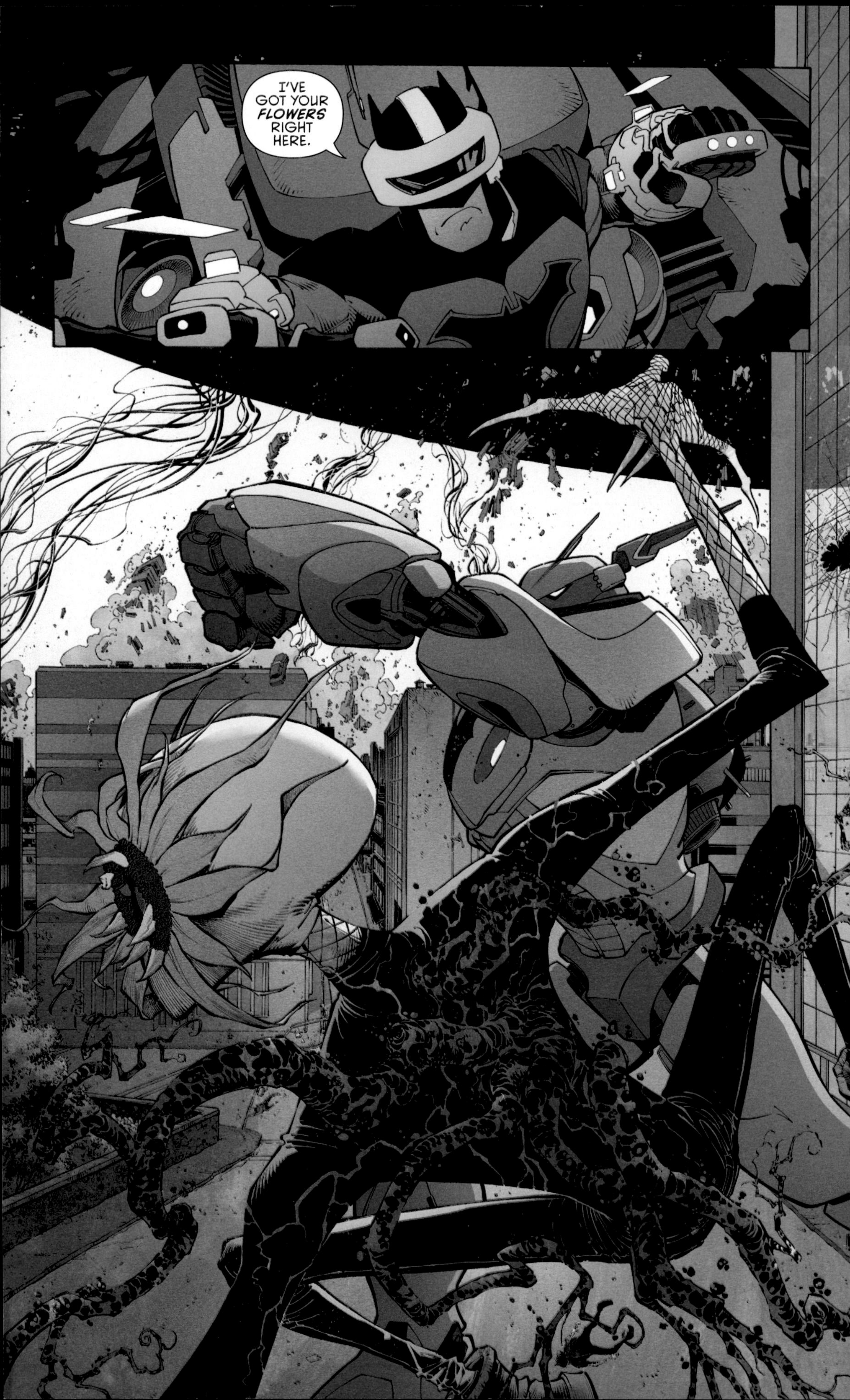
I'VE GOT YOUR *FLOWERS* RIGHT HERE.

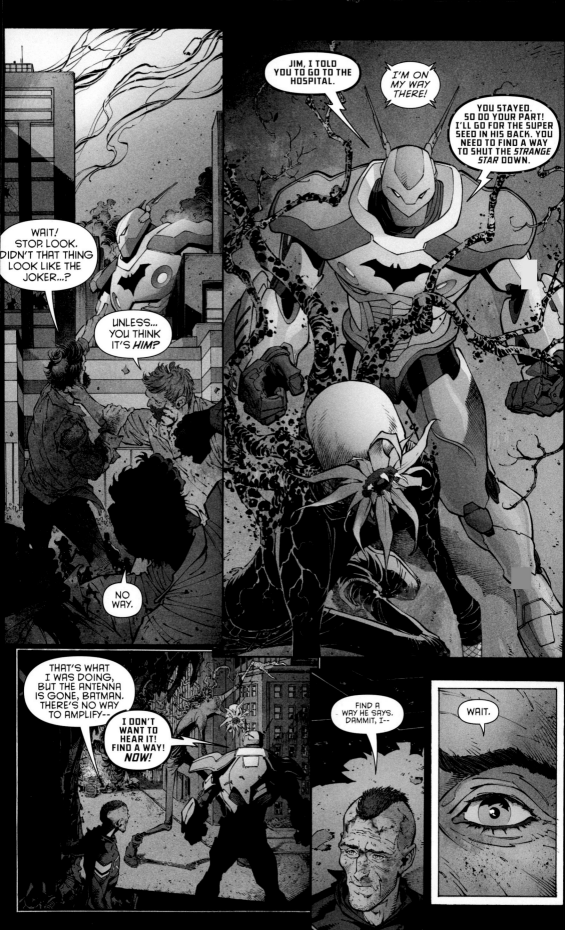

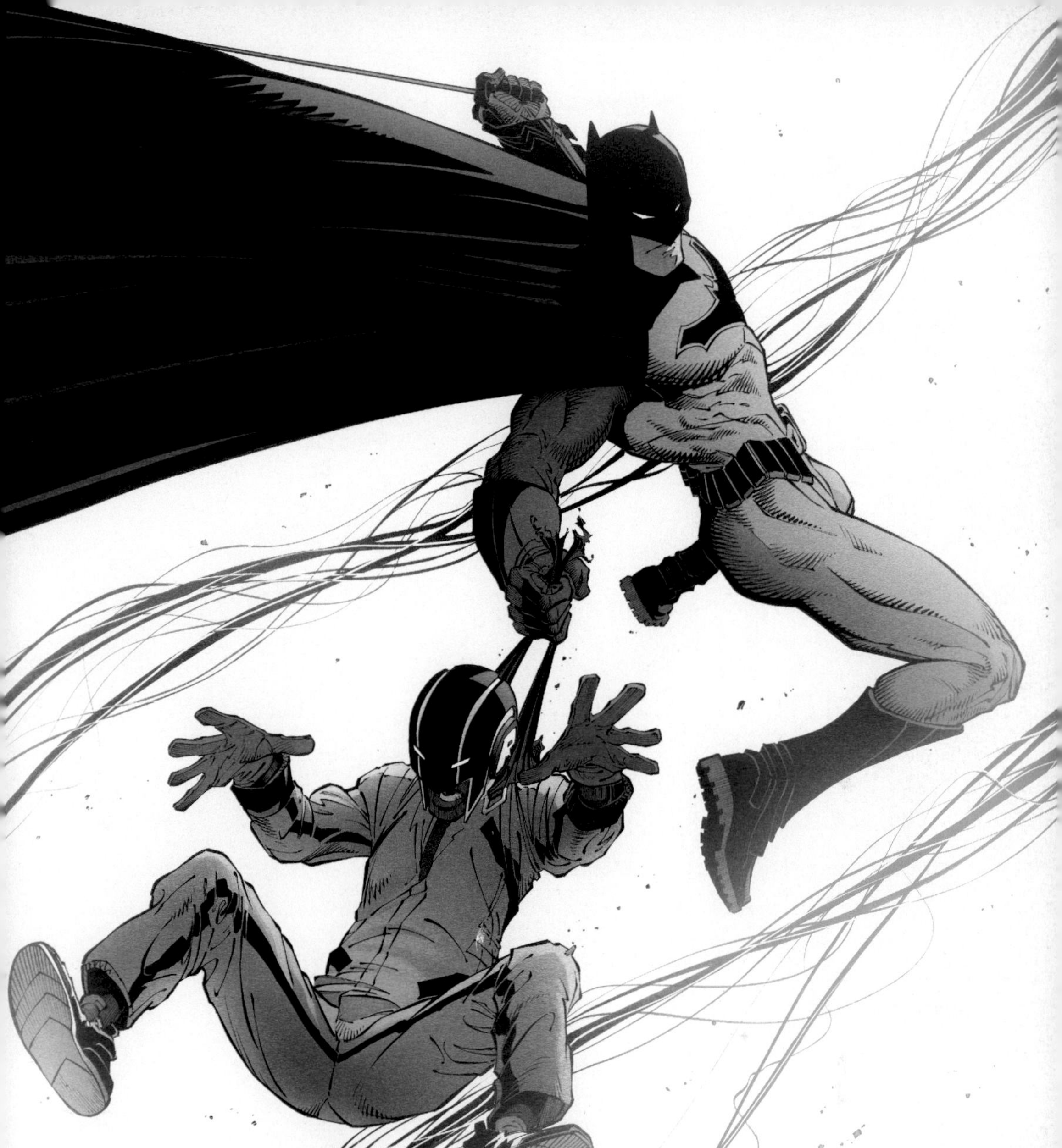

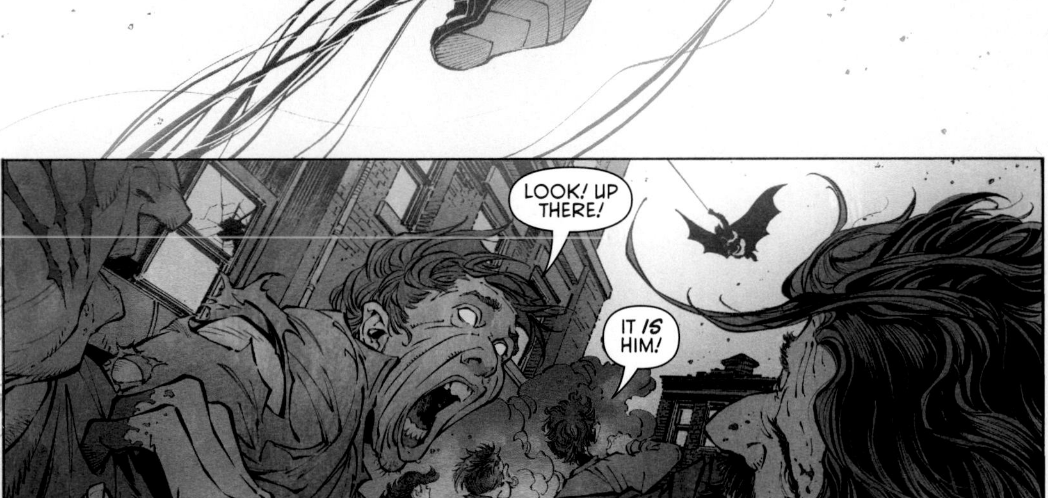
LOOK! UP THERE!
IT IS HIM!

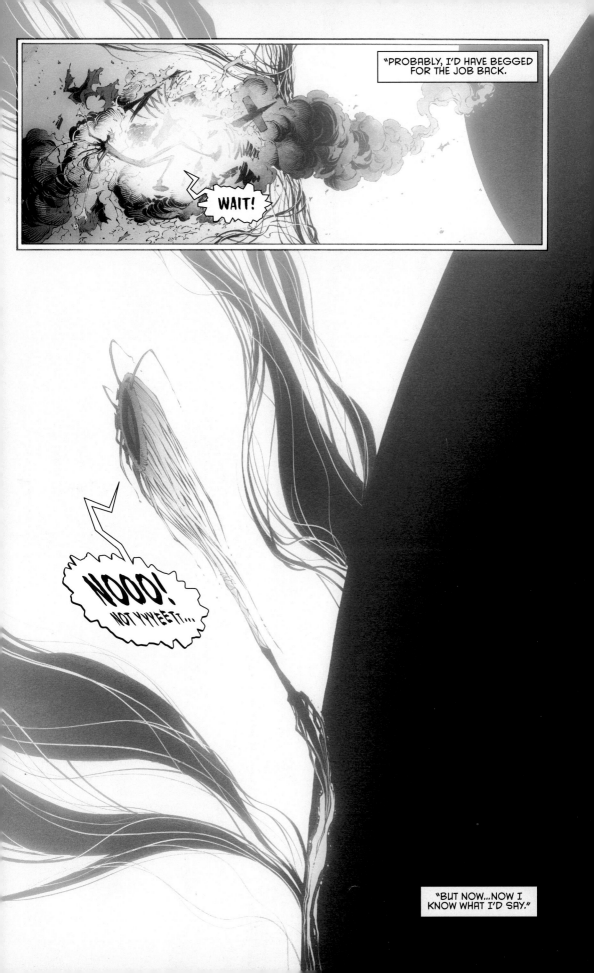

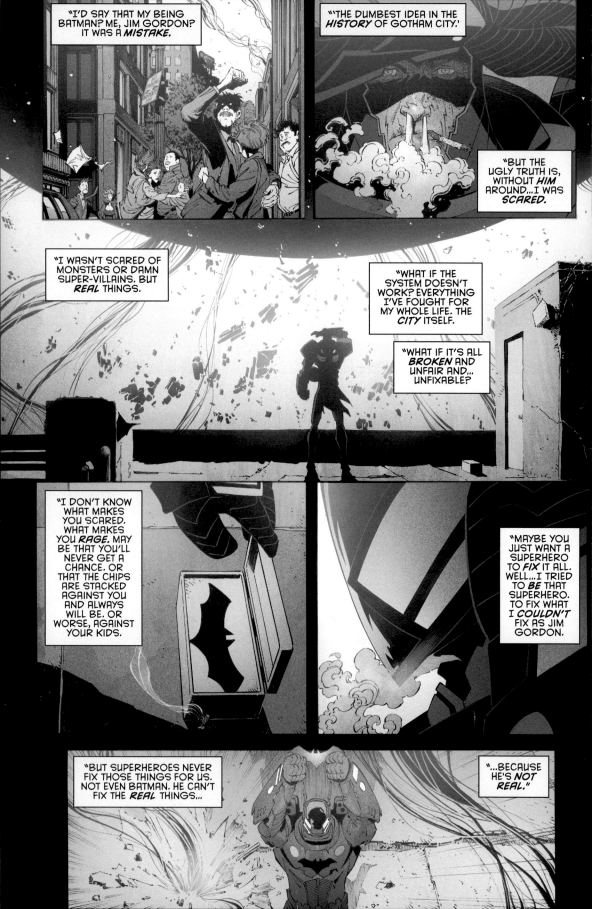

"I'D SAY THAT MY BEING BATMAN? ME, JIM GORDON? IT WAS A *MISTAKE*.

"'THE DUMBEST IDEA IN THE *HISTORY* OF GOTHAM CITY.'

"BUT THE UGLY TRUTH IS, WITHOUT *HIM* AROUND...I WAS *SCARED*.

"I WASN'T SCARED OF MONSTERS OR DAMN SUPER-VILLAINS. BUT *REAL* THINGS.

"WHAT IF THE SYSTEM DOESN'T WORK? EVERYTHING I'VE FOUGHT FOR MY WHOLE LIFE. THE *CITY* ITSELF.

"WHAT IF IT'S ALL *BROKEN* AND UNFAIR AND... UNFIXABLE?

"I DON'T KNOW WHAT MAKES YOU SCARED. WHAT MAKES YOU *RAGE*. MAYBE THAT YOU'LL NEVER GET A CHANCE. OR THAT THE CHIPS ARE STACKED AGAINST YOU AND ALWAYS WILL BE. OR WORSE, AGAINST YOUR KIDS.

"MAYBE YOU JUST WANT A SUPERHERO TO *FIX* IT ALL. WELL...I TRIED TO *BE* THAT SUPERHERO. TO FIX WHAT I *COULDN'T* FIX AS JIM GORDON.

"BUT SUPERHEROES NEVER FIX THOSE THINGS FOR US. NOT EVEN BATMAN. HE CAN'T FIX THE *REAL* THINGS...

"...BECAUSE HE'S *NOT REAL*."

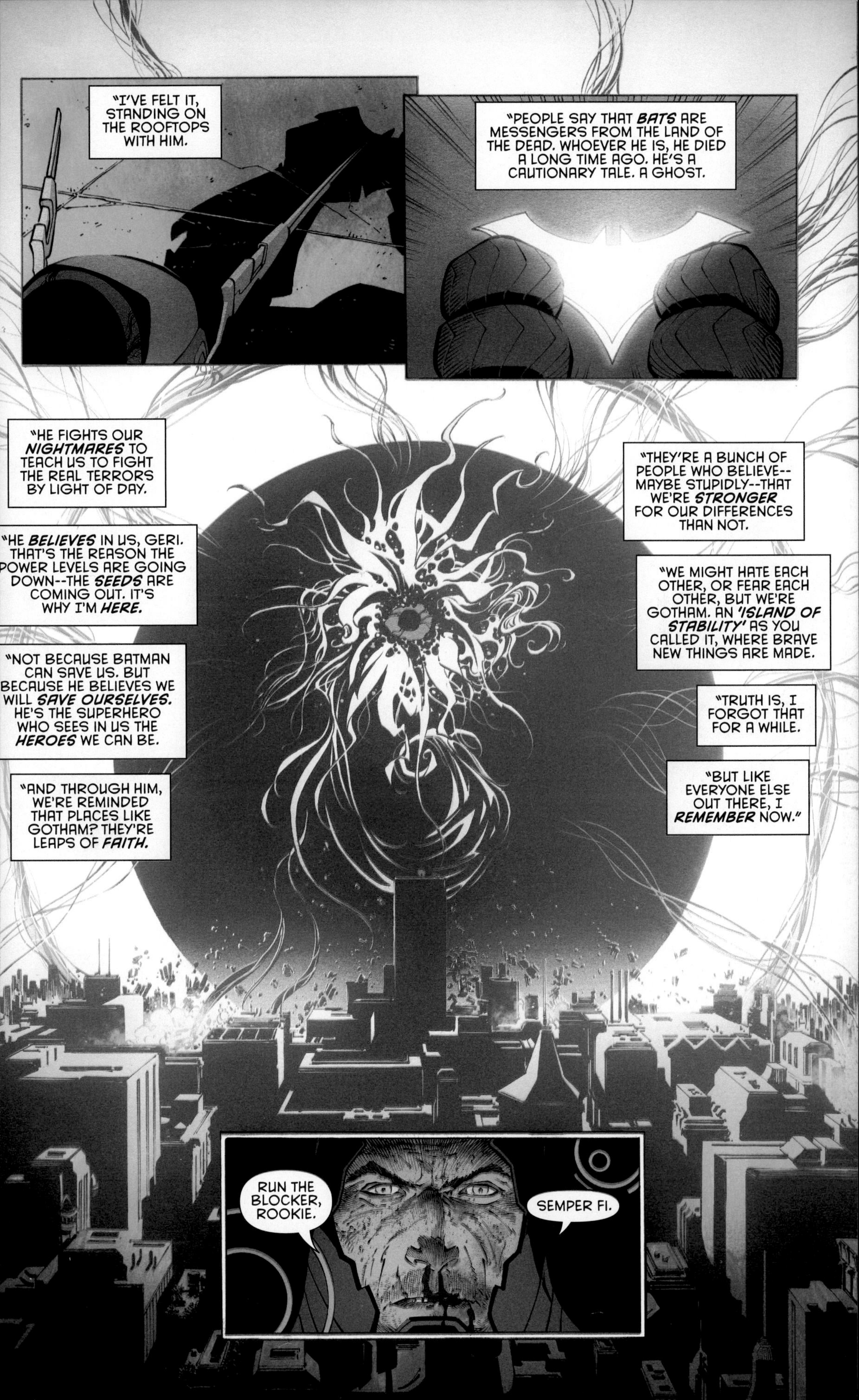
"I'VE FELT IT, STANDING ON THE ROOFTOPS WITH HIM.
"PEOPLE SAY THAT BATS ARE MESSENGERS FROM THE LAND OF THE DEAD. WHOEVER HE IS, HE DIED A LONG TIME AGO. HE'S A CAUTIONARY TALE. A GHOST.
"HE FIGHTS OUR NIGHTMARES TO TEACH US TO FIGHT THE REAL TERRORS BY LIGHT OF DAY.
"HE BELIEVES IN US, GERI. THAT'S THE REASON THE POWER LEVELS ARE GOING DOWN--THE SEEDS ARE COMING OUT. IT'S WHY I'M HERE.
"NOT BECAUSE BATMAN CAN SAVE US. BUT BECAUSE HE BELIEVES WE WILL SAVE OURSELVES. HE'S THE SUPERHERO WHO SEES IN US THE HEROES WE CAN BE.
"AND THROUGH HIM, WE'RE REMINDED THAT PLACES LIKE GOTHAM? THEY'RE LEAPS OF FAITH.
"THEY'RE A BUNCH OF PEOPLE WHO BELIEVE--MAYBE STUPIDLY--THAT WE'RE STRONGER FOR OUR DIFFERENCES THAN NOT.
"WE MIGHT HATE EACH OTHER, OR FEAR EACH OTHER, BUT WE'RE GOTHAM. AN 'ISLAND OF STABILITY' AS YOU CALLED IT, WHERE BRAVE NEW THINGS ARE MADE.
"TRUTH IS, I FORGOT THAT FOR A WHILE.
"BUT LIKE EVERYONE ELSE OUT THERE, I REMEMBER NOW."
RUN THE BLOCKER, ROOKIE.
SEMPER FI.

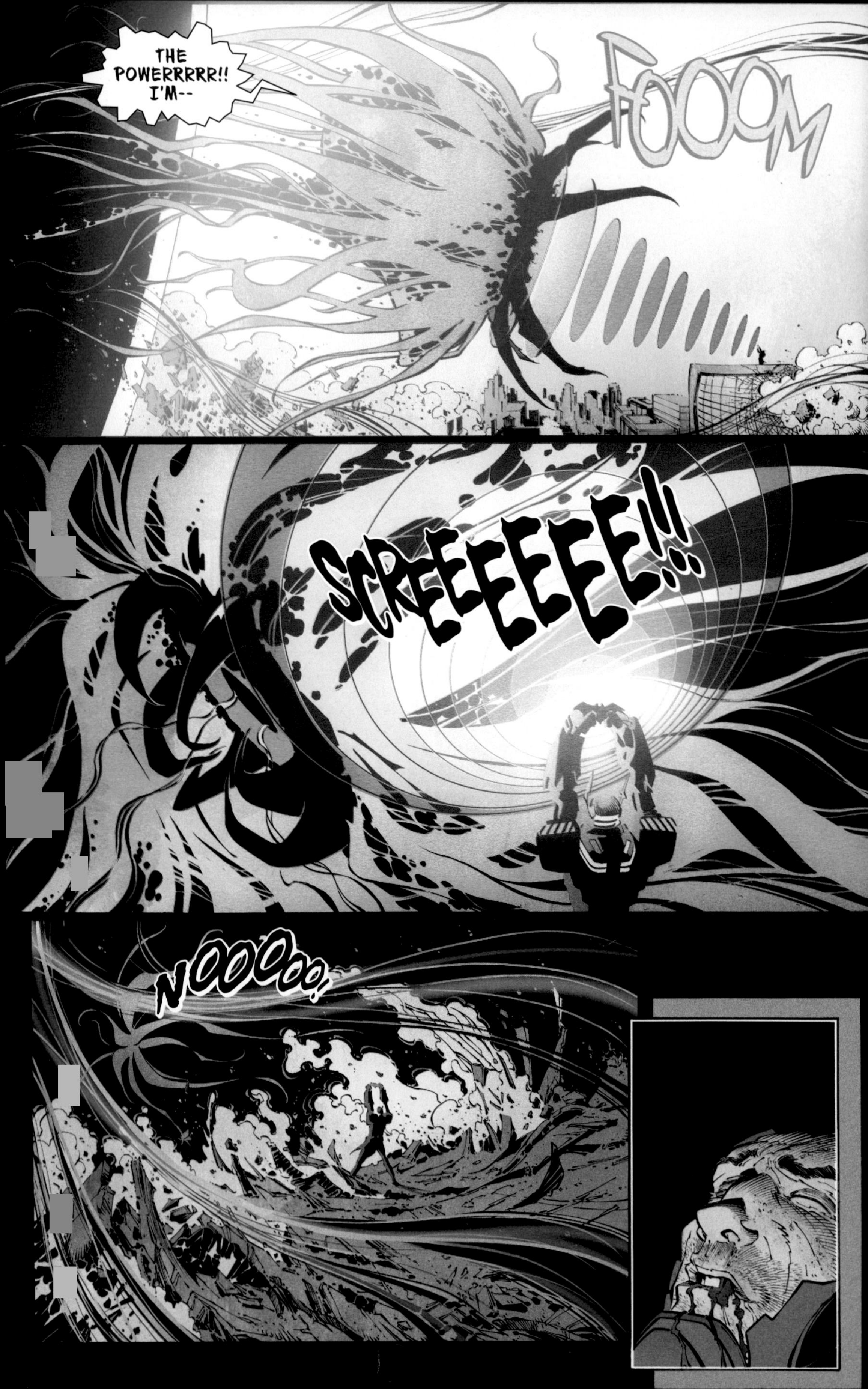
THE POWERRRRR!! I'M--
FOOOM
SCREEEEEE!!!
NOOOooo!

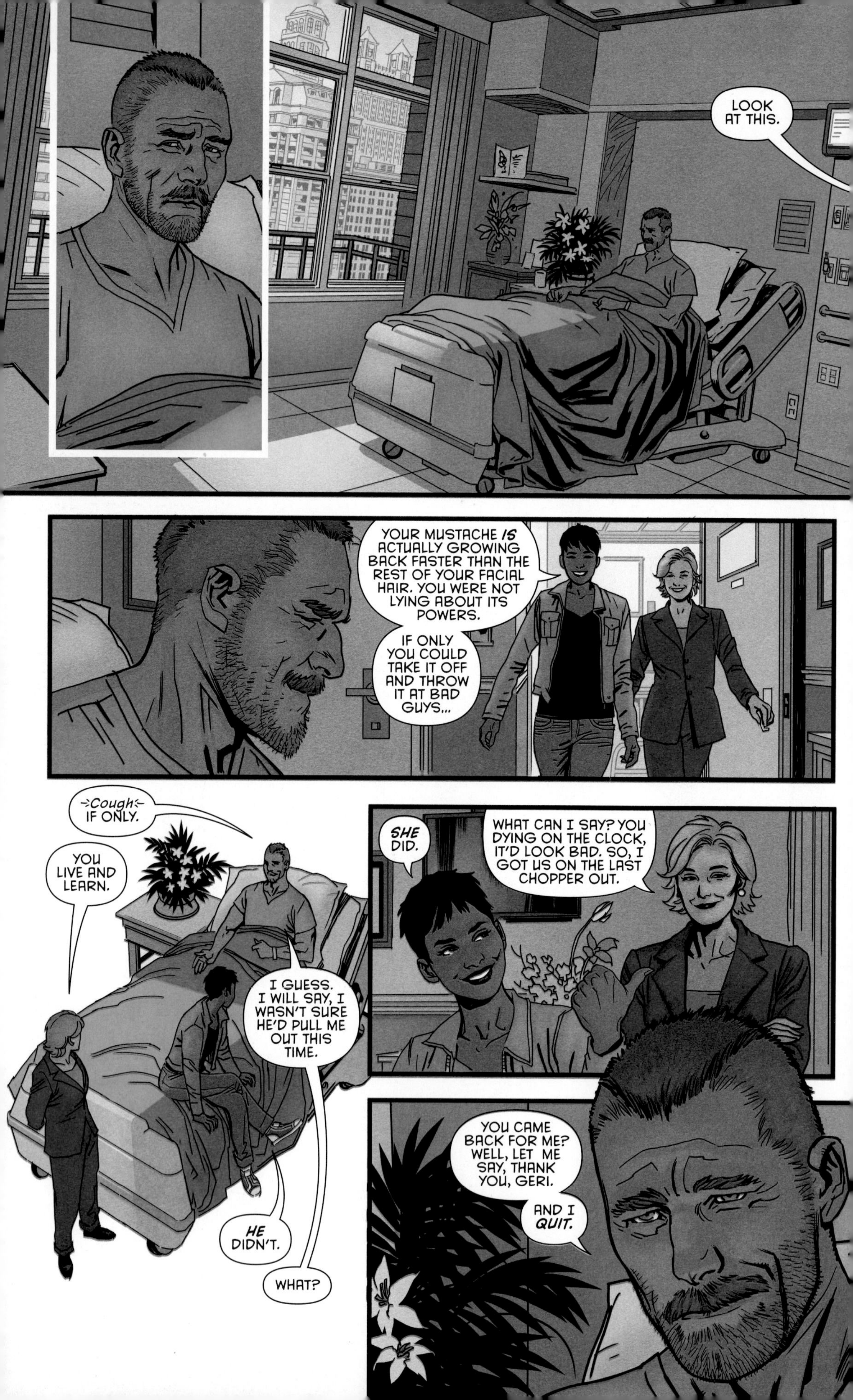
LOOK AT THIS.
YOUR MUSTACHE *IS* ACTUALLY GROWING BACK FASTER THAN THE REST OF YOUR FACIAL HAIR. YOU WERE NOT LYING ABOUT ITS POWERS.
IF ONLY YOU COULD TAKE IT OFF AND THROW IT AT BAD GUYS...
Cough IF ONLY.
YOU LIVE AND LEARN.
I GUESS. I WILL SAY, I WASN'T SURE HE'D PULL ME OUT THIS TIME.
HE DIDN'T.
WHAT?
SHE DID.
WHAT CAN I SAY? YOU DYING ON THE CLOCK, IT'D LOOK BAD. SO, I GOT US ON THE LAST CHOPPER OUT.
YOU CAME BACK FOR ME? WELL, LET ME SAY, THANK YOU, GERI.
AND I *QUIT.*

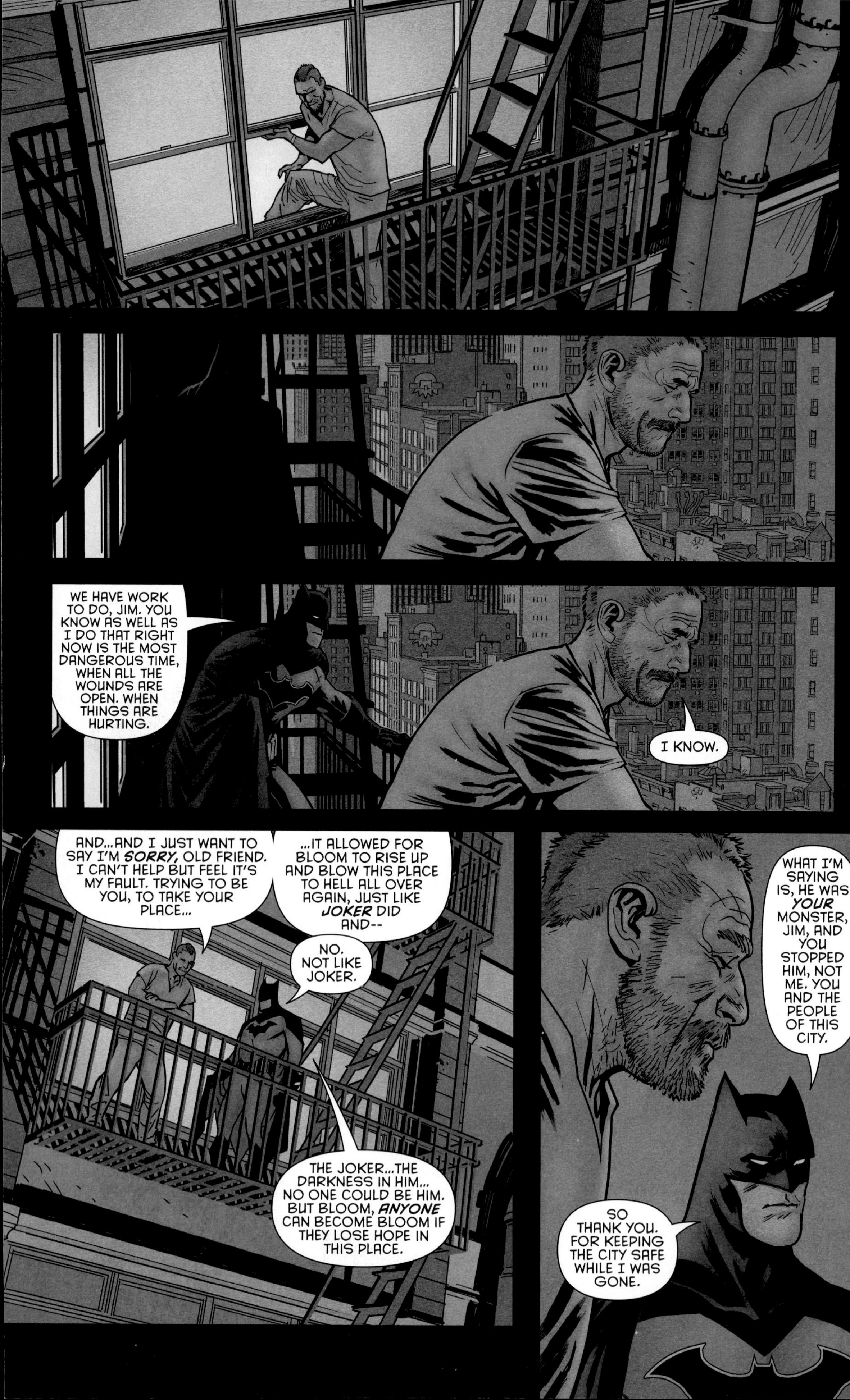
WE HAVE WORK TO DO, JIM. YOU KNOW AS WELL AS I DO THAT RIGHT NOW IS THE MOST DANGEROUS TIME, WHEN ALL THE WOUNDS ARE OPEN. WHEN THINGS ARE HURTING.
I KNOW.
AND...AND I JUST WANT TO SAY I'M *SORRY,* OLD FRIEND. I CAN'T HELP BUT FEEL IT'S MY FAULT. TRYING TO BE YOU, TO TAKE YOUR PLACE...
...IT ALLOWED FOR BLOOM TO RISE UP AND BLOW THIS PLACE TO HELL ALL OVER AGAIN, JUST LIKE *JOKER* DID AND--
NO. NOT LIKE JOKER.
THE JOKER...THE DARKNESS IN HIM... NO ONE COULD BE HIM. BUT BLOOM, *ANYONE* CAN BECOME BLOOM IF THEY LOSE HOPE IN THIS PLACE.
WHAT I'M SAYING IS, HE WAS *YOUR* MONSTER, JIM, AND YOU STOPPED HIM, NOT ME. YOU AND THE PEOPLE OF THIS CITY.
SO THANK YOU. FOR KEEPING THE CITY SAFE WHILE I WAS GONE.

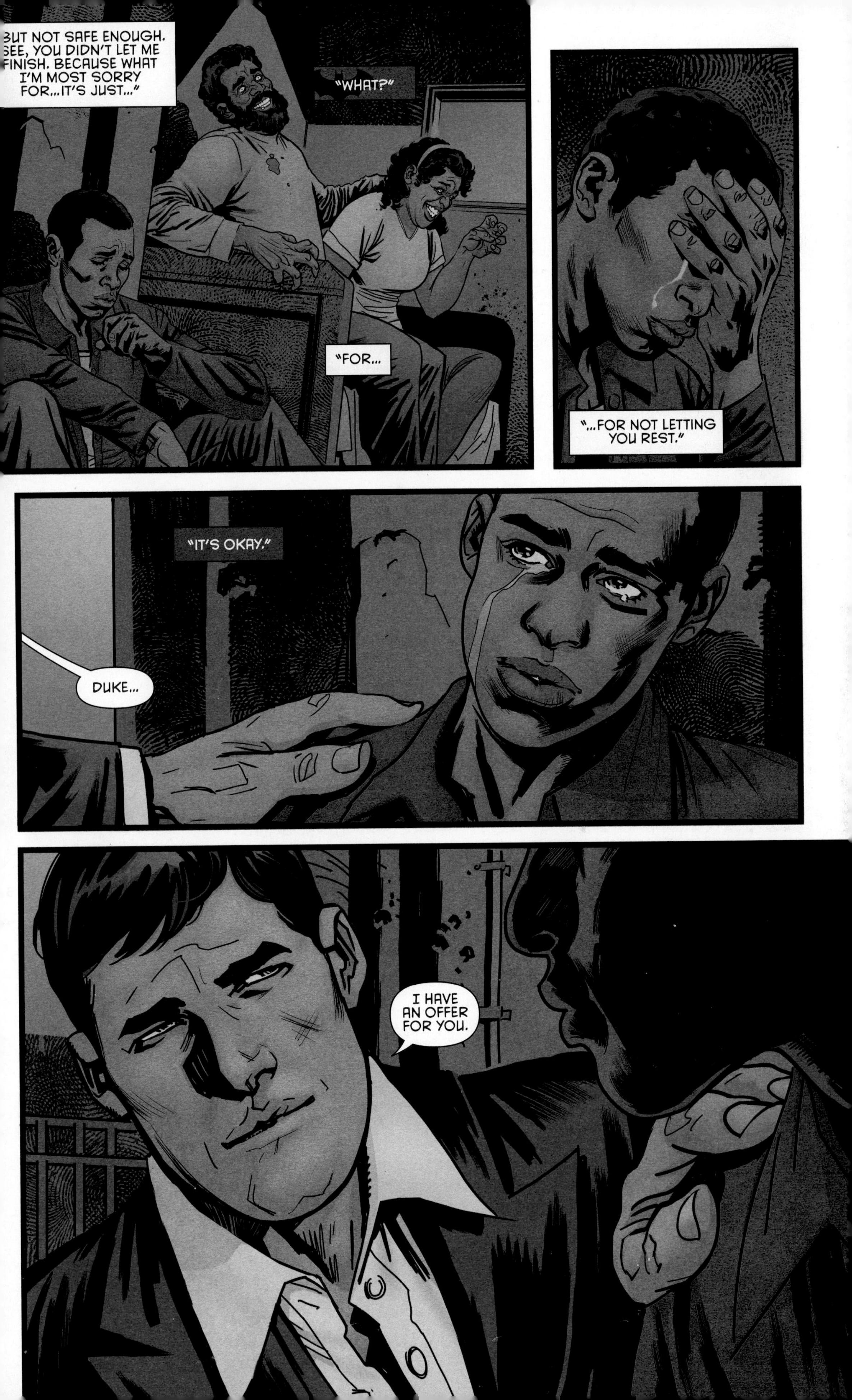
BUT NOT SAFE ENOUGH. SEE, YOU DIDN'T LET ME FINISH. BECAUSE WHAT I'M MOST SORRY FOR...IT'S JUST..."
"WHAT?"
"FOR...
"...FOR NOT LETTING YOU REST."
"IT'S OKAY."
DUKE...
I HAVE AN OFFER FOR YOU.

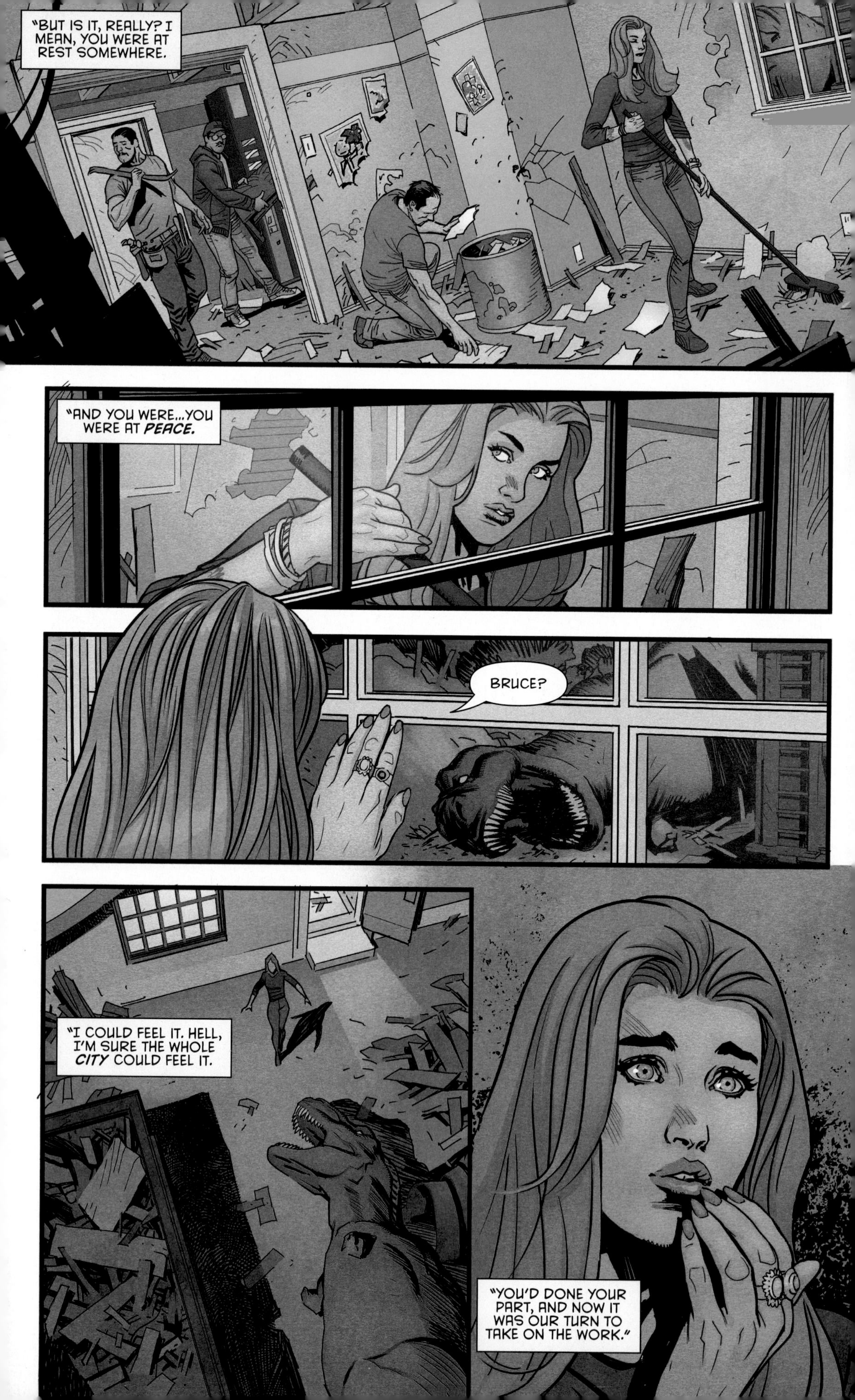
"BUT IS IT, REALLY? I MEAN, YOU WERE AT REST SOMEWHERE.
"AND YOU WERE...YOU WERE AT *PEACE.*
BRUCE?
"I COULD FEEL IT. HELL, I'M SURE THE WHOLE *CITY* COULD FEEL IT.
"YOU'D DONE YOUR PART, AND NOW IT WAS OUR TURN TO TAKE ON THE WORK."

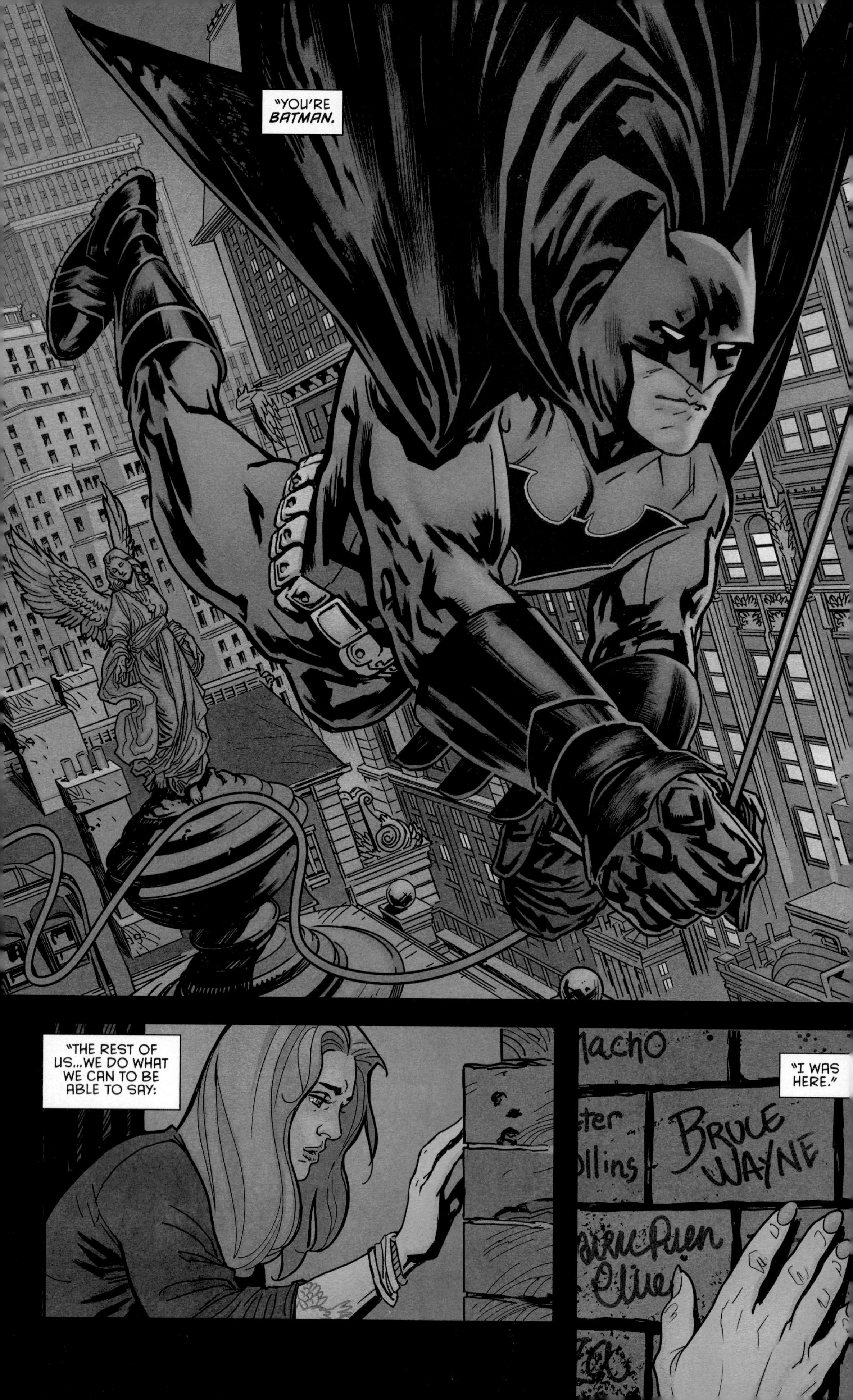
"YOU'RE BATMAN.
"THE REST OF US...WE DO WHAT WE CAN TO BE ABLE TO SAY:
BRUCE WAYNE
"I WAS HERE."

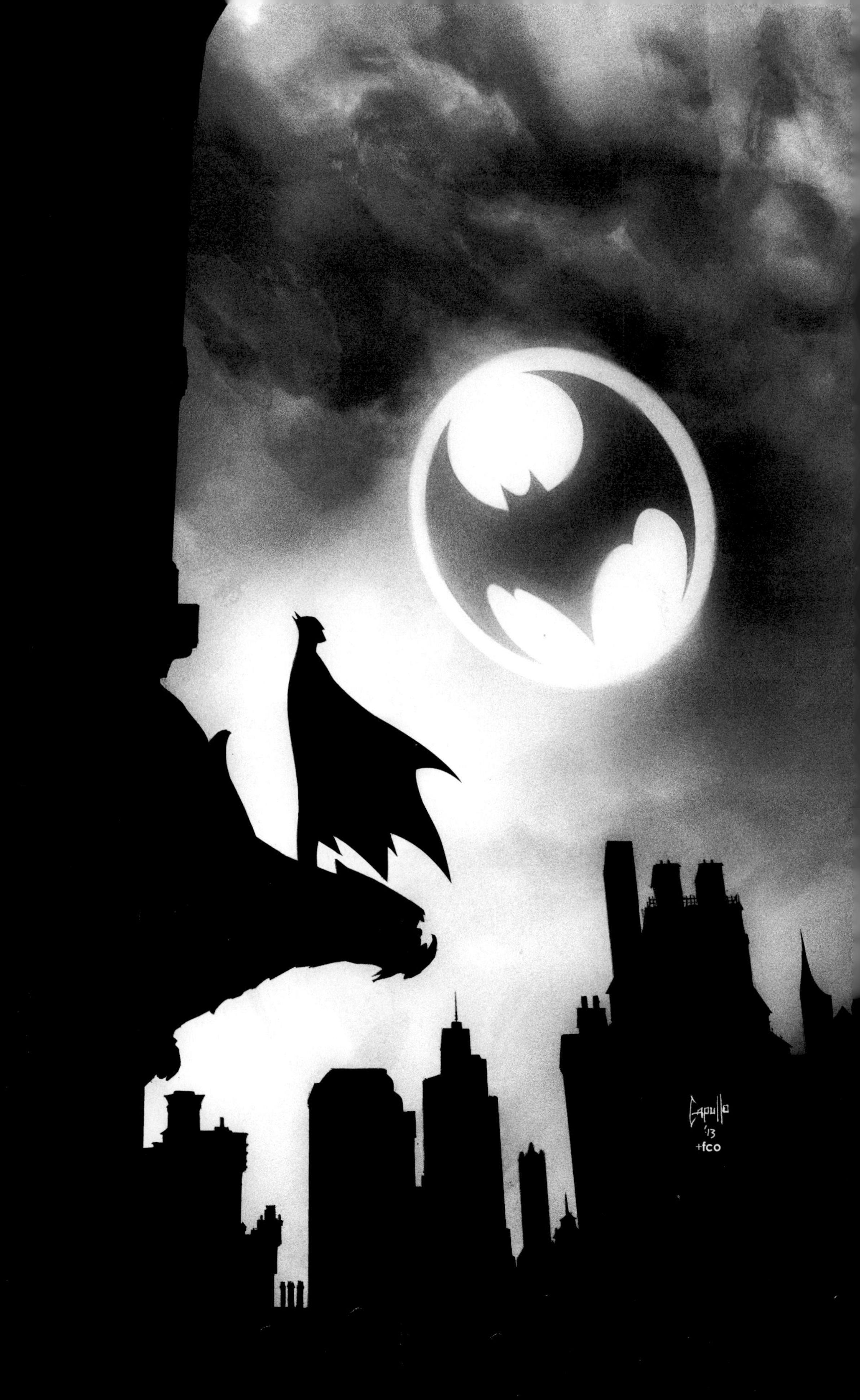
Capullo '13
+fco

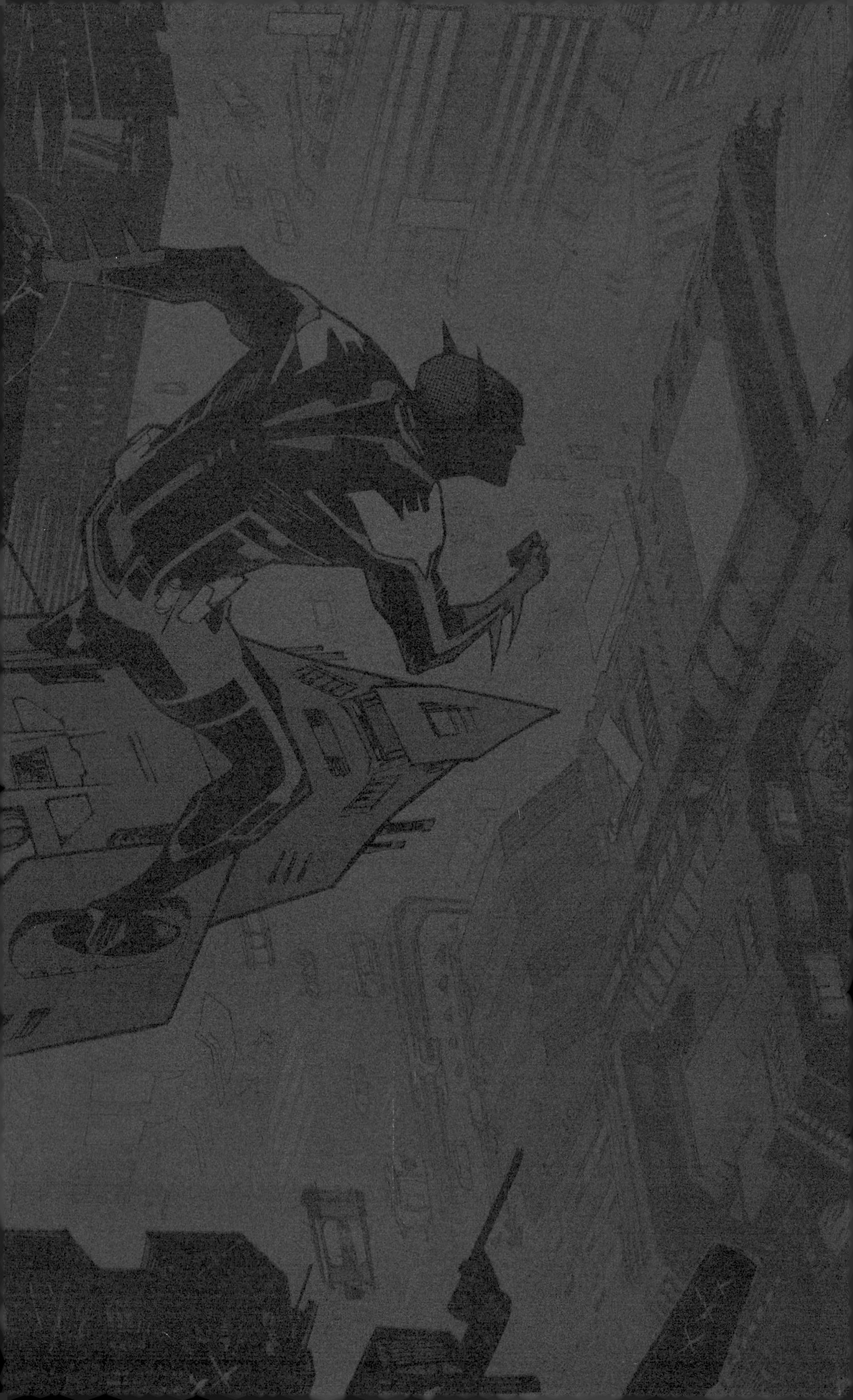

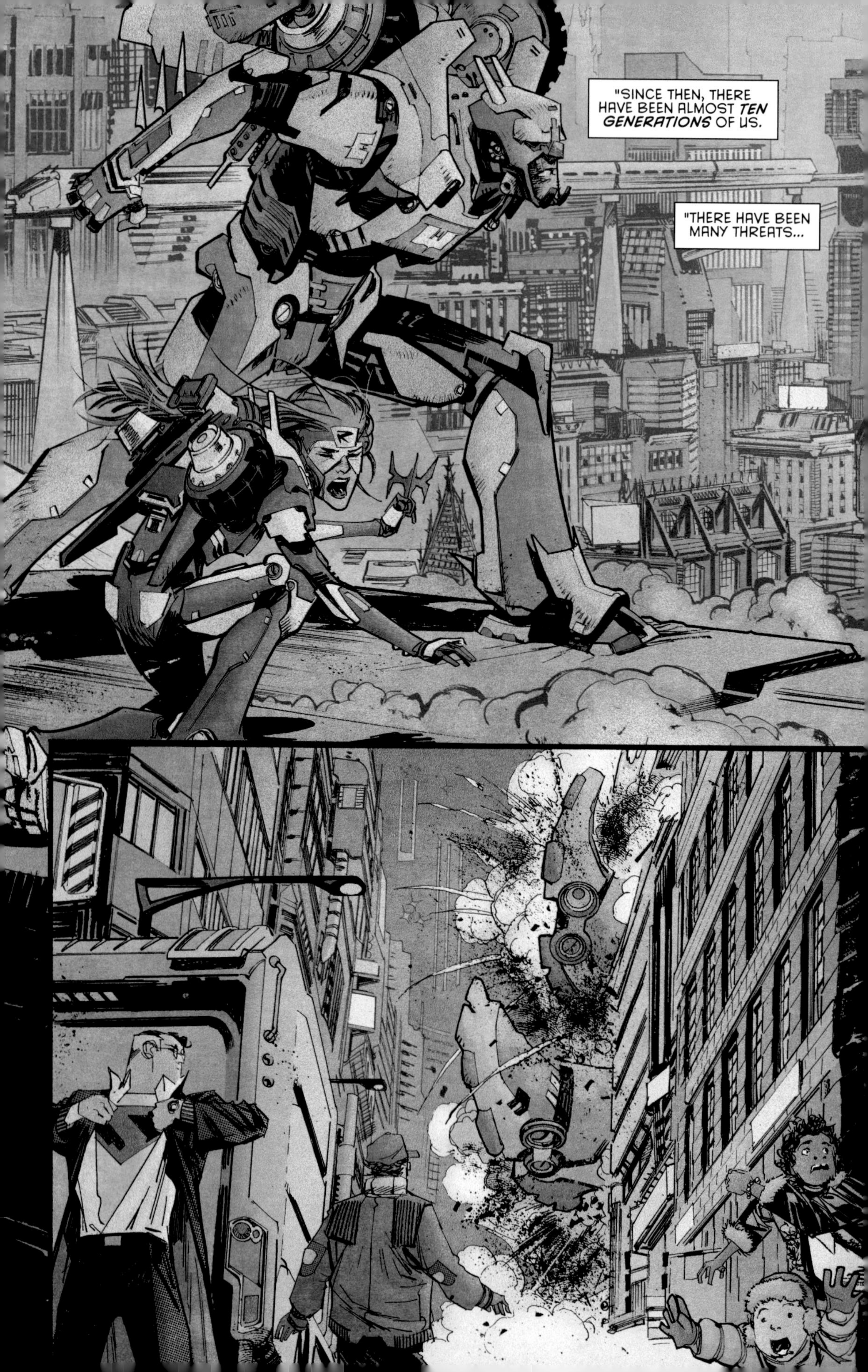
"SINCE THEN, THERE HAVE BEEN ALMOST TEN GENERATIONS OF US.
"THERE HAVE BEEN MANY THREATS...

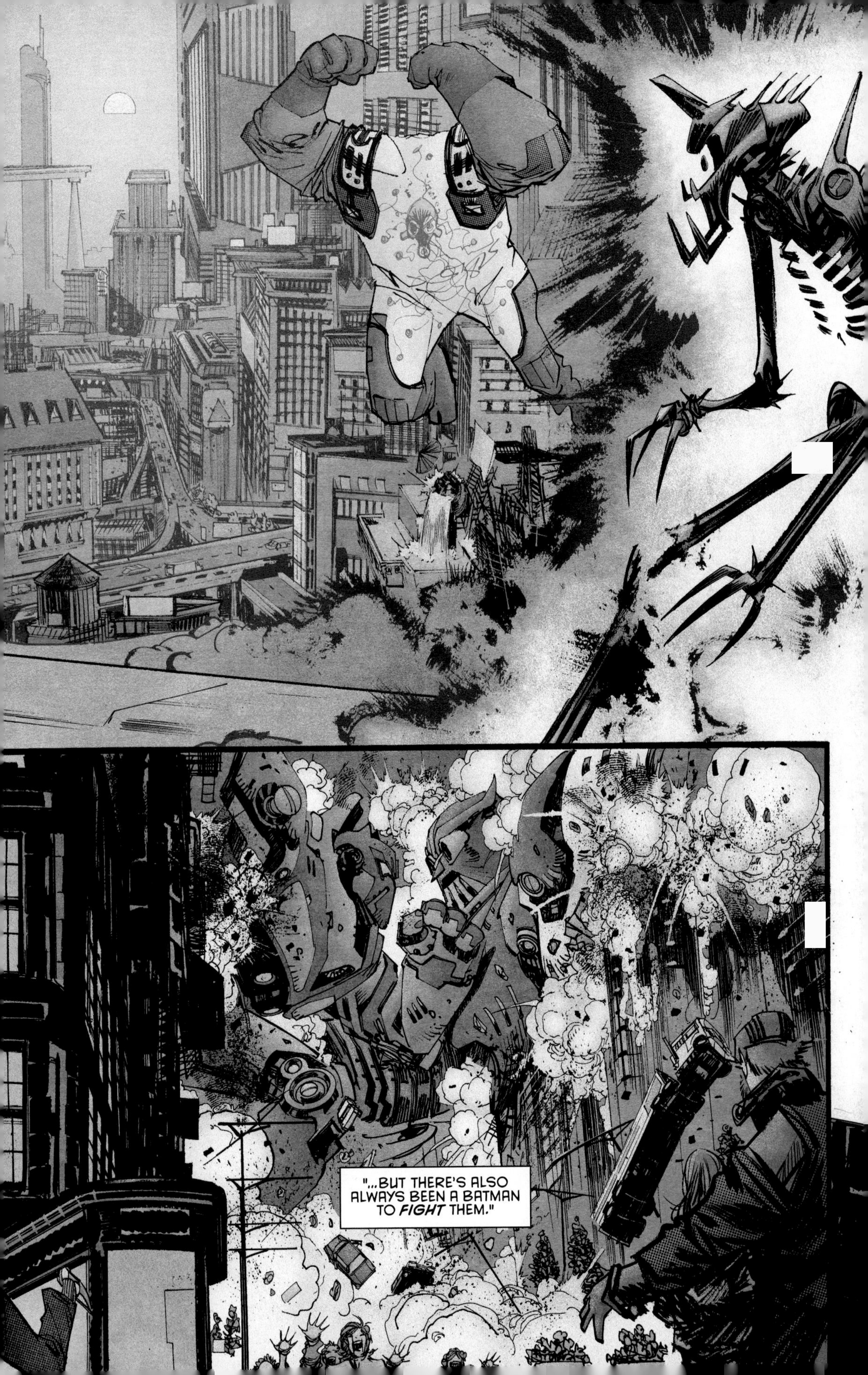
"...BUT THERE'S ALSO ALWAYS BEEN A BATMAN TO FIGHT THEM."

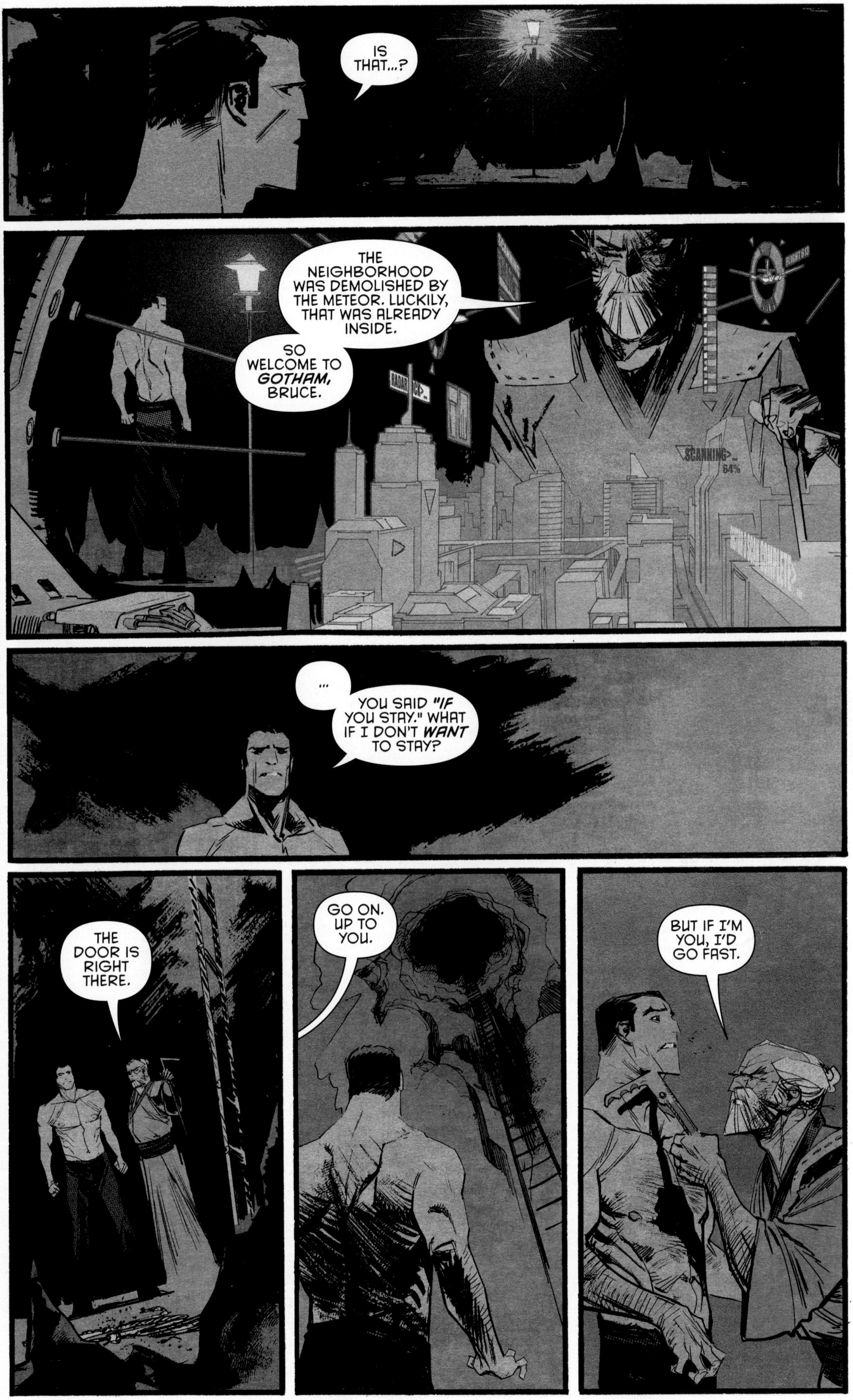
IS THAT...?
THE NEIGHBORHOOD WAS DEMOLISHED BY THE METEOR. LUCKILY, THAT WAS ALREADY INSIDE.
SO WELCOME TO *GOTHAM,* BRUCE.
SCANNING>...
64%
...
YOU SAID *"IF* YOU STAY." WHAT IF I DON'T *WANT* TO STAY?
THE DOOR IS RIGHT THERE.
GO ON. UP TO YOU.
BUT IF I'M YOU, I'D GO FAST.

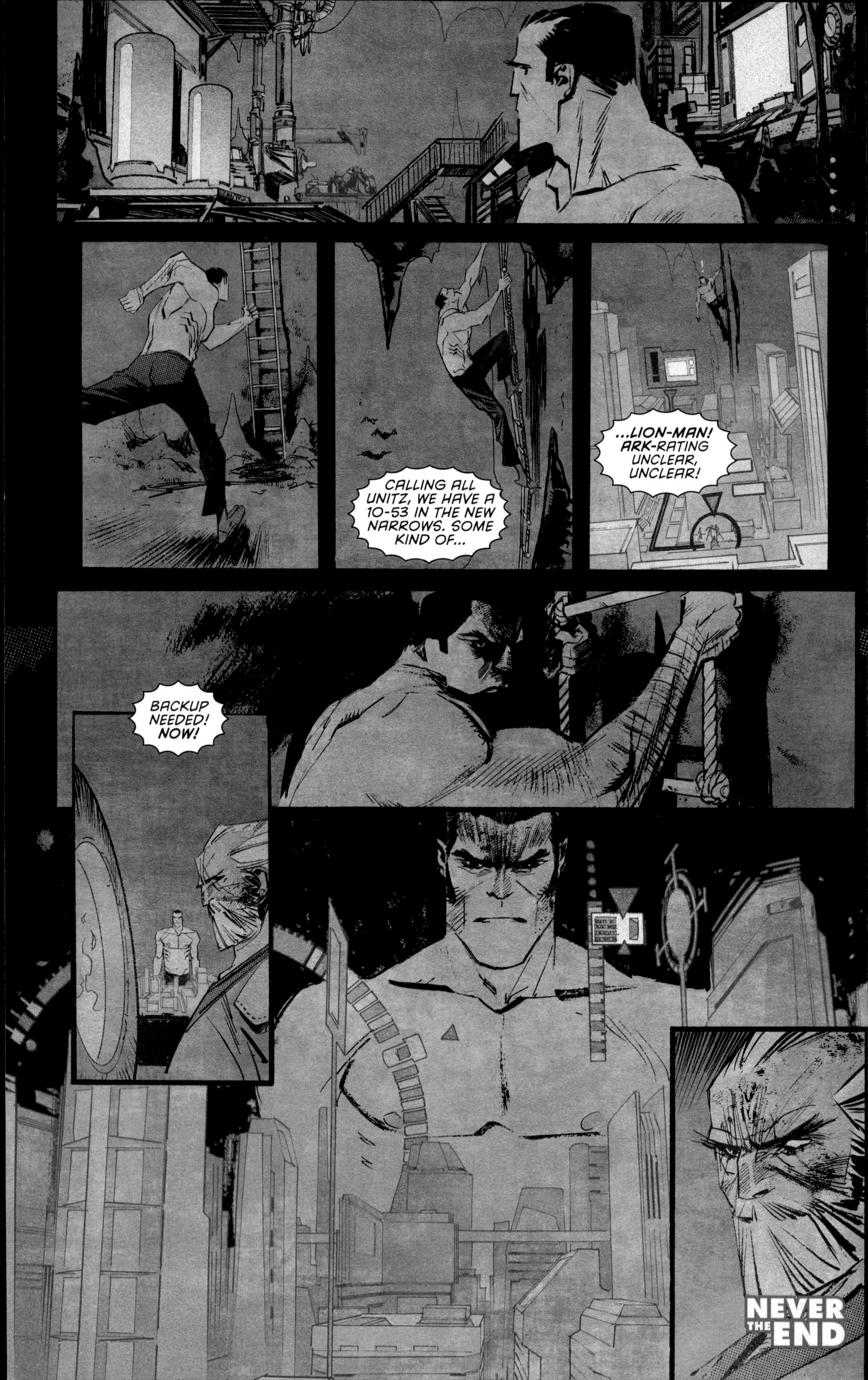

CALLING ALL UNITZ, WE HAVE A 10-53 IN THE NEW NARROWS. SOME KIND OF...
...LION-MAN! ARK-RATING UNCLEAR, UNCLEAR!
BACKUP NEEDED! NOW!
NEVER THE END

VARIANT COVER GALLERY

BATMAN #50/SUPERMAN #50
CONNECTING *BATMAN V SUPERMAN* VARIANTS
BY GABRIELE DELL'OTTO

BATMAN #50/SUPERMAN #50
CONNECTING *BATMAN V SUPERMAN* VARIANTS
BY SEAN MURPHY & DAVE MCCAIG

BATMAN #50/SUPERMAN #50
CONNECTING *BATMAN V SUPERMAN* VARIANTS
BY JOSH MIDDLETON

BATMAN #50
BATMAN V SUPERMAN CONVENTION EXCLUSIVE
VARIANT BY DAVID FINCH,
MATT BANNING & JUNE CHUNG

BATMAN #50/SUPERMAN #50
CONNECTING *BATMAN V SUPERMAN* VARIANTS
BY GUILLEM MARCH

BATMAN #50/SUPERMAN #50
CONNECTING *BATMAN V SUPERMAN* VARIANTS
BY DAVE JOHNSON & DAVE MCCAIG

BATMAN #50/SUPERMAN #50
CONNECTING *BATMAN V SUPERMAN* VARIANTS
BY PATRICK GLEASON,
MICK GRAY & JOHN KALISZ

BATMAN #50/SUPERMAN #50
CONNECTING BATMAN V SUPERMAN VARIANTS
BY TIM SALE & BRENNAN WAGNER

BATMAN #50/SUPERMAN #50
CONNECTING *BATMAN V SUPERMAN* VARIANTS
BY AMANDA CONNER & PAUL MOUNTS

BATMAN #50
BATMAN V SUPERMAN VARIANT BY PAUL POPE

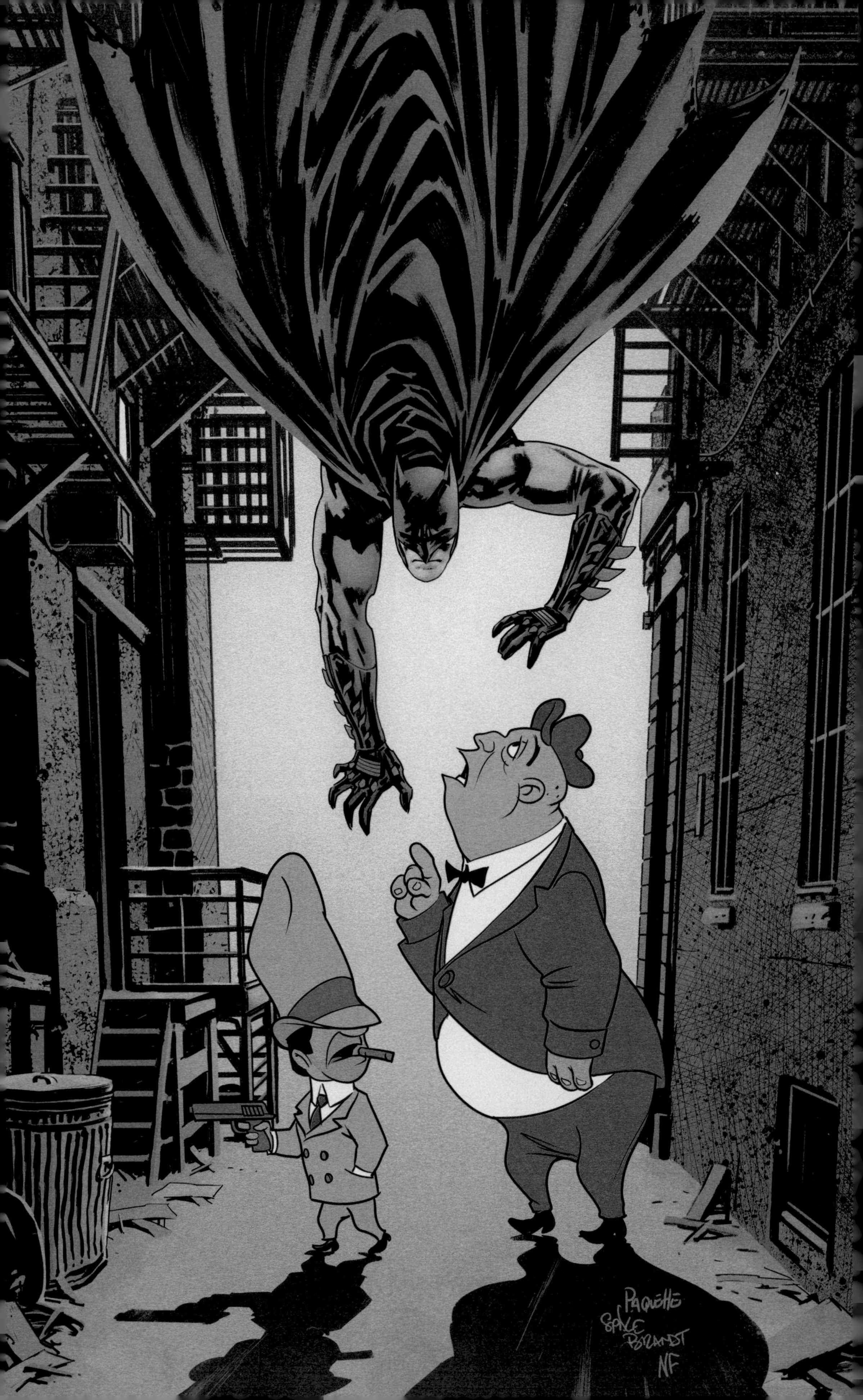

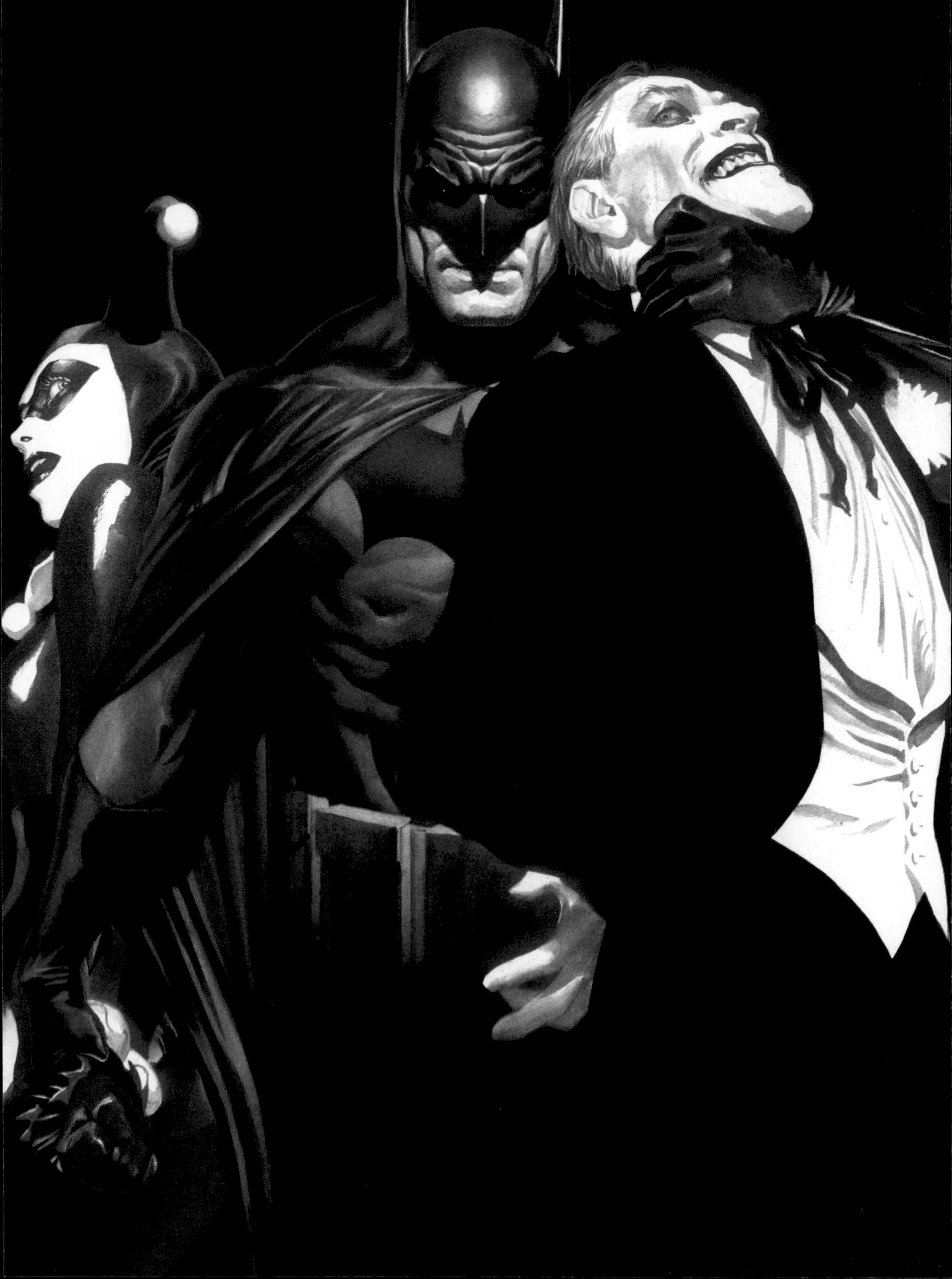

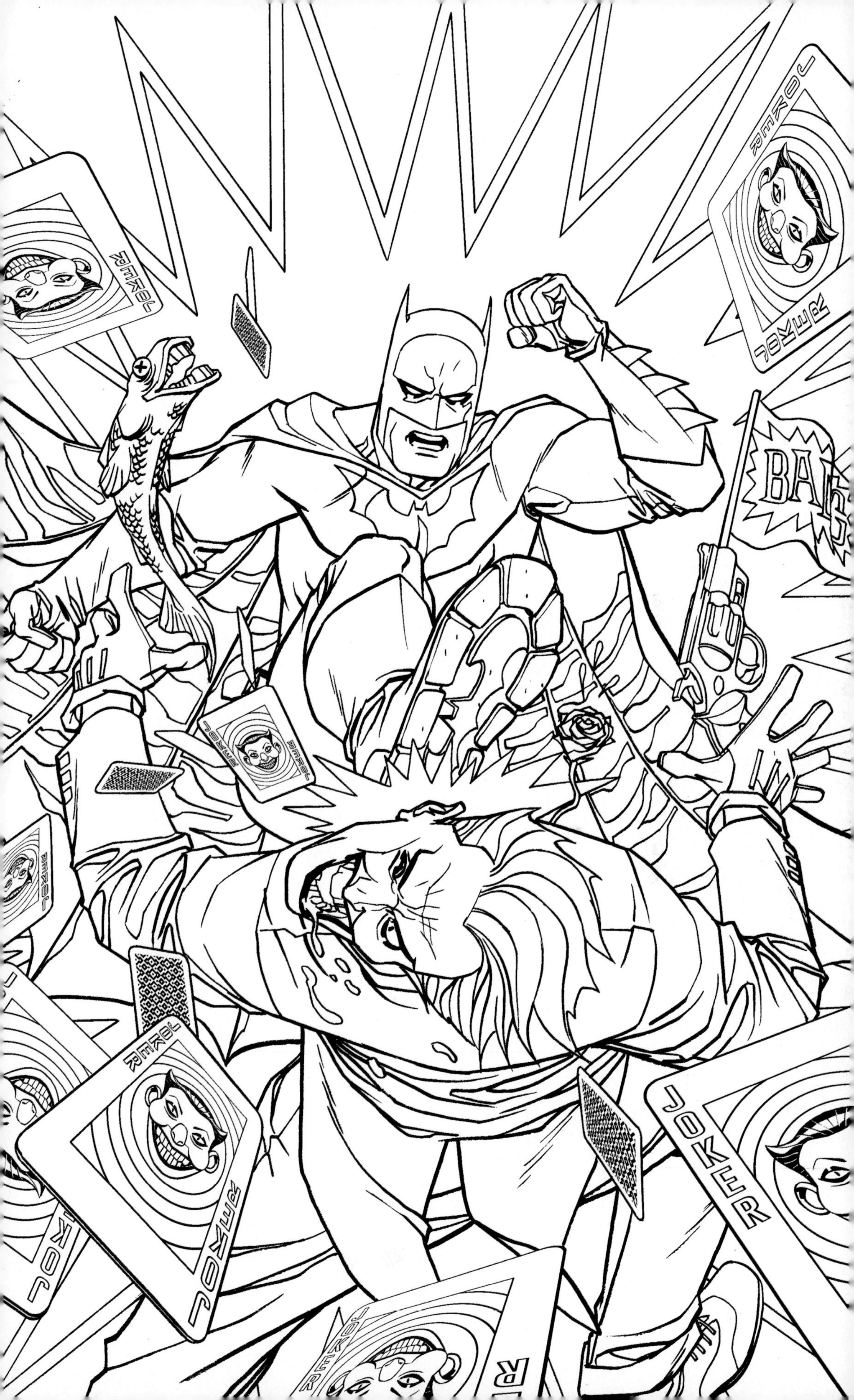
JOKER

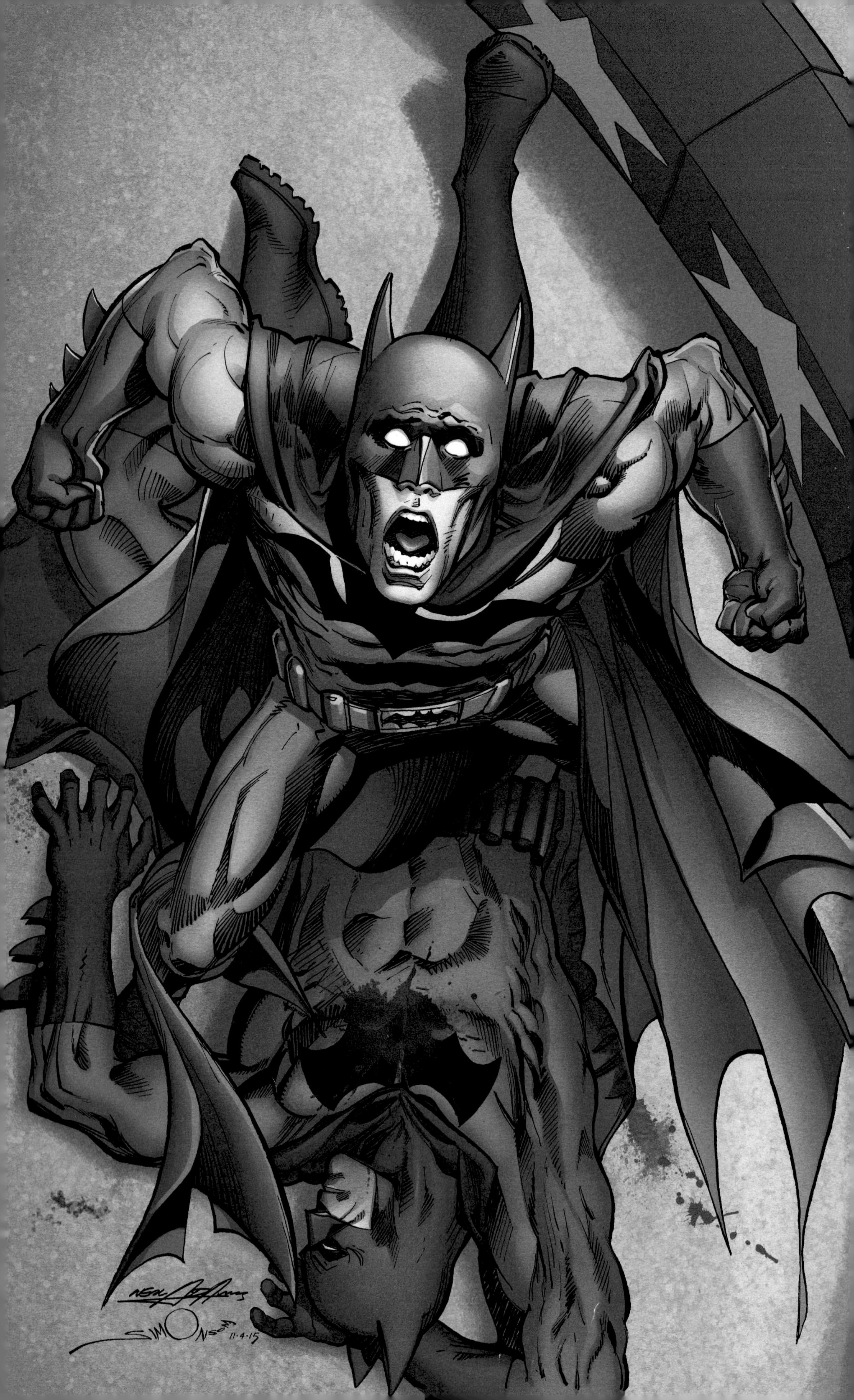

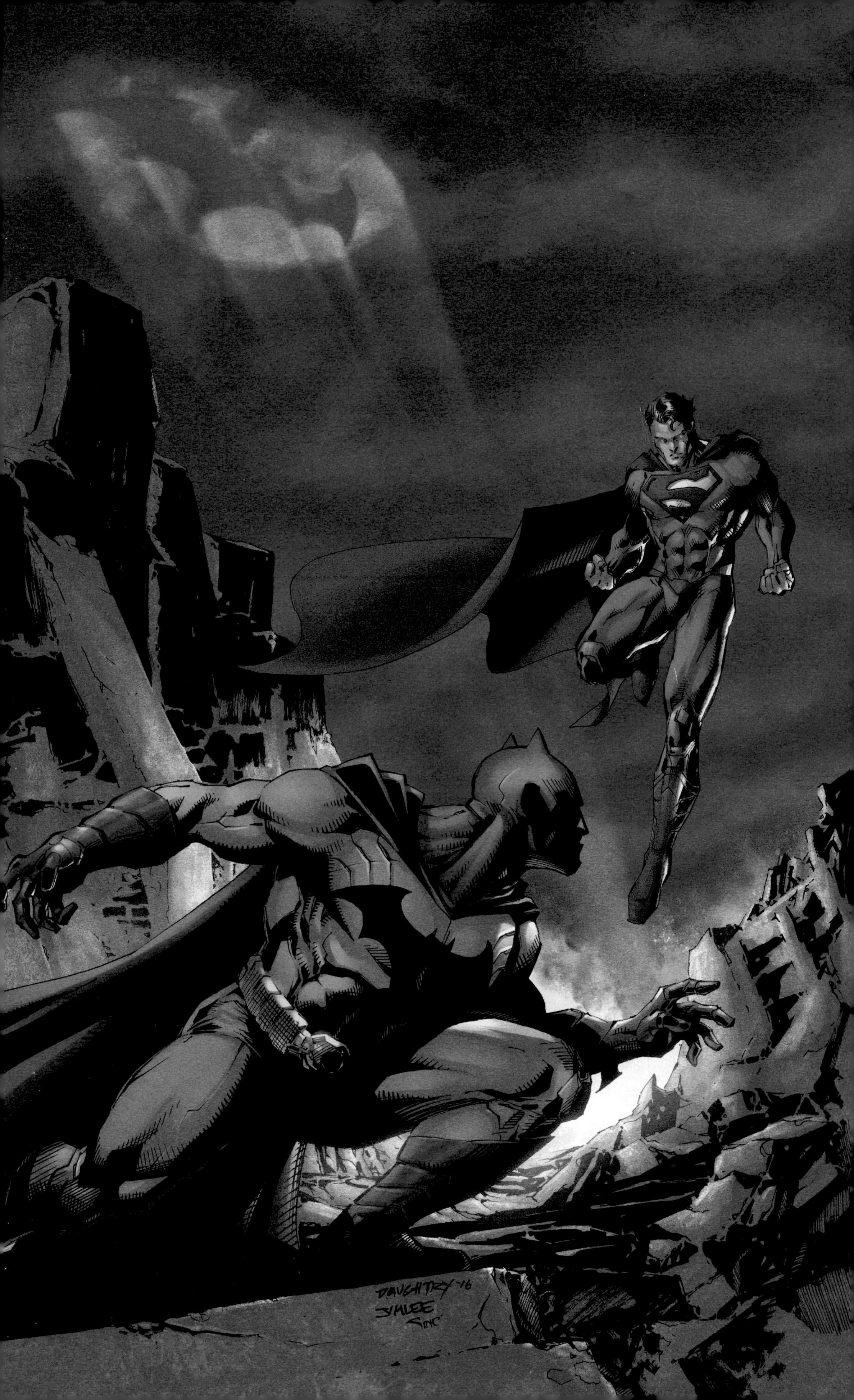
DAUGHTRY '16
JIMLEE

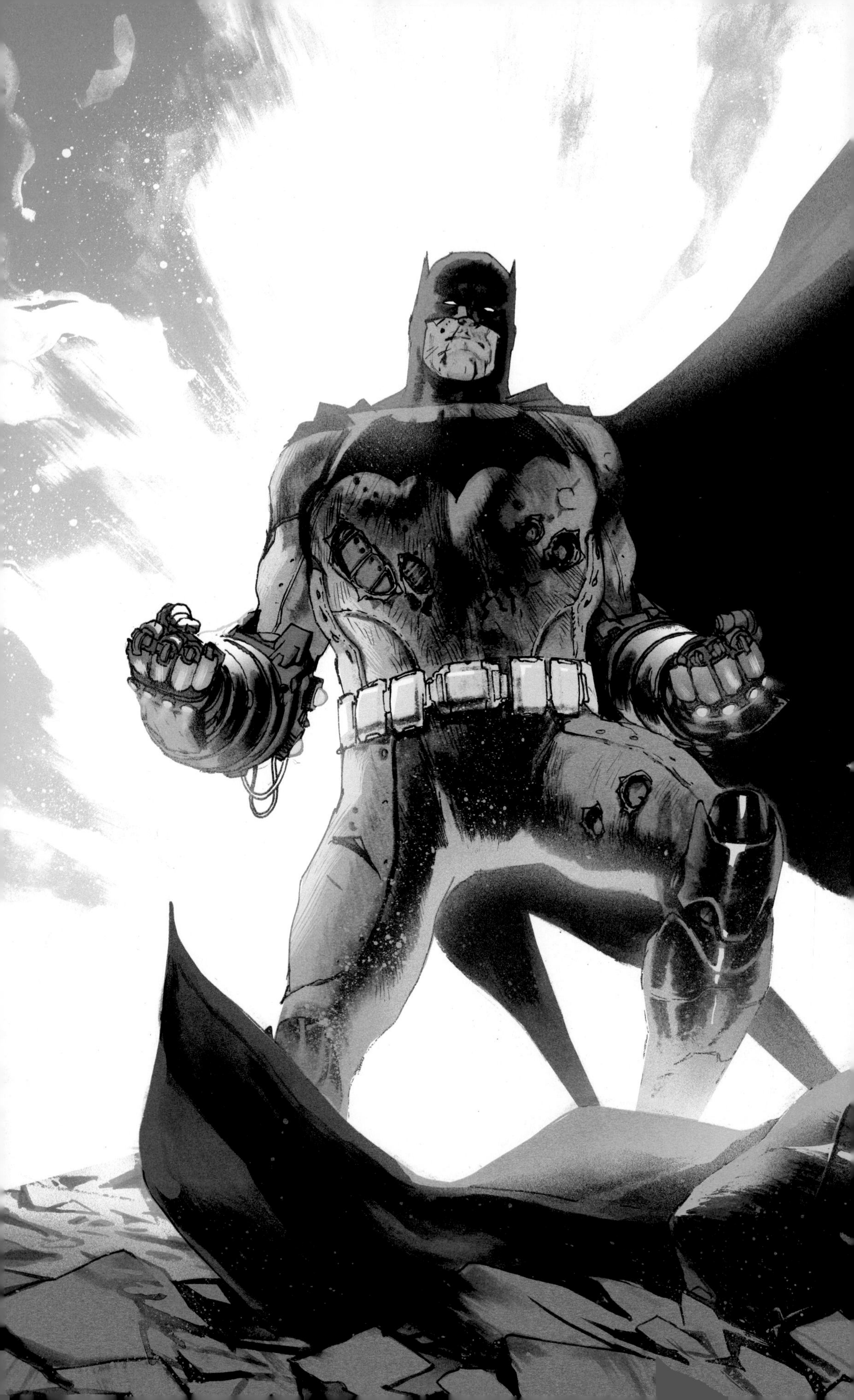

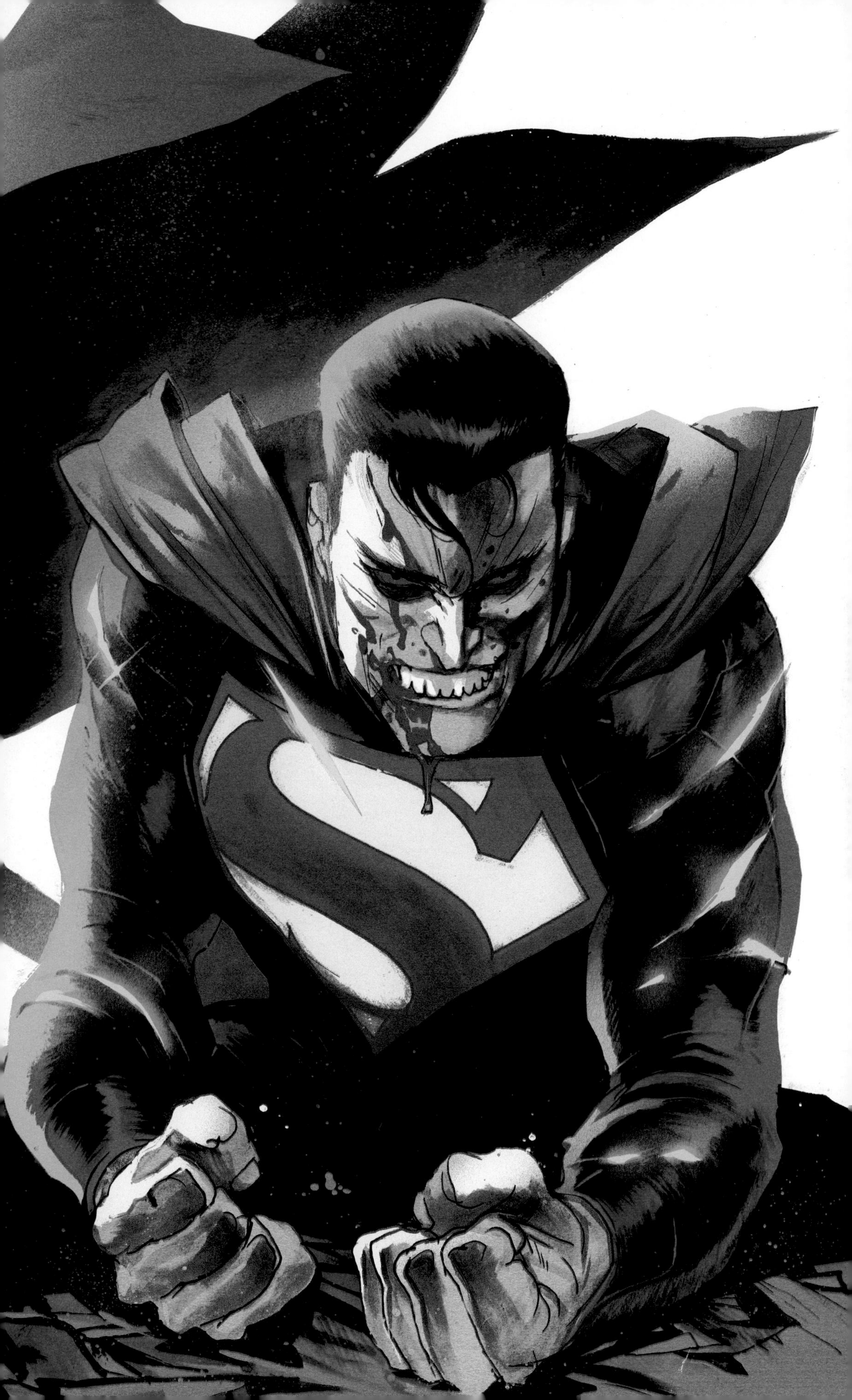

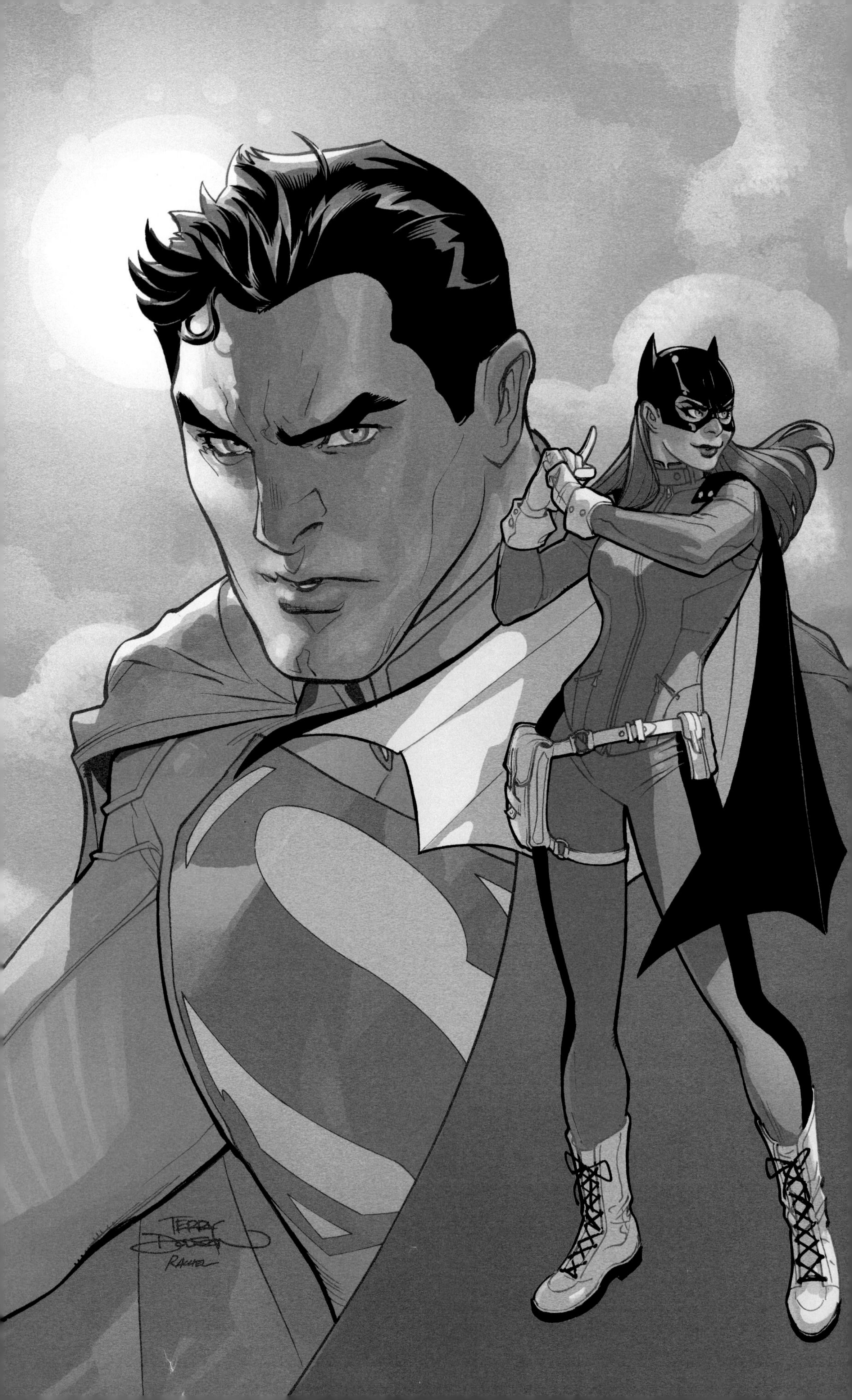
TERRY DODSON
RACHEL

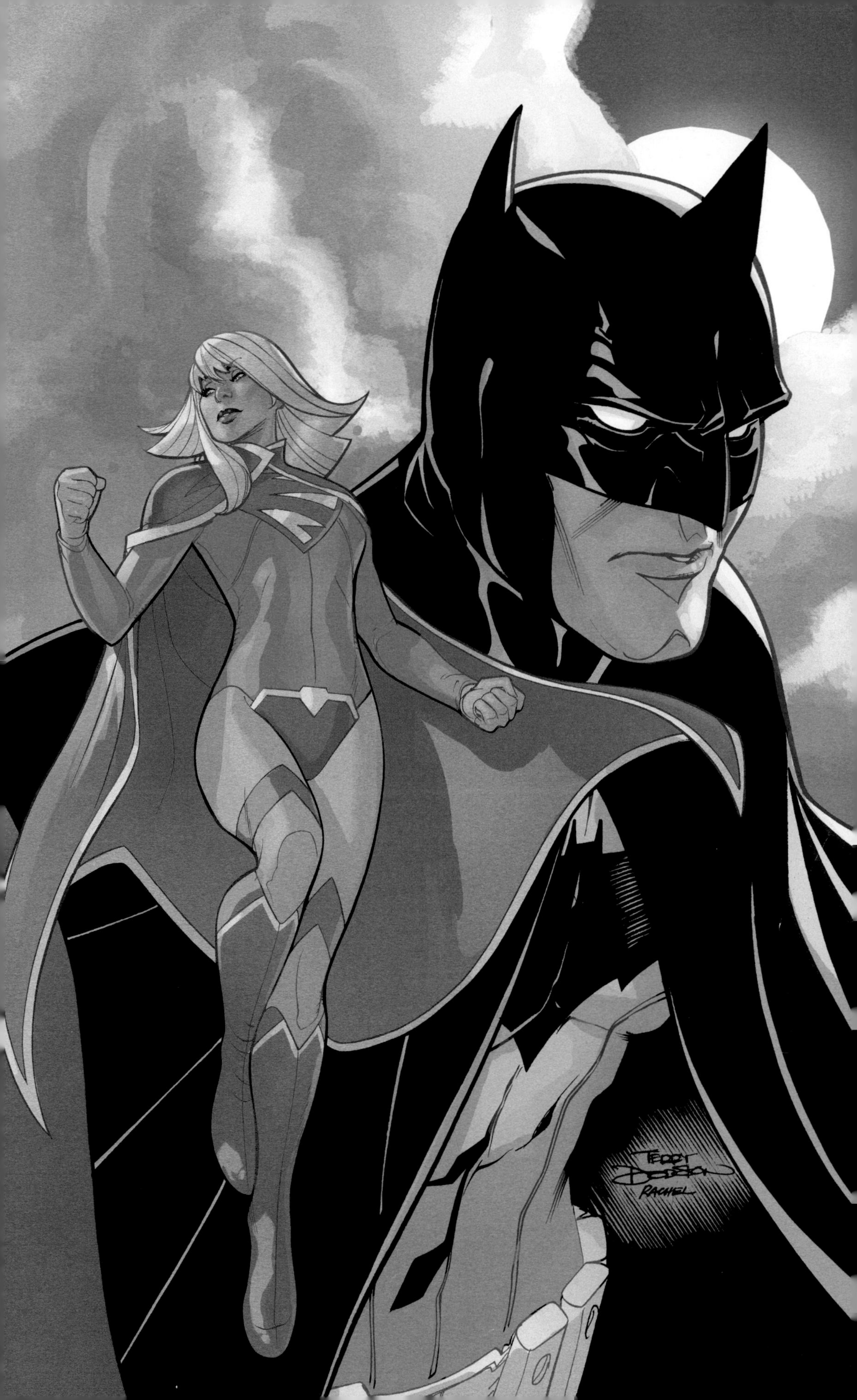
TERRY DODSON
RACHEL

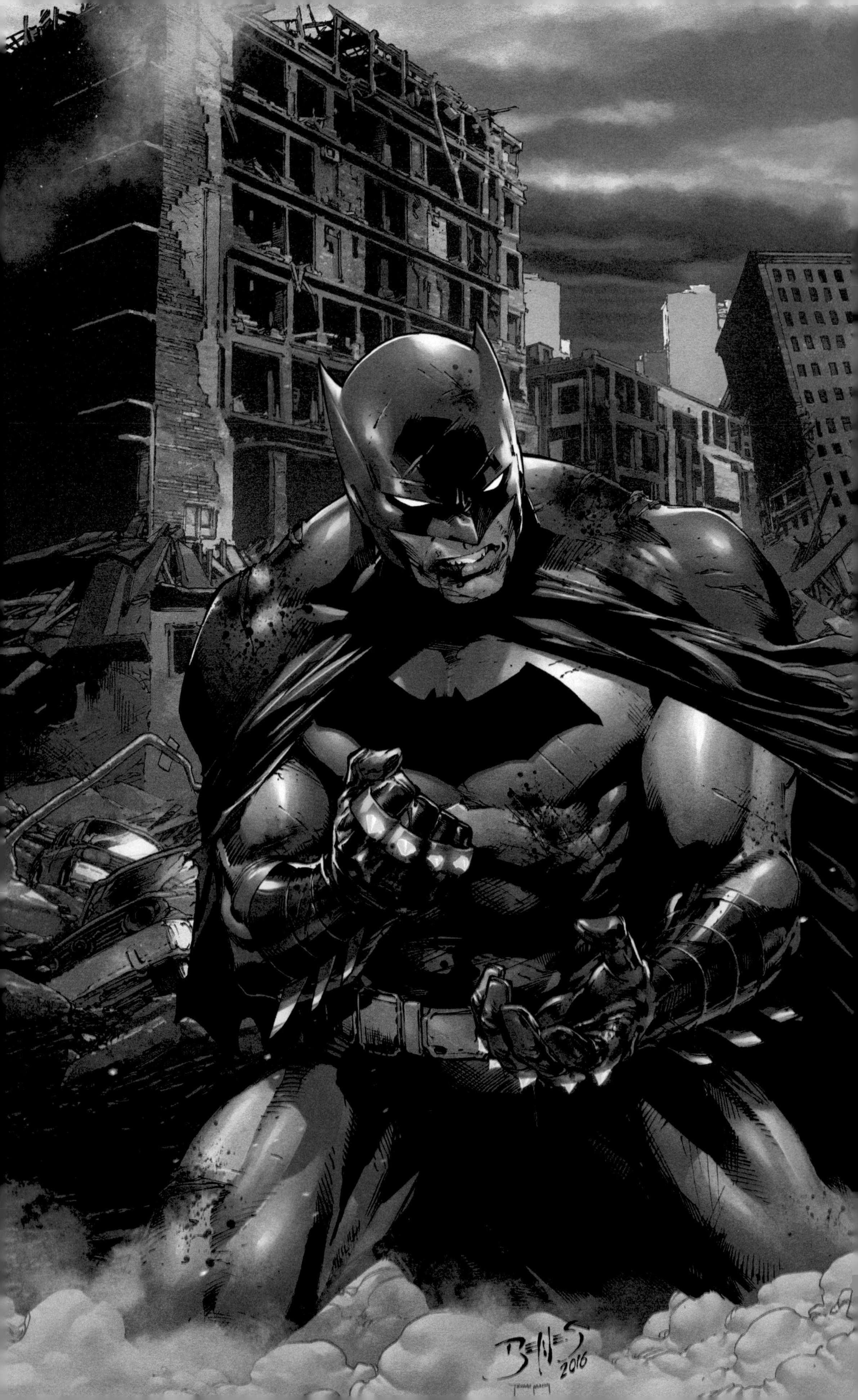

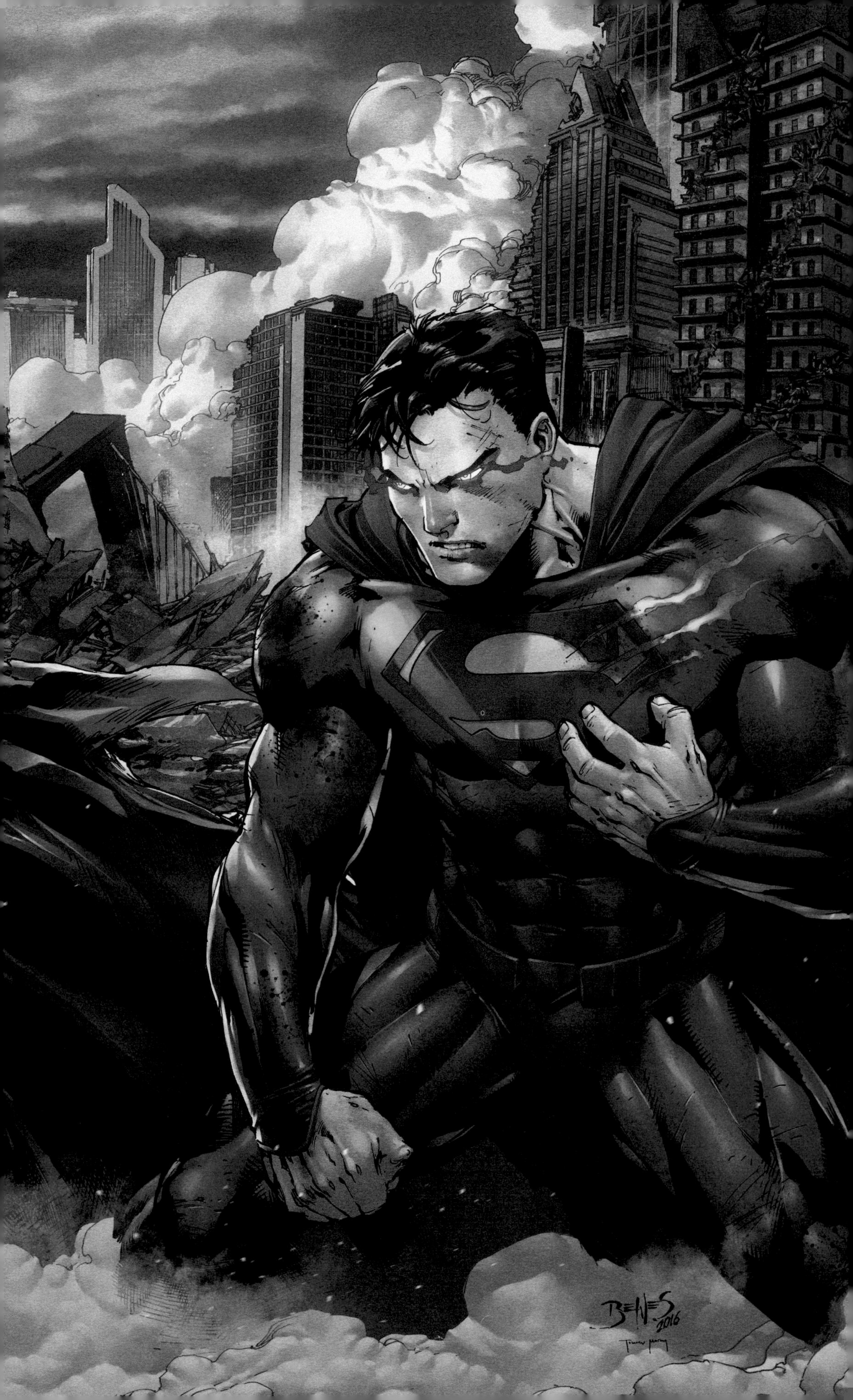
BENES
2016

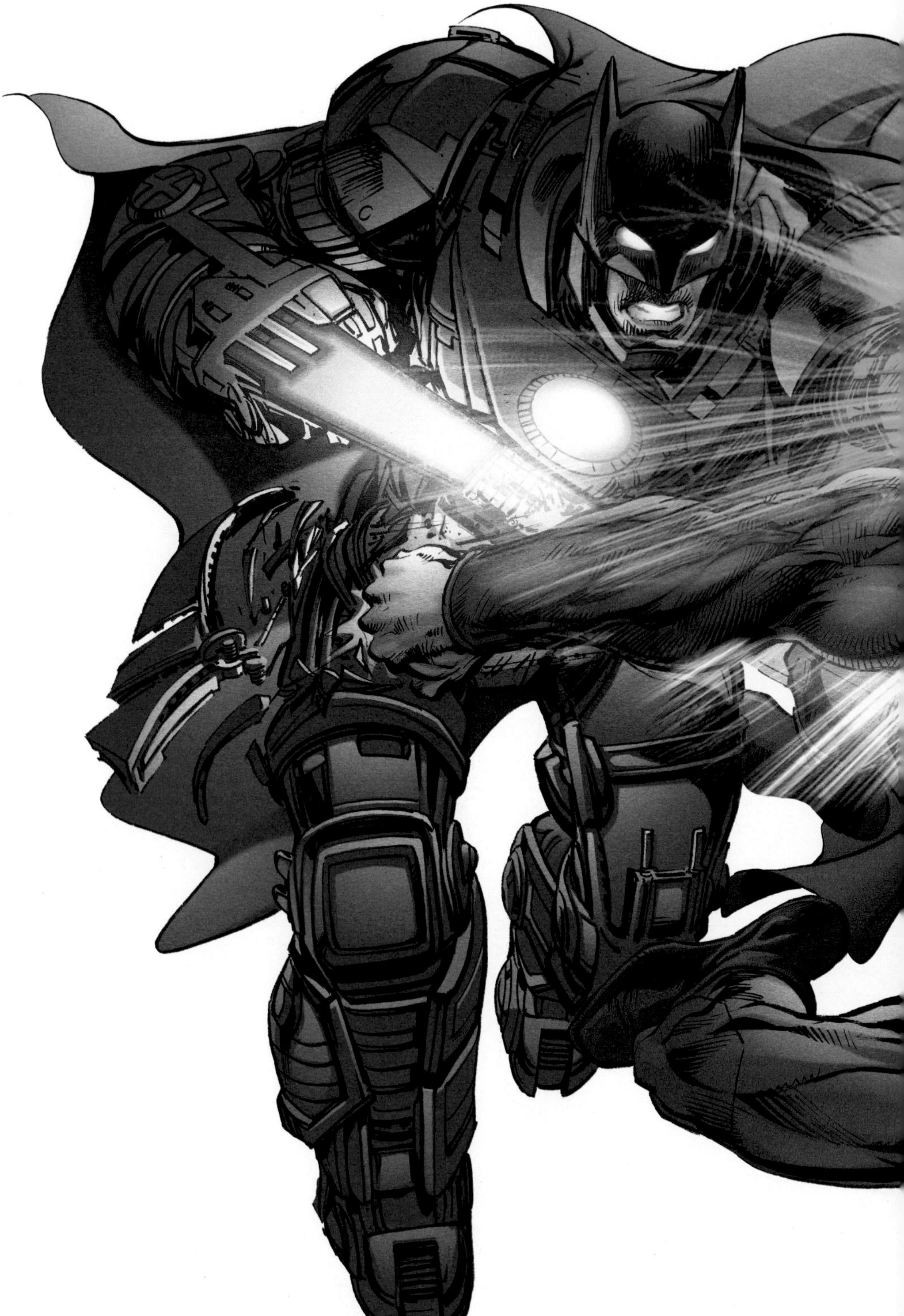

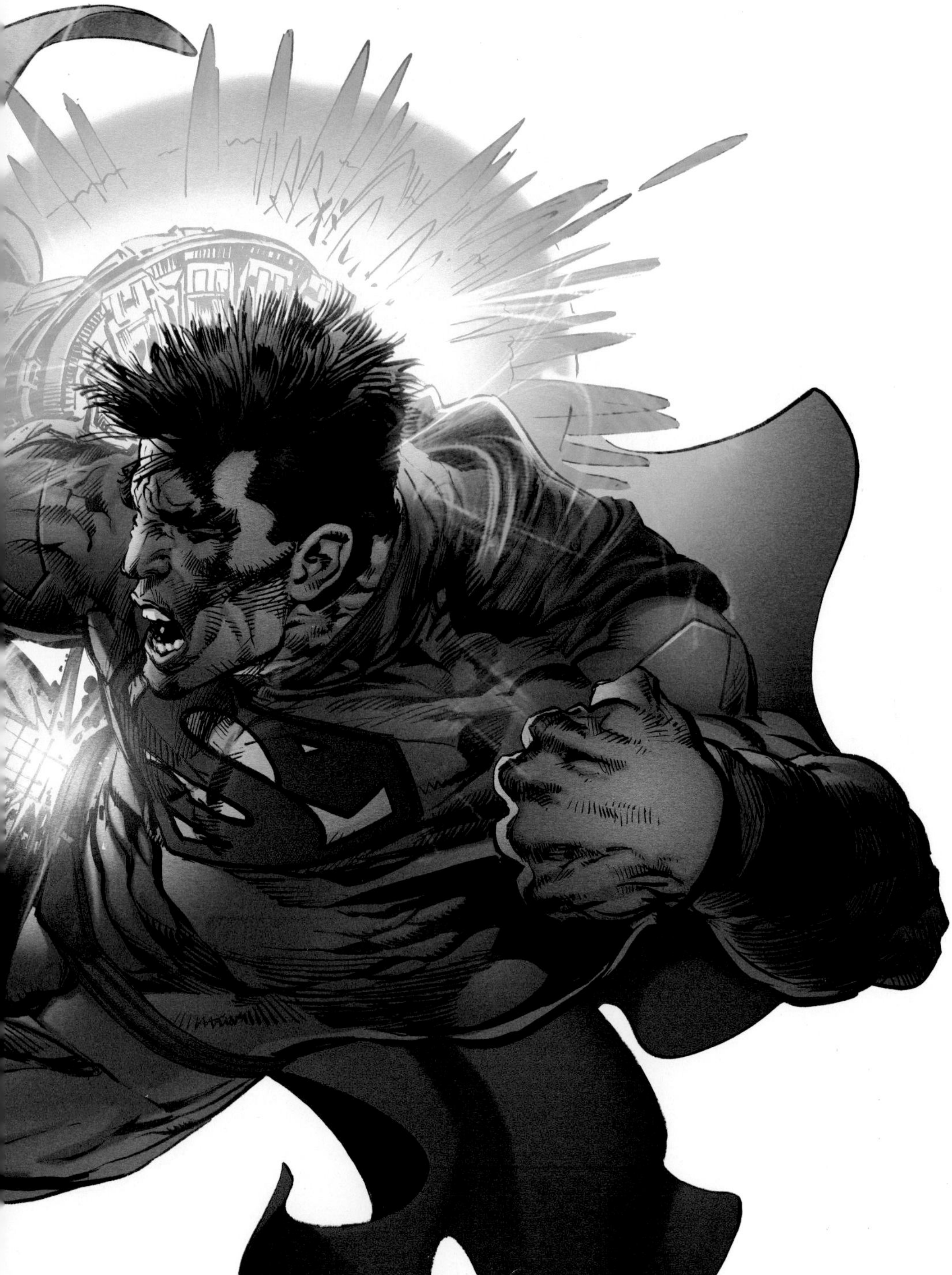

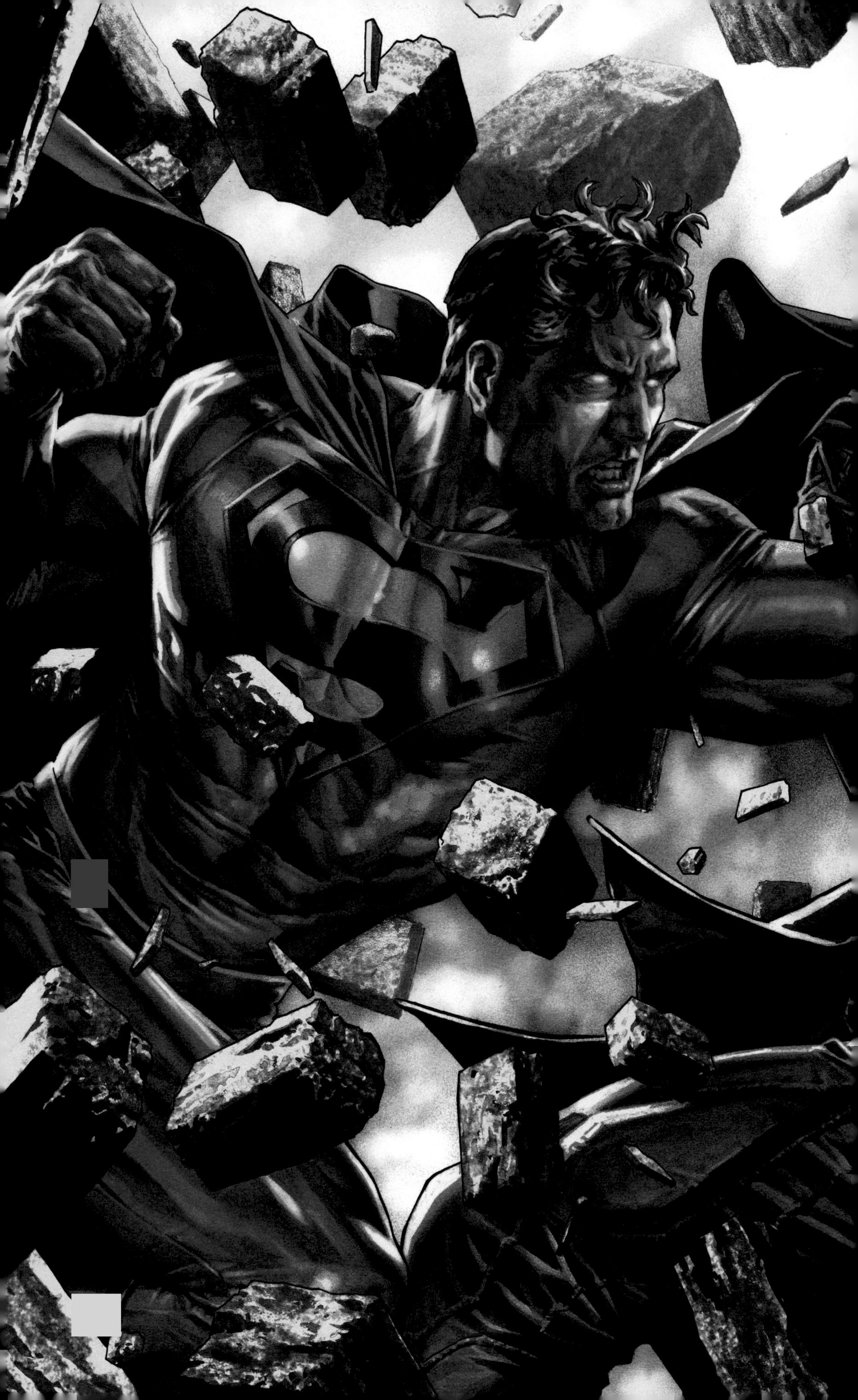

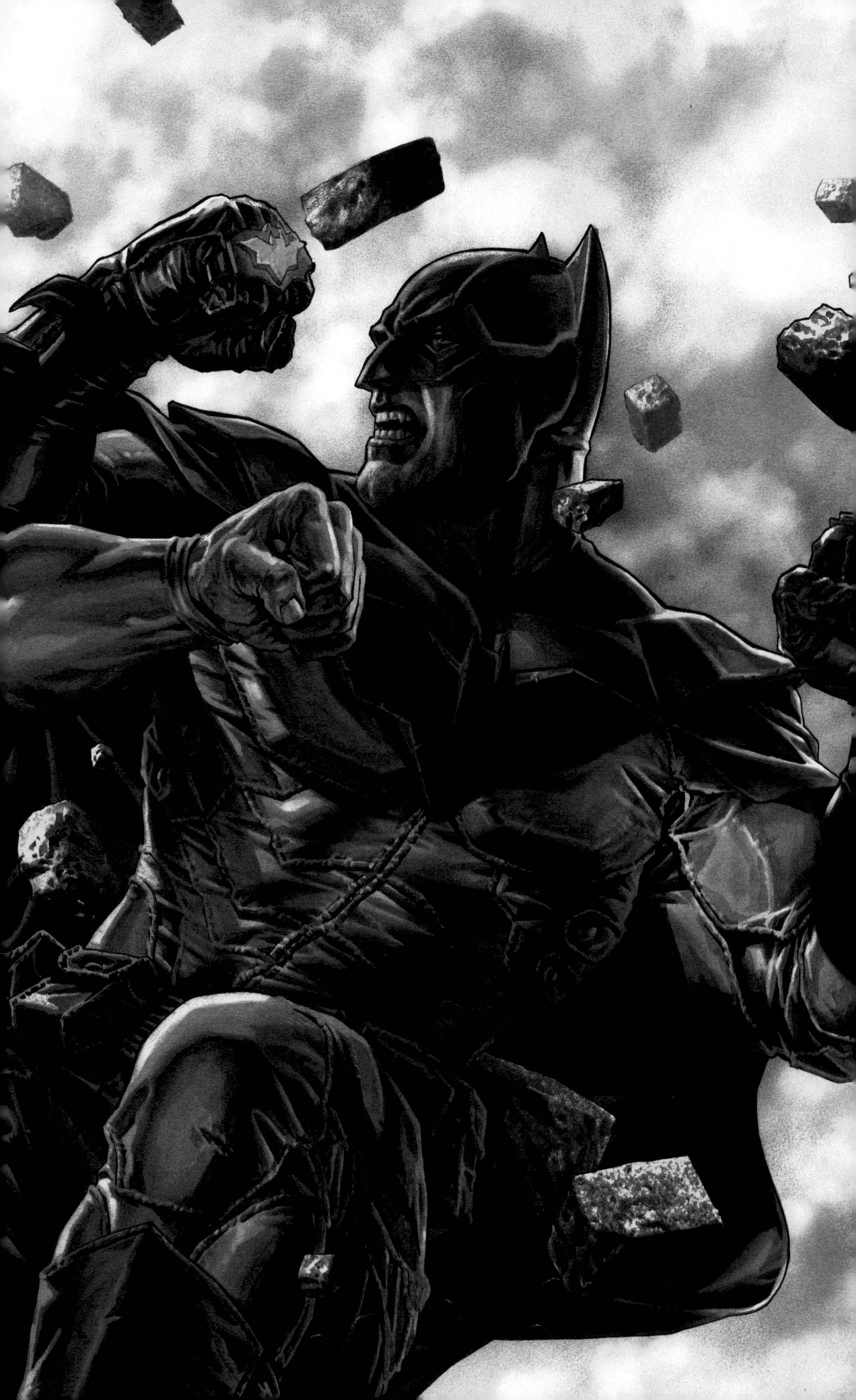

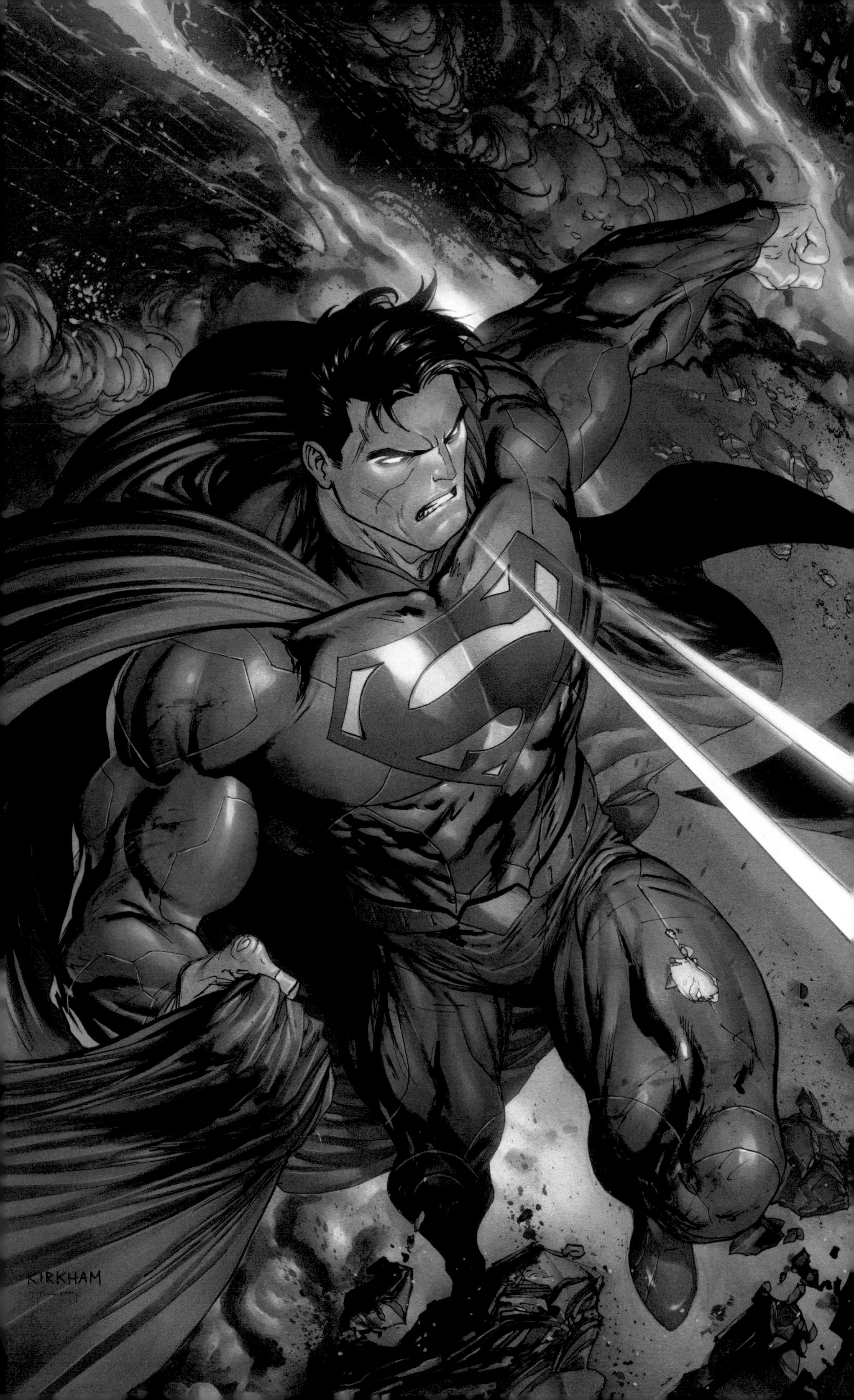
KIRKHAM

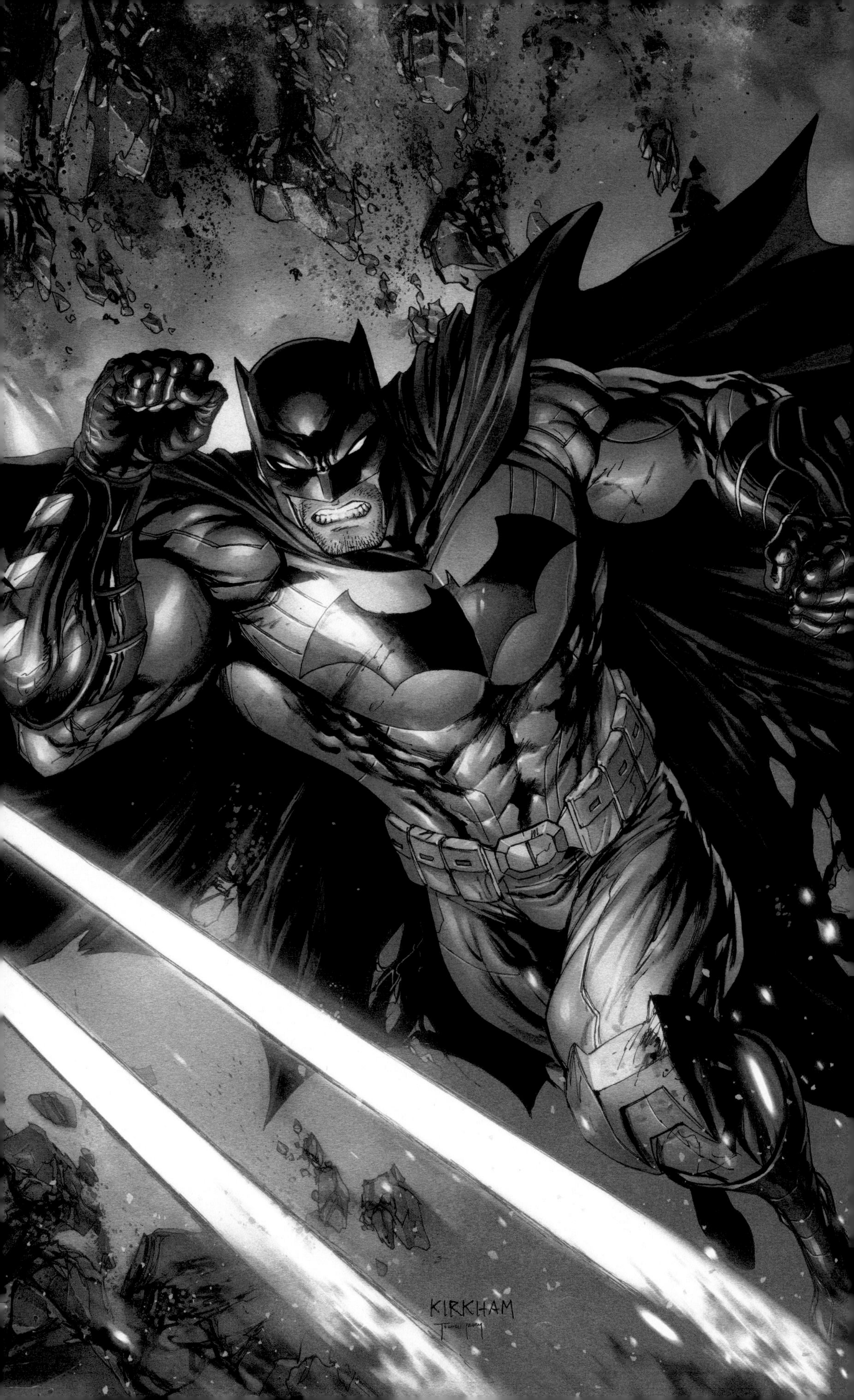
KIRKHAM

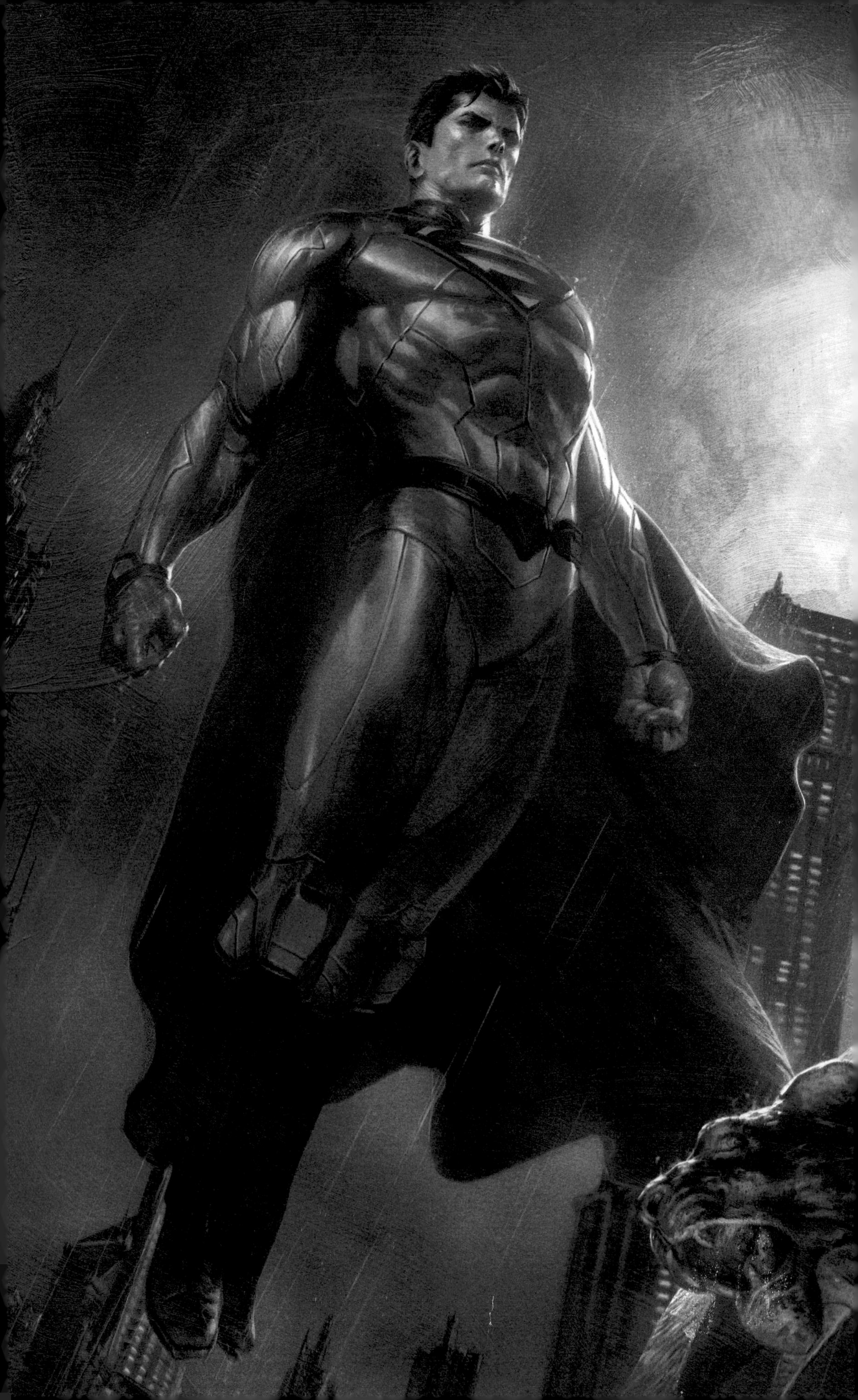

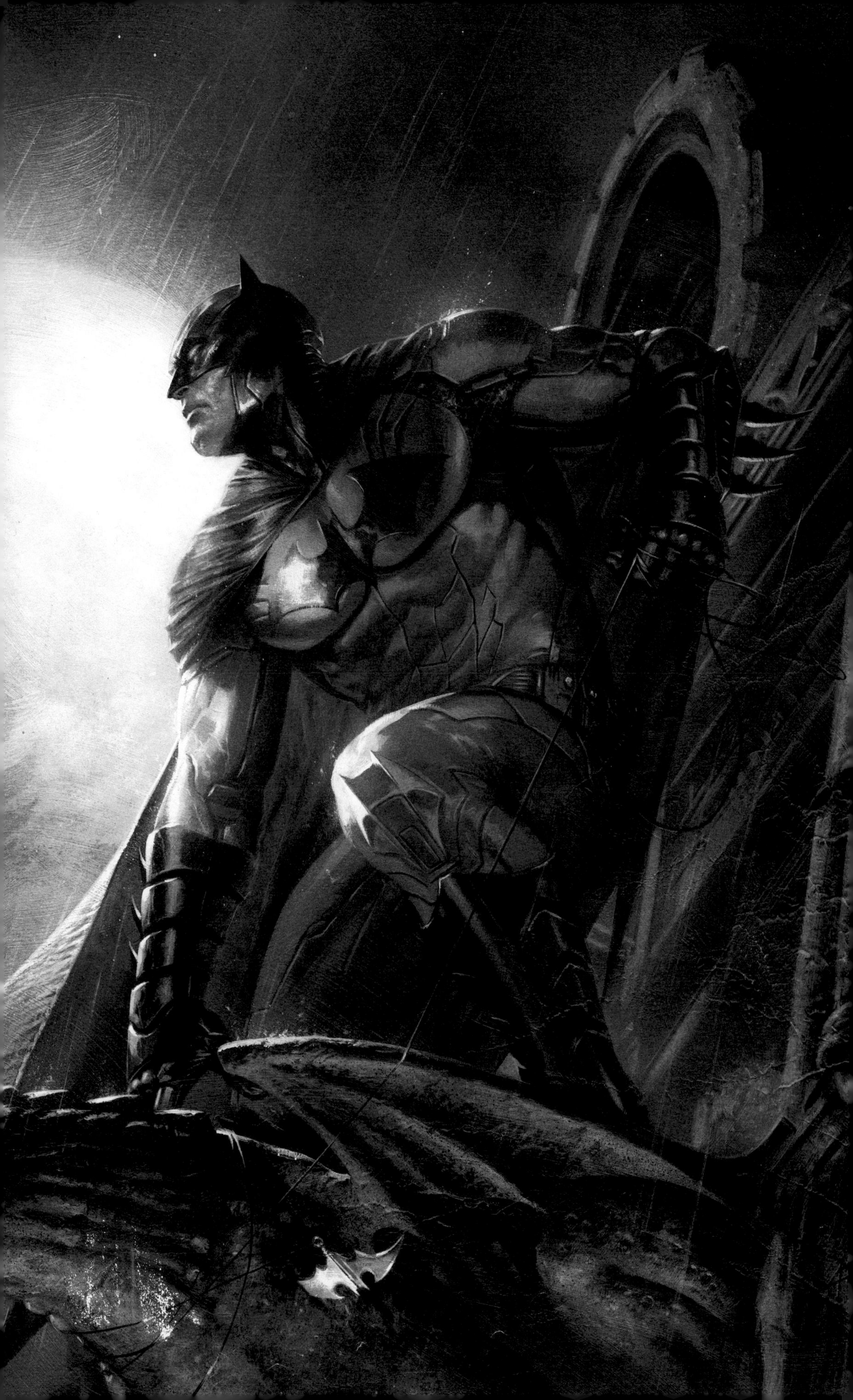

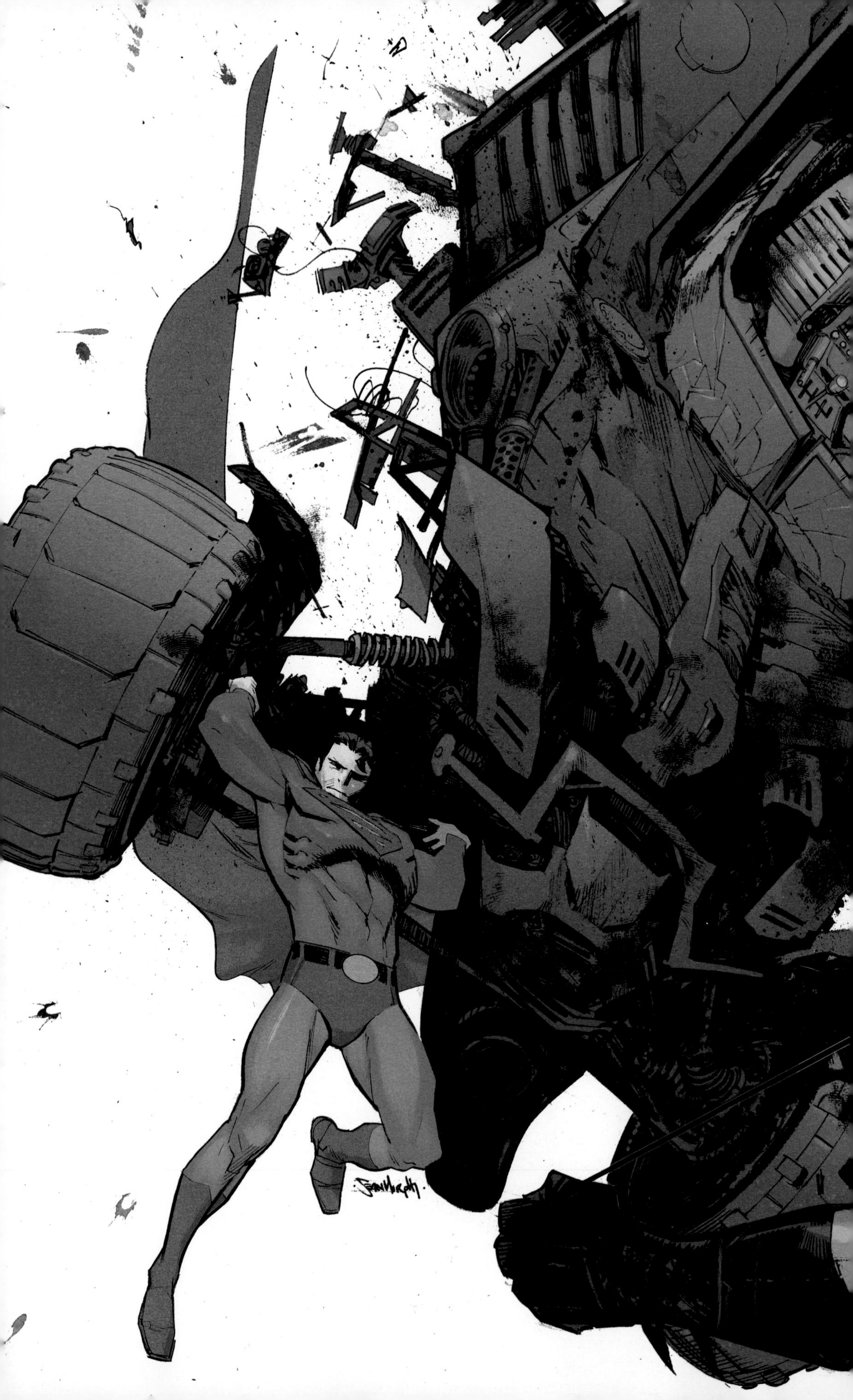

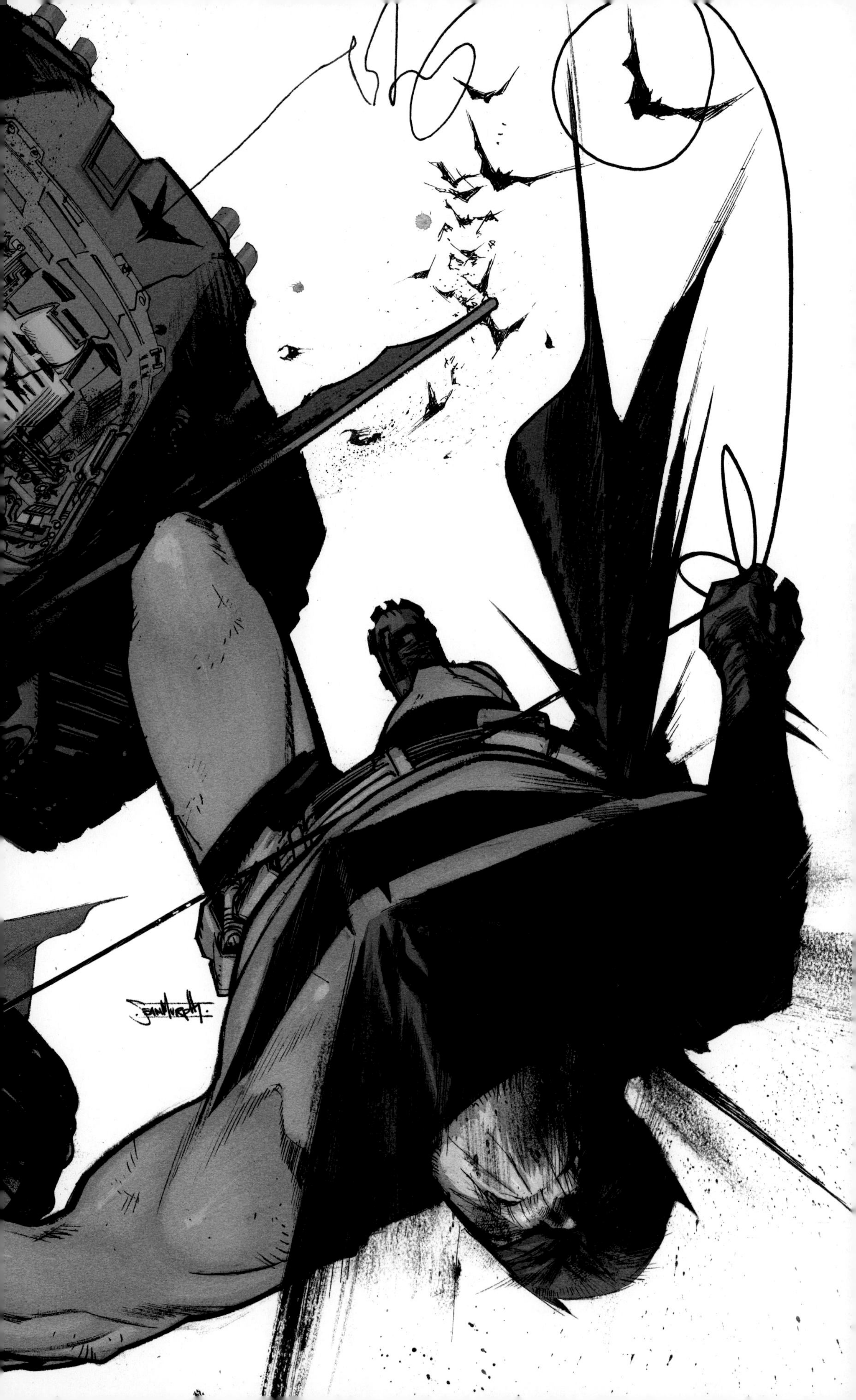

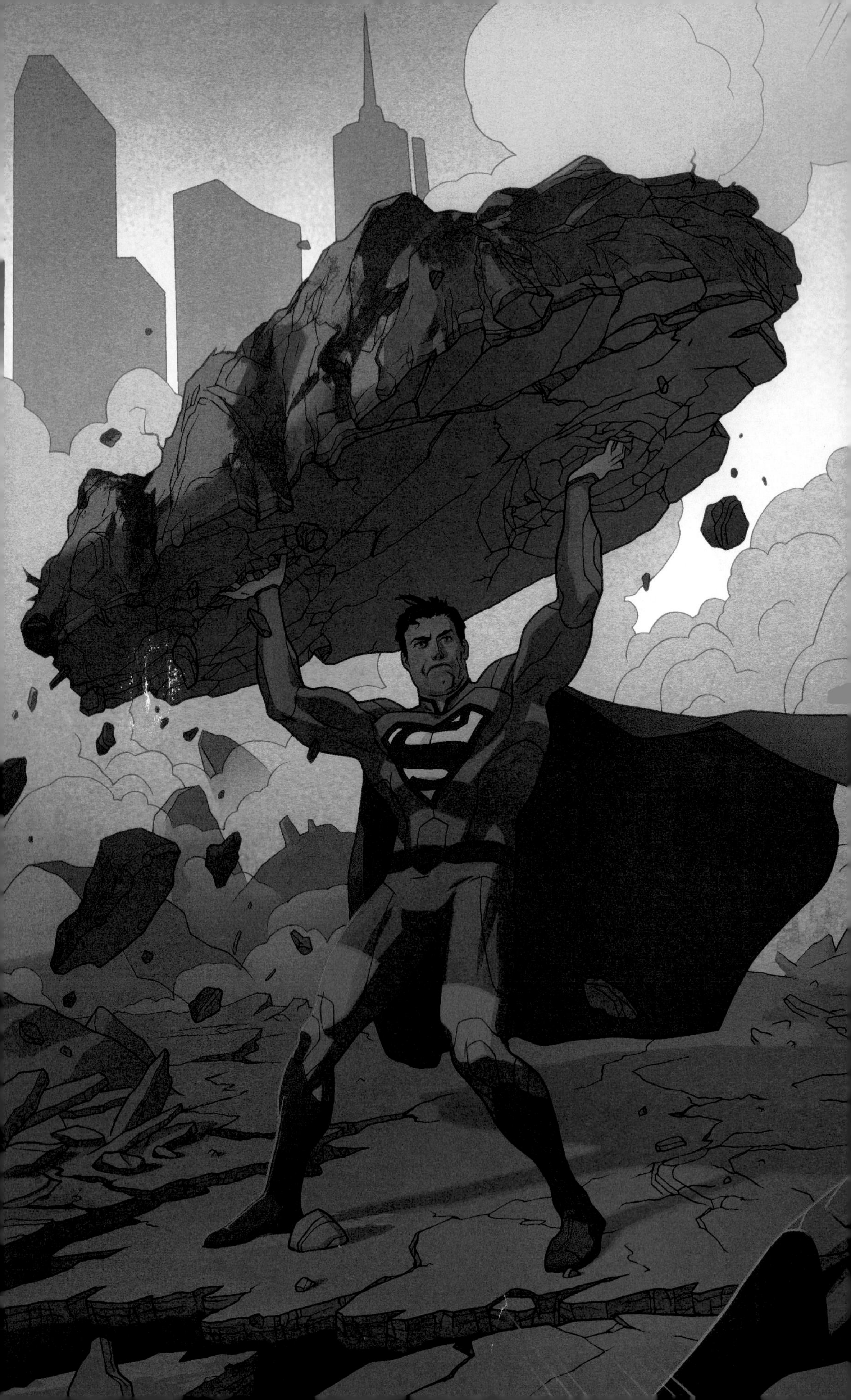

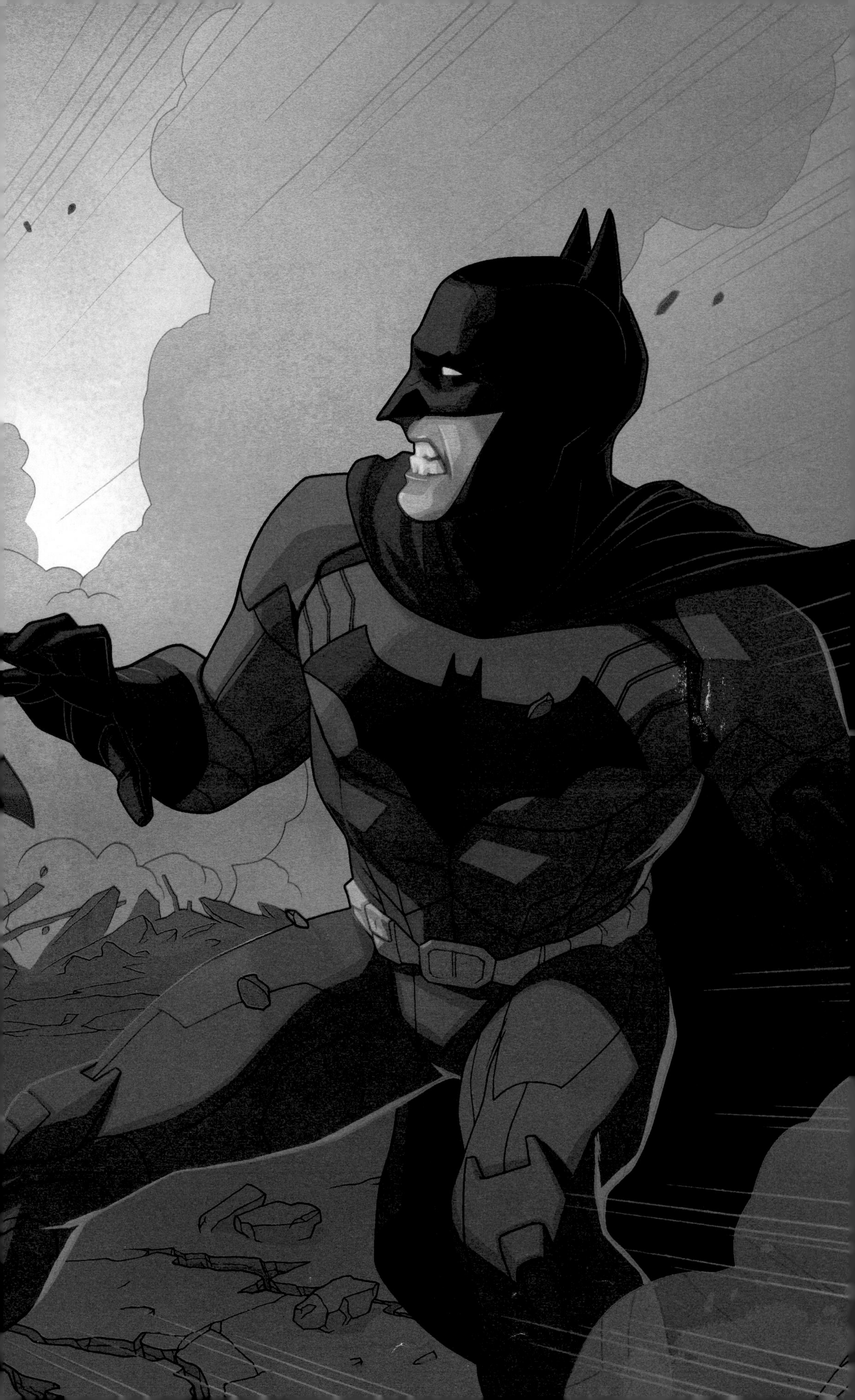

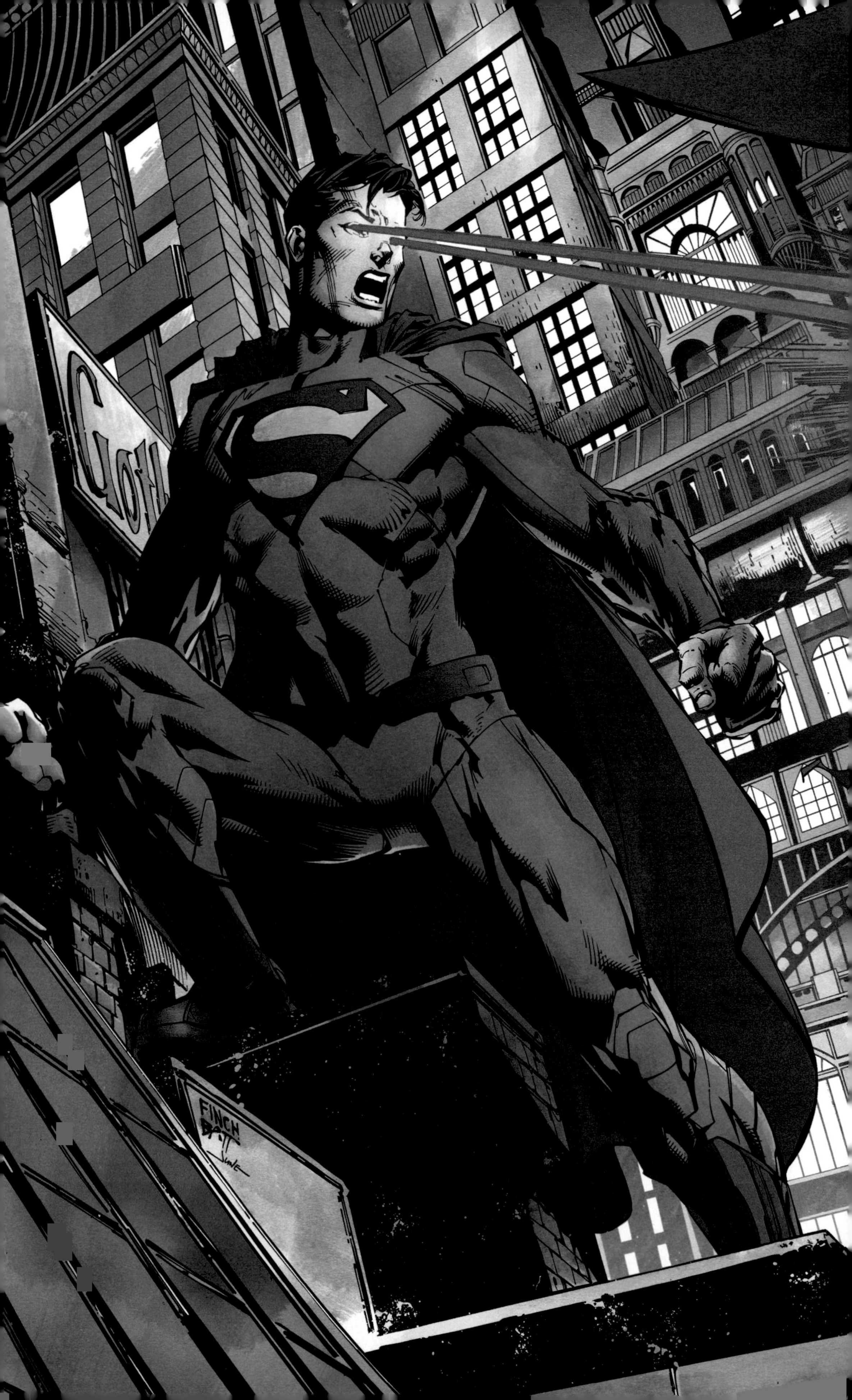

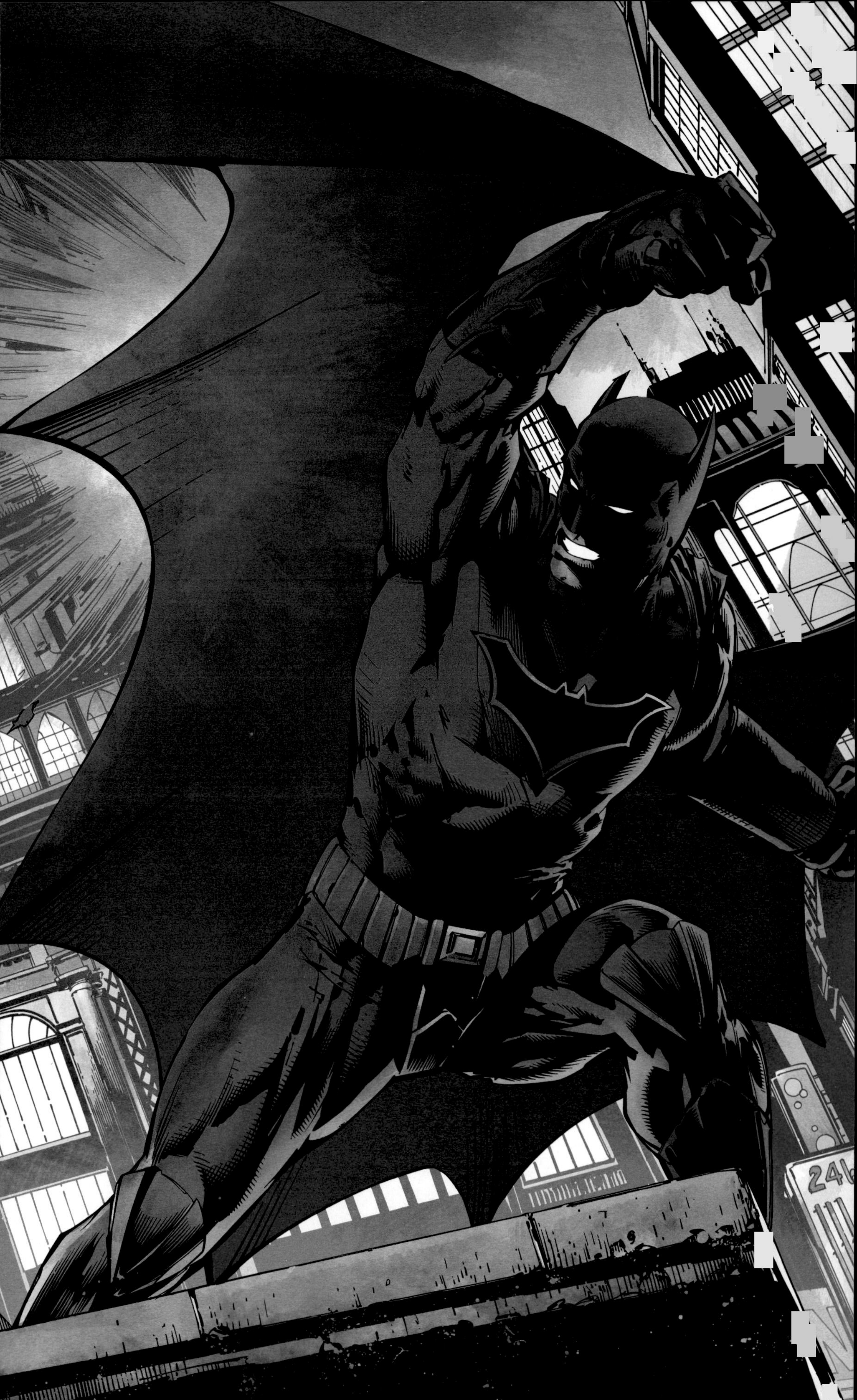

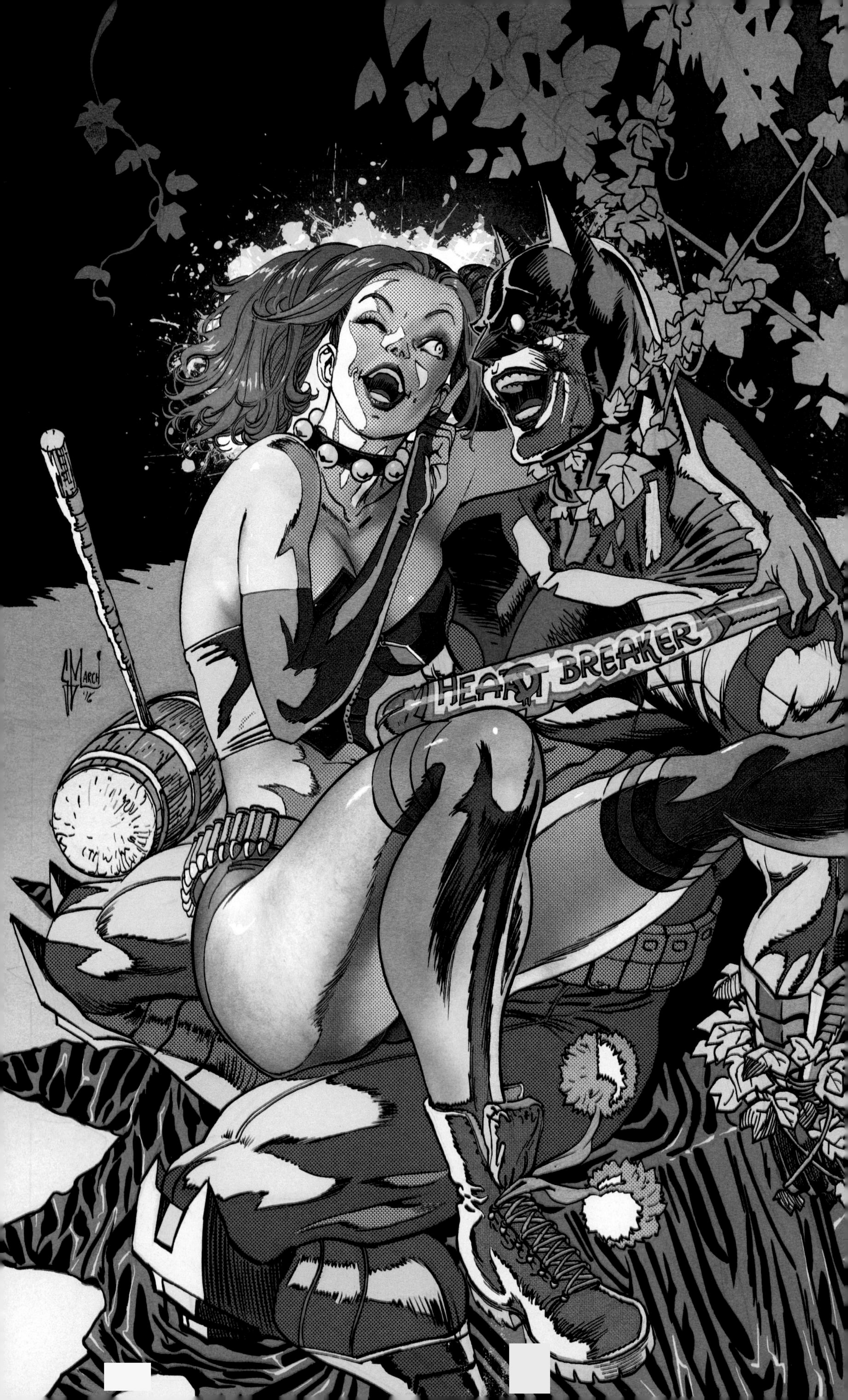
HEART BREAKER

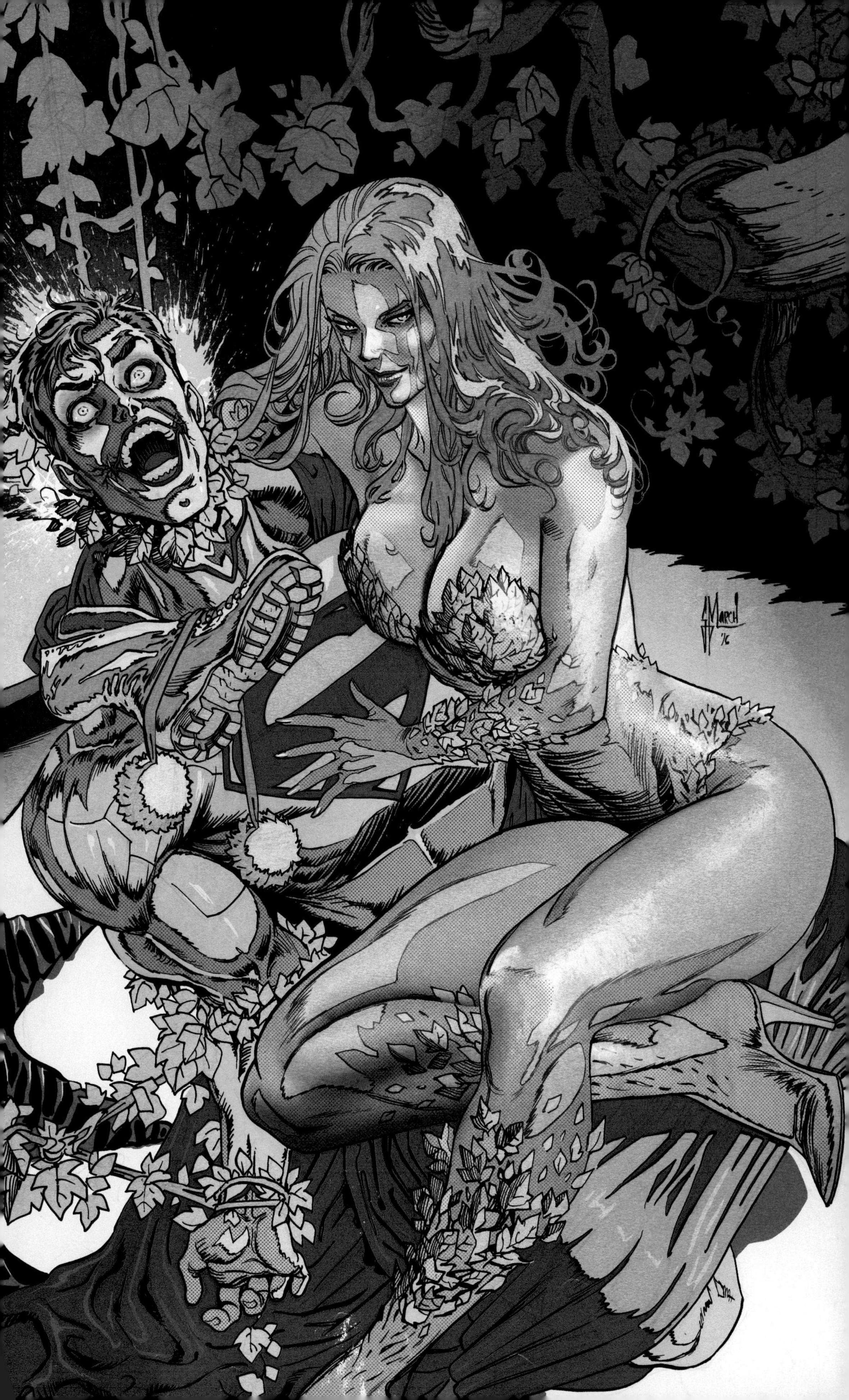

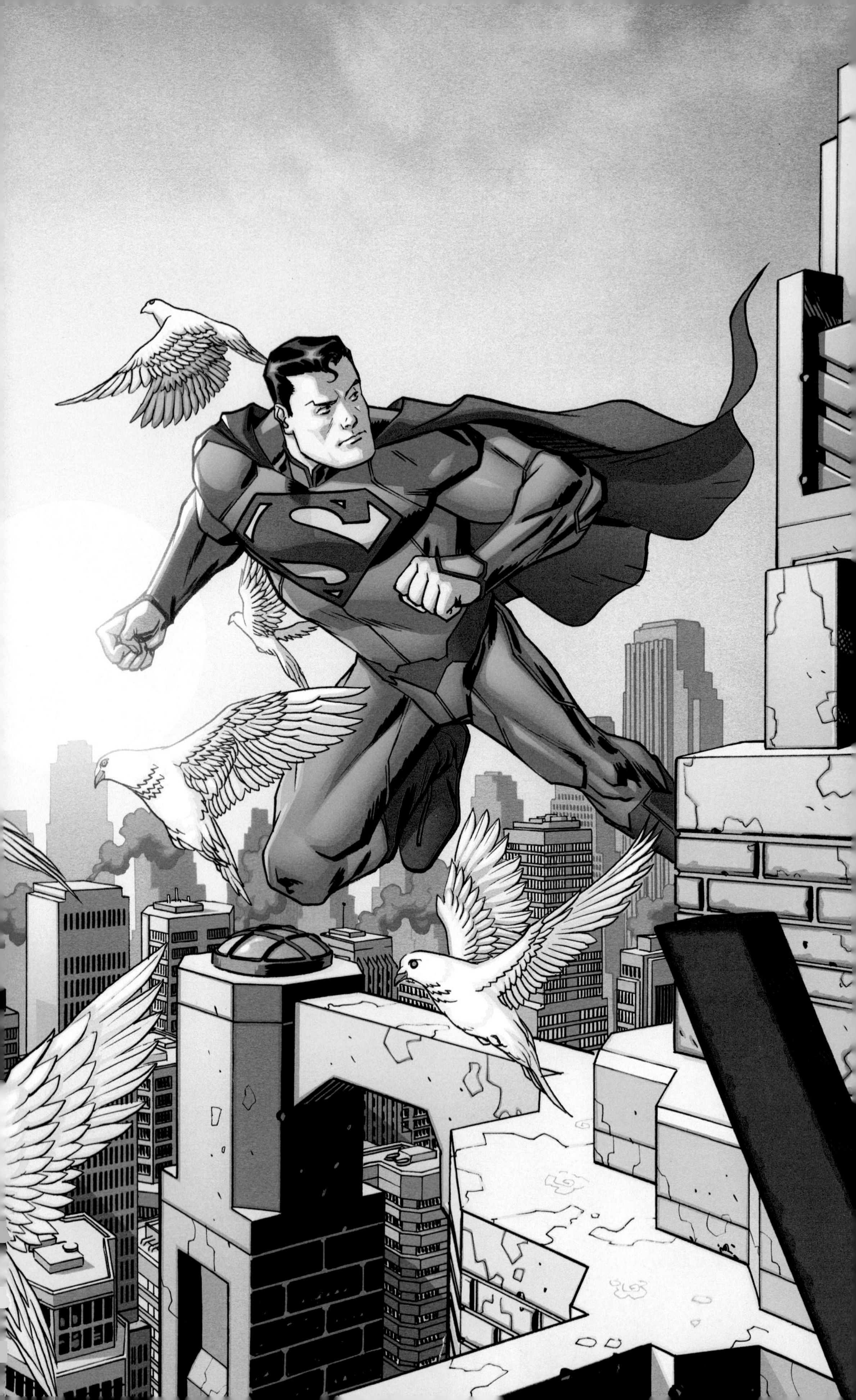

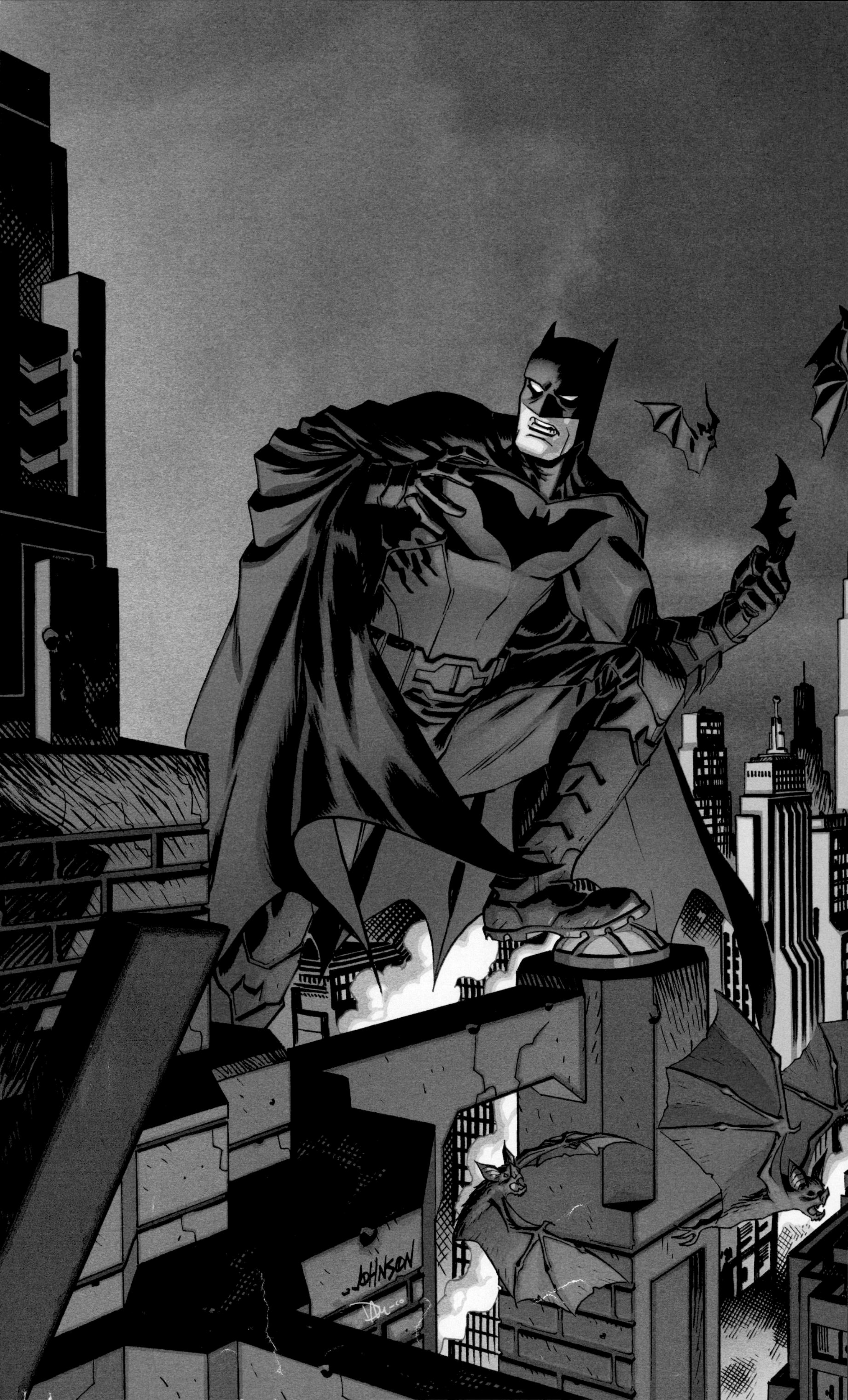
JOHNSON

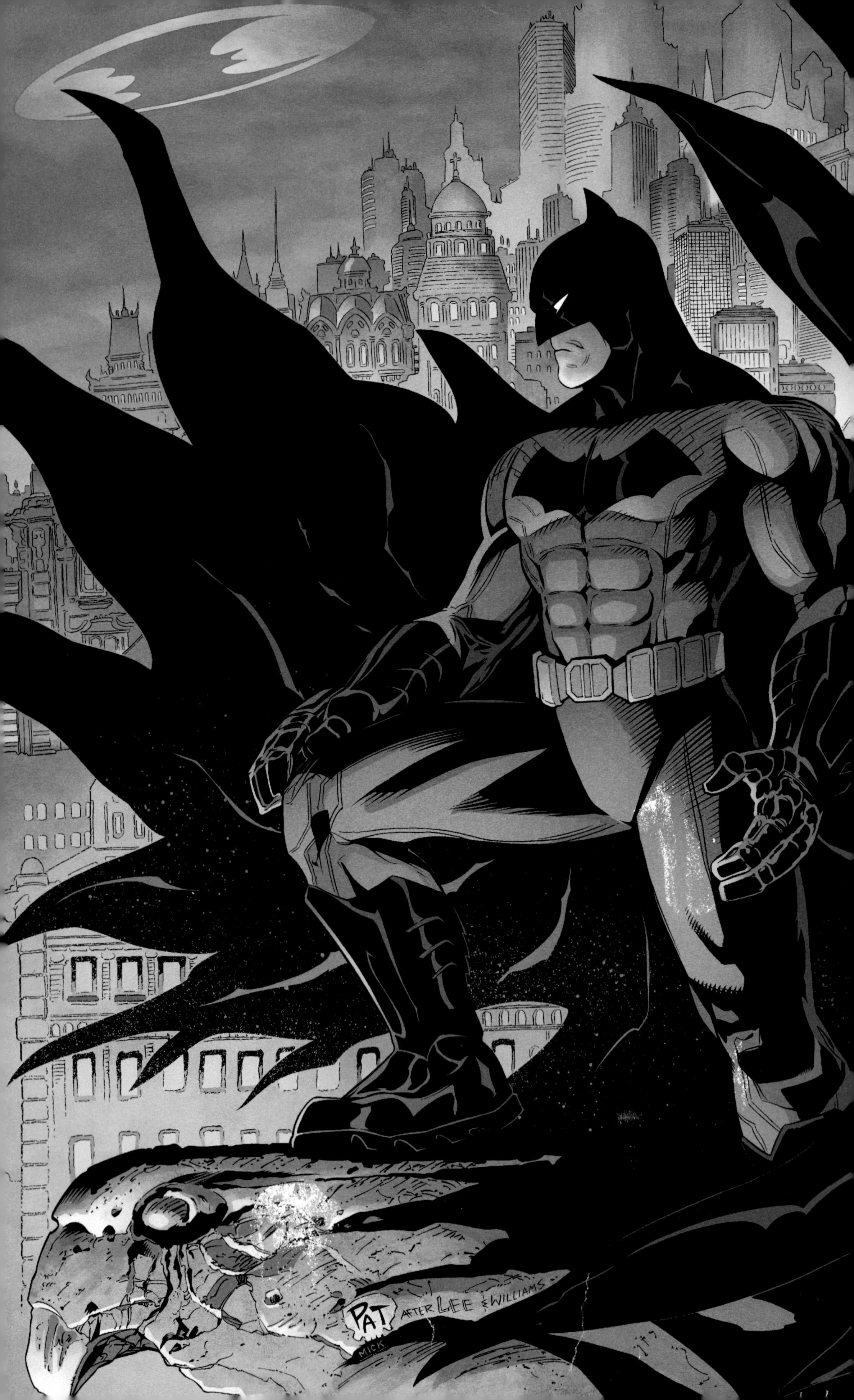
PAT! AFTER LEE & WILLIAMS
MICK

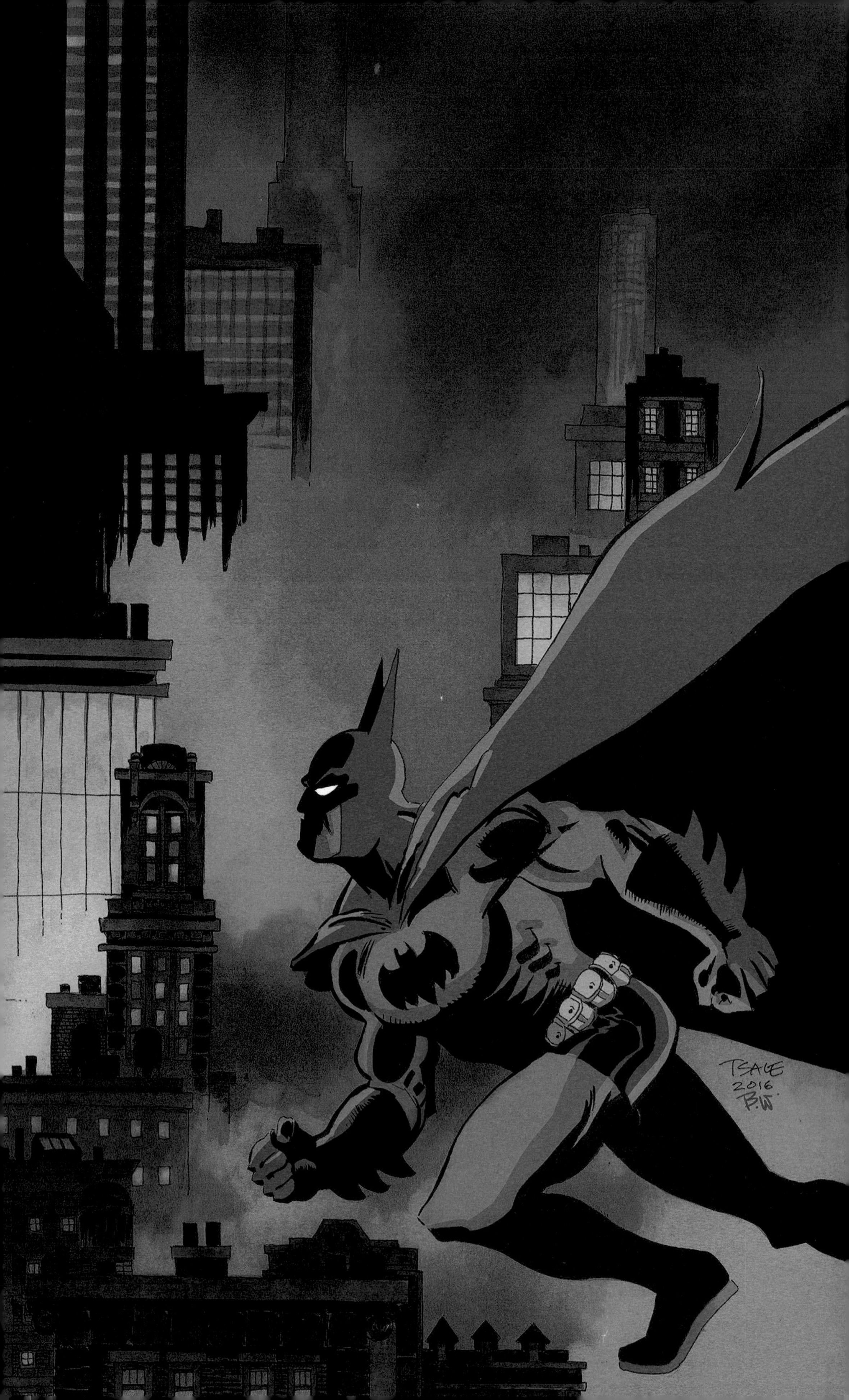
TSALE
2016
B.W.

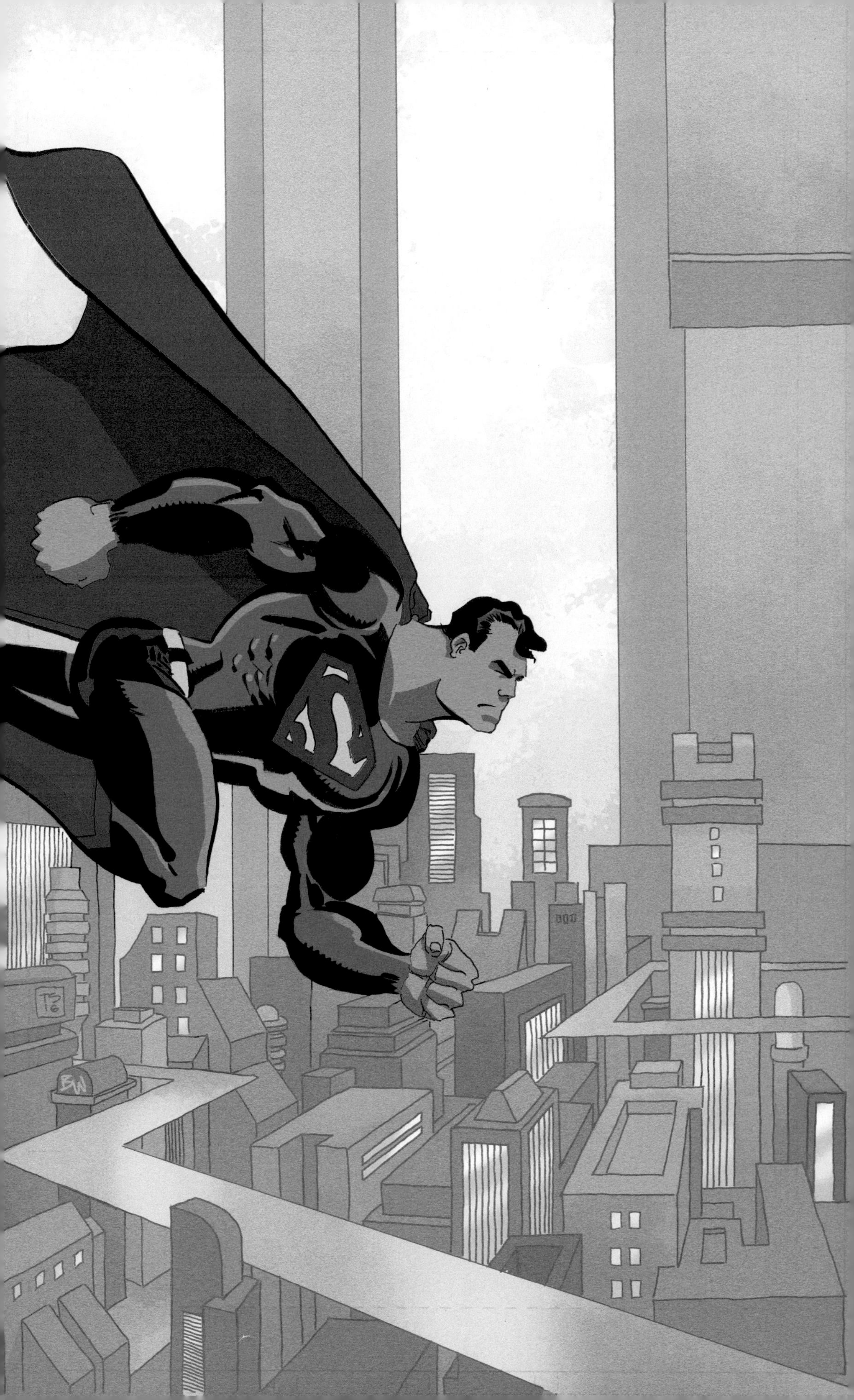

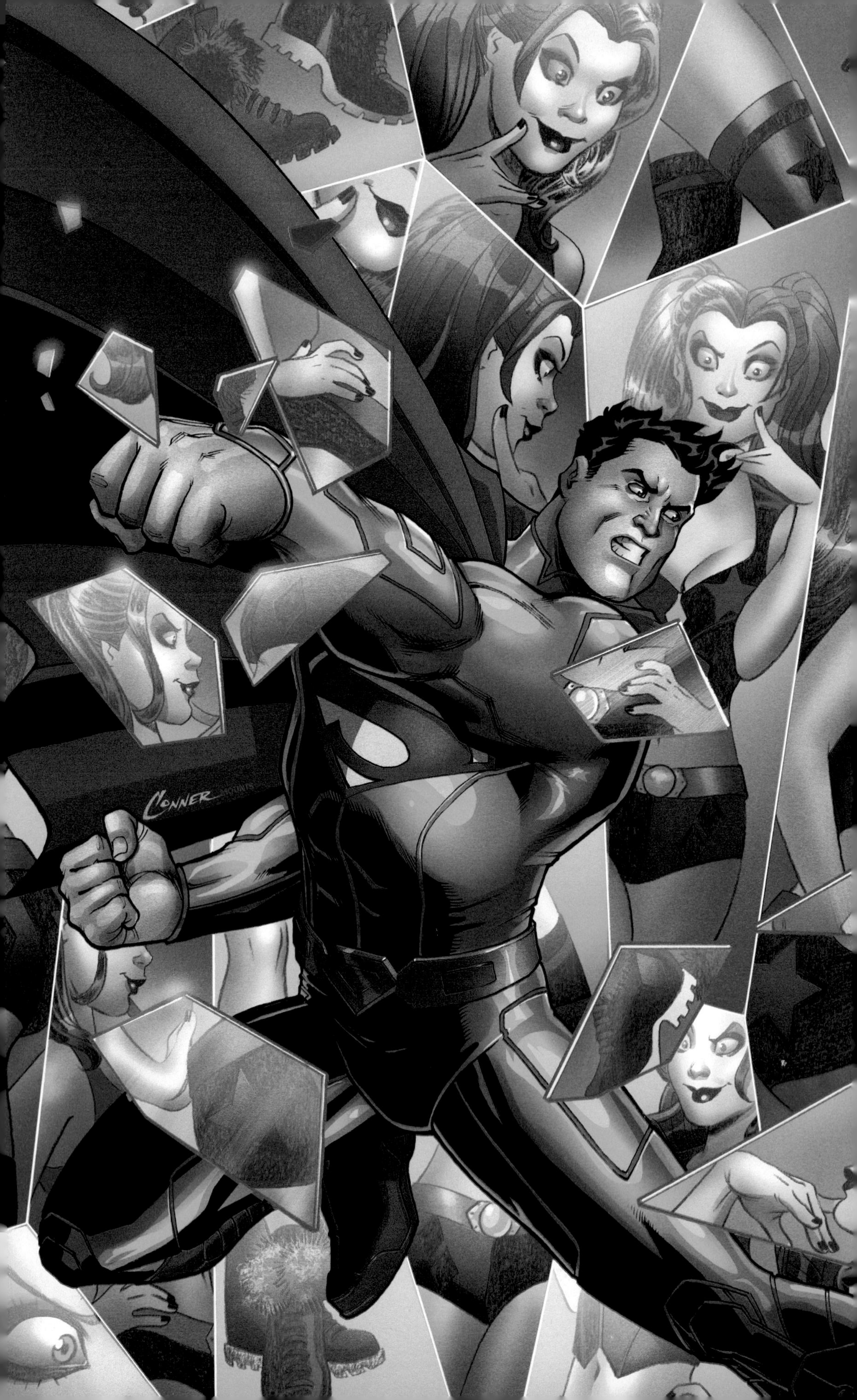
CONNER

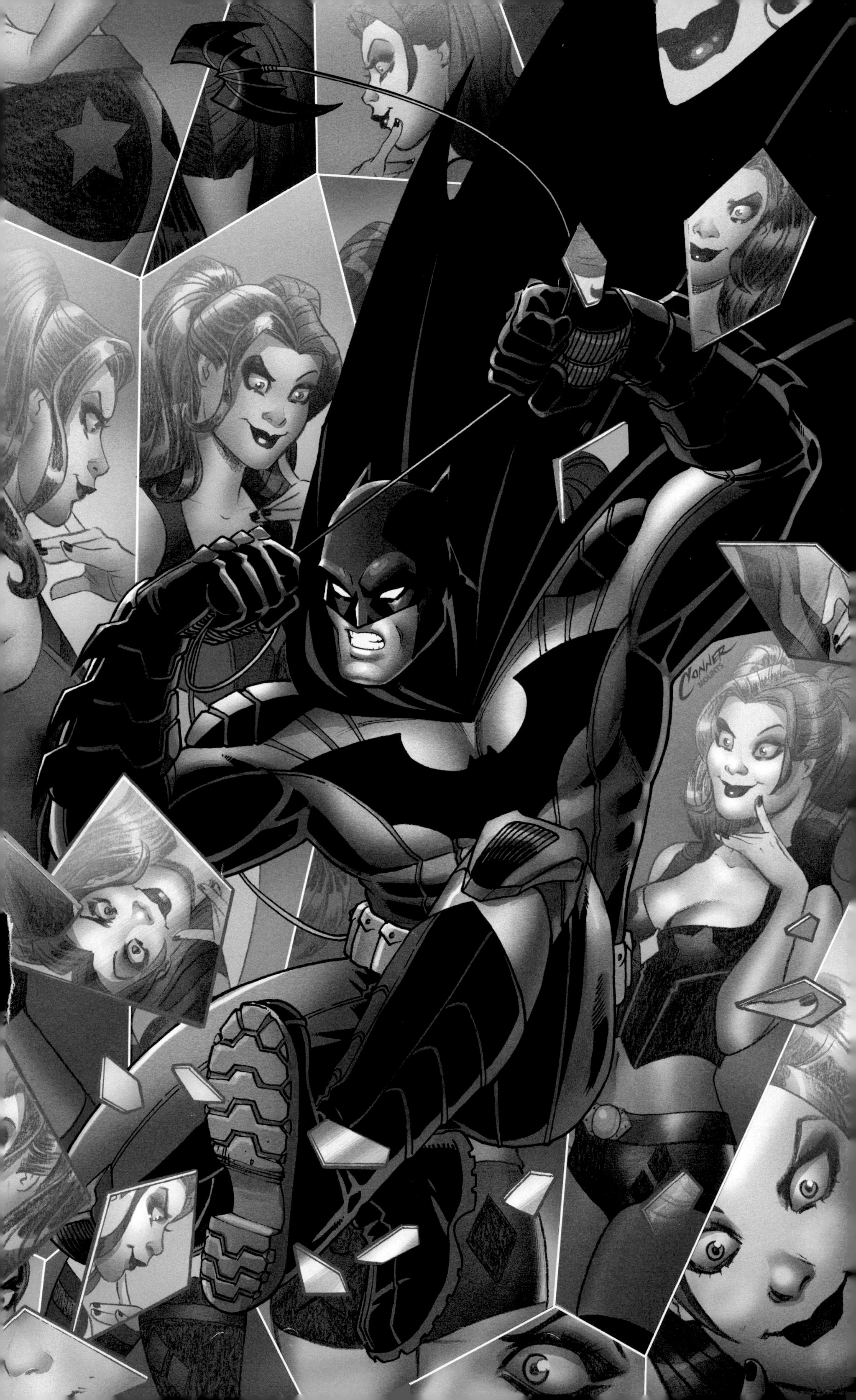
CONNER
MOUNTS

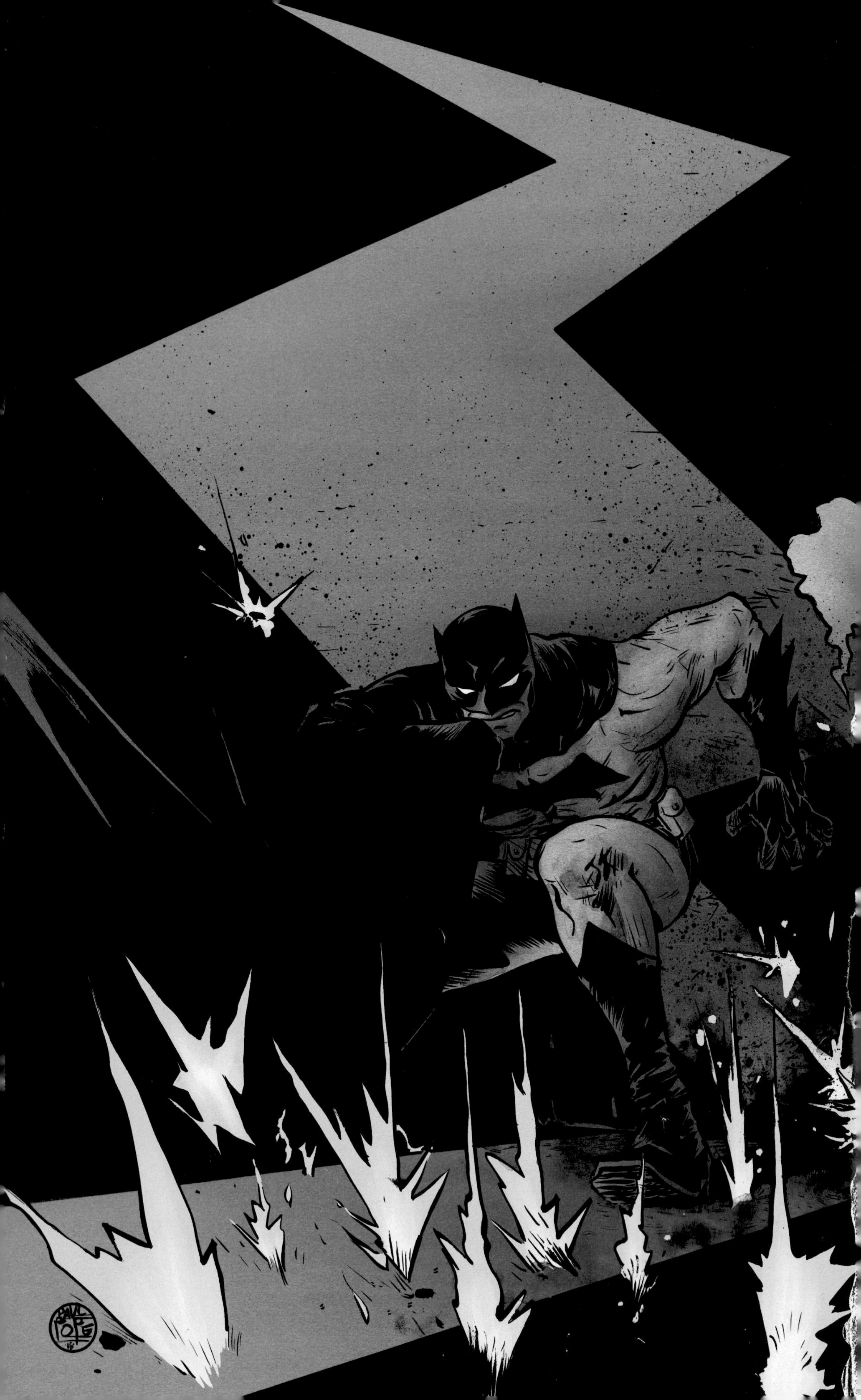